THE
MIDDLE
AGES

THE
MIDDLE
AGES

EVERYDAY LIFE
IN MEDIEVAL EUROPE

JEFFREY L. SINGMAN

STERLING
New York

STERLING
New York

An Imprint of Sterling Publishing
387 Park Avenue South
New York, NY 10016

STERLING and the distinctive Sterling logo are registered trademarks
of Sterling Publishing Co., Inc.

This Sterling edition published in 2013.

© 1999 by Jeffrey L. Singman

Please see page 309 for image credits.

This edition published by arrangement with ABC-CLIO
130 Cremona Drive Suite C,
Santa Barbara, CA 93117-5505, USA.

ISBN 978-1-4549-0905-7

Distributed in Canada by Sterling Publishing
c/o Canadian Manda Group, 165 Dufferin Street
Toronto, Ontario, Canada M6K 3H6
Distributed in the United Kingdom by GMC Distribution Services
Castle Place, 166 High Street, Lewes, East Sussex, England BN7 1XU
Distributed in Australia by Capricorn Link (Australia) Pty. Ltd.
P.O. Box 704, Windsor, NSW 2756, Australia

For information about custom editions, special sales, and premium and corporate purchases,
please contact Sterling Special Sales at 800-805-5489 or specialsales@sterlingpublishing.com.

Manufactured in China

2 4 6 8 10 9 7 5 3

www.sterlingpublishing.com

Frontispiece: PEASANTS WORK FARMLAND *outside the gates of a medieval castle in this
illustration from the* Grimani Breviary, *a famous Flemish illuminated manuscript produced
ca. 1515–1520.*

CONTENTS

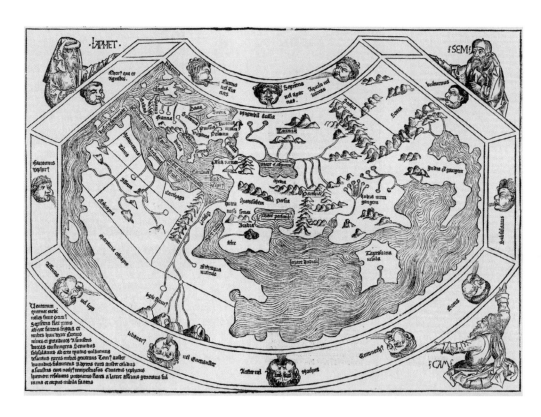

INTRODUCTION

OVER HALF A MILLENNIUM AFTER THE CLOSE OF THE MIDDLE Ages, the period continues to exercise a unique emotive power over Western culture. Our attitude is ambivalent but never detached. A governmental system we dislike is termed "medieval," yet we continue to be drawn to tales of King Arthur and Robin Hood. We consider the Middle Ages a barbaric time, yet they furnish some of our most enduring icons: the knight in shining armor, the idealized noble lady, the king upon his throne. The Middle Ages somehow remain with us in a way that other historical periods do not.

Our interest in things medieval is not an idle fancy. In many respects, the Middle Ages represent the point of origin of modern Western culture. They began with the confluence of three distinct cultural strands: the classical civilization of imperial Rome, the barbarian culture of the Germanic tribes in the north, and the near-eastern traditions imported into Europe with the advent of Christianity. Further back, we find the elements of modern Western culture only in fragmentary form, but in the Middle Ages all the main pieces come into place. The medieval world is at times alien and remote, yet it always resonates within us.

Of course, fascination and understanding are two quite different things. The sorts of images of the medieval world that abound in popular culture prove that our perception of the Middle Ages is mythic rather than historical. The transition from popular stereotypes of the Middle Ages to a real understanding of the period is not easy to make, and the difficulty is aggravated by a shortage of introductory information. There are a number of outstanding children's books on the Middle Ages that offer a vivid look at what life was like in the period,

ONE OF THE EARLIEST PRINTED MAPS, *created in Nuremberg, Germany by Hartmann Schedel in 1493. The engraving, which presents the world as it was known just prior to Christopher Columbus's voyage to the New World and the rounding of the Cape of Good Hope by Bartolomeu Dias, reveals many medieval notions about the earth. For example, the Indian Ocean is shown in its land-locked, pre-discovery state, and the inclusion of Noah's sons Japhet, Shem, and Ham in the corners indicates a theology-centered mindset.*

and there are also plenty of advanced texts on specific aspects of medieval life that provide a comparable level of detail. But there is surprisingly little at an intermediate level-books that offer both a broad picture and informative details of medieval life for readers who are not children but who are not generally familiar with the medieval world. I can speak with feeling about the lack of such resources, having missed them during my own education. As a high school, college, and graduate student, it was always easy to find general works on medieval political institutions, and there were plenty of books on specific topics relating to ordinary life, but I lacked a good introduction to medieval society that offered a sense of how this world worked from the ground up. As with my other titles in this series, I have tried to offer here a book that I would have wanted for myself.

Approaching the Medieval World

Medieval people naturally did not think of themselves as being in the middle (in Latin, medium ævum, the middle age). Authors of the period speak of *nos moderni*, "we modern people." The Middle Ages were invented after the fact, by historians during the Renaissance who saw the period as an unfortunate interregnum between the splendors of the classical age and the glories of the present. This threefold division of European history into ancient, medieval, and modern has since become canonical. It is not without validity. Certainly there was a profound, although not abrupt, disjuncture between the Middle Ages and what came before, and during the latter part of the fifteenth century there were a number of revolutionary developments—notably the introduction of the printing press and the European discovery of the New World—that ultimately changed the shape of European society and culture at every level. Yet we should not forget that the canonical system of historical periods can obscure other significant historical junctures. The rise of the money economy, banking, and credit in the eleventh to thirteenth centuries was among the most important occurrences in Europe's economic history. The fourteenth century witnessed the death of a third of the population from the Black Death, the single most dramatic demographic event that has ever befallen Europe, and one that undermined the balance of power that had sustained medieval feudalism.

Medievalists commonly divide the Middle Ages into three periods, termed the early, High (or central), and late Middle Ages. The early Middle Ages begins with the fall of the Western Roman Empire—not a single datable event but a long process of decline, although for convenience we may place it around the year 500. They end in about the eleventh century, when Europe once more achieved a degree of political stability that permitted a new flourishing of intellectual and economic life. The early Middle Ages were marked by a high incidence of warfare due to the lack of strong central governments; urban activity was limited; and written culture was almost exclusively in the hands of the church, itself largely dominated by the monastic element. In the High Middle Ages, extending roughly from the eleventh to the early fourteenth century, there was a dramatic reemergence of urban life and an increasing sophistication in secular culture, with a corresponding decline in the importance of monasticism. The late Middle Ages, from the early fourteenth to the late fifteenth century, began with a series of population catastrophes of which the most serious was the Black Death of 1347–1350; also in this period a number of developments in military technique and technology undermined the supremacy of the knight on the battlefield. These events disrupted the traditional power relations of feudal Europe, and the late Middle Ages were characterized by a weakening of traditional feudal structures and an ongoing series of social and religious crises that reflected the inability of the church and feudal society to handle a substantially changed environment.

Overall, the Middle Ages cover about a millennium of human history. Their geographical scope is no less broad. Even a fairly restricted definition of medieval Europe that includes only those areas owing allegiance to the Catholic Church would still range from Portugal to Poland, and from Sicily to Scandinavia. A book that tried to cover daily life comprehensively across so many years and so many regions would be so diffuse as to lose most of its meaning. Instead, this book will focus on a narrower span of time, the High Middle Ages, particularly the years from 1100 to 1300. Sitting between the early and late Middle Ages, this period offers a particularly full picture of medieval life. In 1100, the traditions of the feudal and manorial systems were still largely in place, although beginning to weaken under the pressures of an increasingly monetarized economy. By 1300, all the major new institutions of the Middle Ages, such as the universities and mendicant orders, had established themselves, and the dynamics of feudal society had not yet been disrupted by the population losses that were soon to follow. Two hundred years, however, is still a substantial stretch (imagine trying to write about daily life from 1800 to 2000), therefore I will try to suggest something of the processes of change at work within the period, even if the details cannot be covered.

To narrow the geographic scope, this book will concentrate on the feudal heartland of northwestern Europe: in modern terms, northern France, the German-speaking areas west of the Rhine, the Low Countries, and England. These areas shared a similar historical profile. All had been part of the Roman Empire and were conquered by Germanic invaders in the third to fifth centuries, who set up kingdoms of their own in their new lands and eventually adopted Roman Christianity. Mediterranean Europe, particularly Italy and Spain, shared much of this historical profile but retained more continuity with Roman traditions, and was subject to significant influence from the Arabic world; as a result, Mediterranean society was markedly different in many ways from that of the north, looking back to the Roman past and forward to the Renaissance future as well as participating in the feudal culture of the Middle Ages. Some reference also will be made to regions outside the core area, both to supplement information lacking for the core areas and to suggest something of the diversity of medieval culture within Europe.

As with my previous works in this series, this present book is heavily informed by my own interest and experience in the practice of living history. Broadly speaking, living history may be defined as any attempt at a concrete re-creation of an aspect of historical life. In this sense, the performers of early music or artists practicing medieval techniques of calligraphy are participating in living history. In its most comprehensive form, living history involves an attempt to portray an entire historical milieu by impersonating an individual who lived or might have lived in the past. Living history is not an alternative to traditional historical scholarship. Without the source studies and rigorous analysis of the conventional historian, it quickly slips into mere fantasy. From the point of view of the practitioner, it does not so much answer questions about the past as pose them. The particular strength of living history is that it reminds us that general interpretations of the processes and events of history only have meaning if they can be interpreted with respect to the lives of individual human beings. As Thomas Carlyle wrote in the nineteenth century of the then-new genre of the historical novel:

> These historical novels have taught all men this truth, which looks like a truism, yet was unknown to writers of history and others, till so taught: that the bygone ages of the world were actually filled with living men, not by protocols, state papers, controversies, and abstractions of men.[1]

The influence of living history on this book will be immediately evident in the inclusion of a certain amount of hands-on material—games, recipes, songs. To use the past as a source for cultural enrichment in the present is certainly a valid undertaking, and in an age when folk crafts and folk culture have been displaced by industrial production and commercial entertainment, it is natural for us to look to history to help us rediscover how to create. The re-creation of specific aspects of historical culture also offers a point of communion with the past: a modern person playing a medieval game is coming as close to a real experience of history as the realities of time will allow.

At a more subtle level, the practice of living history pervades the perspective of this book as a whole. Living history encourages us to approach the past through the concrete and the individual. It suggests that we imagine ourselves in the position of a historical person, arrange our data around us, and see whether the world we have reconstructed appears credible and coherent. This distinctive focus and point of view helps to test our interpretation of the past. Our portrait of the historical milieu needs to be convincing from the perspective of the individual, since abstract social structures and processes only become real when they are enacted by individual people. At the same time, because we all experience our world as individuals, a portrait of the past will be more vivid and comprehensible, particularly to a reader unfamiliar with the period, if it can be presented in credible human terms. The influence of the living history perspective can be seen in various ways throughout this book. There is a pervasive emphasis on the basic material realities of medieval life: what people's beds were like, how often they washed, where they defecated. Such matters were long considered beneath the dignity of the historian, but in recent times they have received more attention, and as modern scholarship comes increasingly to recognize the significance of such details in shaping people's sense of their bodies and hence of themselves, we will probably see even more interest in them. The written word always takes us out of our bodies, and no book on the Middle Ages can truly convey the profound physical differences between medieval life and the modern world, but perhaps the prominence I have given to these aspects of medieval life will help remind the reader of their importance in understanding the medieval world.

The emphasis in Chapters 4, 5, 6, and 7 of this book on specific examples of the medieval village, castle, monastery, and town also reflects a living history perspective. This approach is not the sole preserve of living history. It has been heavily favored by social historians in the past few decades and can also be found in the more popular books by Sheila Sancha or Joseph and Frances Gies. It is nonetheless particularly congenial to the living history approach, emphasizing as it does a localized and integrated perspective. This perspective is particularly important because medieval society was itself highly localized. One can see broad social and cultural patterns in the medieval world, but these patterns generally reflected shared heritage and shared circumstances rather than the dissemination of centralized institutions.

The choice of examples in these chapters reflects a range of sometimes competing factors. The need to choose a well-documented setting that represents a wide range of the possibilities of its type weighted the choices in favor of the larger and more important locations. Paris, Cluny, and Dover are all large and prominent examples of their respective settings; only Cuxham can claim to be ordinary, and even this modest village has its shortcomings as an example of its class. Nonetheless, even if these places cannot claim to be typical, they do offer a sense of the characteristic dynamics of their respective settings.

This book falls into three main sections. The first three chapters introduce the reader to the general contours of the medieval experience from three perspectives: social, human, and material. The next four chapters take an in-depth look at four prominent social environments that characterized the medieval world. The final chapter delves into the more speculative areas of medieval people's interaction with the world at large and their characteristic modes of thought.

Technical Notes

An enormous variety of monetary currencies circulated in the Middle Ages. Not only did their value change over time, but price structures were unstable and profoundly different from those of the modern world. Most monetary figures cited in this book are either in English pounds sterling or in French *livres parisis* (Parisian pounds). The structure, purchasing power, and exchange rates of these currencies, along with medieval systems of measure, are discussed in detail toward the end of Chapter 2.

Technical terminology in the Middle Ages tended to be extremely fluid. In an age before dictionaries or mass media, the means for standardization of language were limited, and the medieval tendency toward localism intensifies the difficulty of identifying authoritative terms for specific phenomena. Technical terminology applied to aspects of medieval culture therefore tends to be the creation of the historian, not of the Middle Ages themselves. This does not negate the usefulness or validity of the historian's technical terms—it is merely worth remembering that these terms should ultimately be the tools rather than the subject of analysis. Specialized terms that are unlikely to be familiar to the ordinary reader have been included in a glossary at the end of the text.

Since this book is oriented toward introductory study rather than advanced research, I have tried to keep the apparatus to a minimum. A classified, selected bibliography appears at the end of the book listing some of the most useful general sources on various aspects of the medieval world. Sources on specific settings are listed in footnotes in each of the relevant chapters. In keeping with the introductory purpose of this text, I have tried to emphasize English-language books in the bibliography.

Historical Background

The history of feudal Europe in the High Middle Ages is distinguished more by established and evolving institutions than by decisive political events. The conquest of England in 1066 by William, duke of Normandy, may be regarded as the last echo of the national migrations that characterized the early Middle Ages. In following centuries, the monarchs of Europe strove against overmighty barons at home while competing for dominion with rival powers abroad. Perhaps the single most important figure in these struggles was the pope. During the early Middle Ages, the political power of the papacy had been limited, and control of church affairs lay as much in the hands of local secular authorities as with the church hierarchy. Beginning in the eleventh century, the papacy's efforts to assert control over the church led to conflict with the kings of Europe. Typical of these conflicts was the "investiture controversy" in the Holy Roman Empire. The emperors, heirs to a part of Charlemagne's empire corresponding roughly to the boundaries of modern Germany, had traditionally exercised the right to invest bishops with the insignia of their office. In 1075 Pope Gregory VII forbade this practice, since it implied that the bishops were subject to the emperor's authority. The emperor Henry IV refused to surrender authority over the bishops, who played a significant part in secular as well as ecclesiastical government within the empire. In the ensuing conflict, Henry had his German bishops declare Gregory deposed from the papacy, while Gregory excommunicated Henry and likewise declared him deposed. The princes of the empire took the opportunity to revolt, and Henry was forced to visit the pope as a penitent to have the sanctions lifted. Nonetheless, the conflict between pope and emperor continued: in the twelfth and thirteenth centuries much of it was played out in the city states and kingdoms of Italy, where the two powers vied for influence and authority.

The rivalry between secular and ecclesiastical authorities was slower to emerge in France and England. The medieval kingdom of France covered roughly the same area as the modern state, but in 1100 it was divided into powerful fiefdoms under limited royal control. Among these, the duchy of Normandy was held by the king of England, and English involvement in France increased with the accession of Henry II to the English throne, since Henry was already lord of Anjou and Maine, and by his marriage to Eleanor of Aquitaine had gained authority over most of southwestern France. However, English holdings in France were diminished after Henry's death, while the kings of France managed to increase their control over the kingdom. By 1300 France was considered the most powerful kingdom in Europe, in part thanks to a uniquely stable dynasty that had managed to produce a clear line of male successors for several centuries, as well as by the efforts of the able kings Phillip II (Phillip Augustus), Louis IX

(St. Louis), and Phillip IV (Phillip the Fair), who cultivated relations with the rising urban elites as a counterweight to aristocratic power.

Relations with France dominated much of English history in the High Middle Ages, but the English kings, like the German emperors, also experienced difficulties with the papacy. Relations with the church came to a head under Henry II, whose determination to curtail ecclesiastical liberties within his kingdom brought him into conflict with the Archbishop of Canterbury, Thomas à Becket; this dispute led to Becket's murder by some of Henry's knights in 1170. Henry's son John wrangled with the pope over the election of the Archbishop of Canterbury and was eventually forced into a humiliating submission. John also embroiled himself in war with the king of France, and his failure in this war, along with the expense incurred, helped provoke a rebellion of the English barons. The barons allied themselves with the French king, and compelled the king to agree to the Magna Carta, a charter restricting royal authority that has come to symbolize the rights of the governed in the English-speaking world. Civil strife persisted during the reign of John's son Henry III, but at the end of the thirteenth century, Henry's son Edward I managed to expand the authority of the English king, especially by his conquest of Wales, while his summoning of England's first complete Parliament in 1295 offered an enduring model for consensual government.

Much of the political history of Europe in this period is a catalogue of disputes and wars among the European powers, but this was also the age of the Crusades, which often involved unprecedented levels of international cooperation. The First Crusade, declared by the pope in 1095, fell upon an Islamic world divided and unprepared, and within a few short years Jerusalem was captured and a string of crusader states were established along the eastern Mediterranean coast. Subsequent Crusades were either disappointing or disastrous. During the twelfth century the advantage passed to the local Islamic rulers, and by 1300 European holdings in the Holy Land had been entirely swept away. In the end, the most lasting expansion of Christian Europe was not in the Middle East, but in the margins of Europe itself. The Iberian peninsula, once largely under Islamic control, was almost entirely under Christian dominion by 1300, while on the eastern shores of the Baltic Sea, German colonists established themselves at the expense of pagan Slavs.

A MEDIEVAL TIMELINE

1st century B.C.	Establishment of Roman Empire
A.D. 3rd century	Germanic tribes begin to invade the Roman Empire
4th century	Roman Empire adopts Christianity
	Roman Empire divides into Eastern and Western Empires
5th century	Western Roman Empire collapses
6th century	St. Benedict establishes his rule for monastic life
8th century	Arabs invade Mediterranean Europe
800	Charlemagne is crowned Holy Roman Emperor by the pope
9th–10th centuries	Viking raids in northern Europe
10th century	Emergence of castles and knights
1095–1099	First Crusade captures Jerusalem and establishes the Crusader States
1147–1149	Second Crusade
ca. 1150	Geoffrey of Monmouth writes his *History of the Kings of Britain*, popularizing the legend of King Arthur
1154	Accession of Henry II of England
1163	Work begins on the cathedral of Notre-Dame in Paris
1170	Murder of Archbishop Thomas Becket in England
1180	Accession of Phillip II of France (Phillip Augustus)
1187	Saladin captures Jerusalem from Christians
1189	Accession of Richard I of England (Richard the Lionhearted)
1189–1192	Third Crusade recaptures Acre but fails to take Jerusalem
1199	Accession of King John of England
ca. 1200	Emergence of banks in Italy
	Emergence of the University of Paris

1

MEDIEVAL SOCIETY

W E ARE INCLINED TODAY TO ROMANTICIZE THE MIDDLE AGES as a time when things were simpler, but in reality medieval society was highly complex. Modern societies are structured by documents and constitutions, and many of their pivotal relationships are defined by abstract institutions like governments and corporations. In the Middle Ages, society was shaped by personal relationships like kinship and patronage; these structures were perpetuated not by abstract institutions but by the personal ties of inheritance. The force of tradition gave these personal relationships some stability, but they were never static. Relationships changed over time in response to changing circumstances, and the actual social structure at any given place and time was an intricate network reflecting a whole history of personal relationships. One peasant might enjoy more rights than his neighbor because one of his forebears had been particularly assertive in his relationship to the manor lord; a baron might be required to provide extra knights for the king's service because his great-grandfather had been a poor negotiator.

The more we study the medieval world, the more complex it becomes. In later chapters of this book we will look at specific settings to see something of the complexity of local conditions, but to understand these settings we need a frame of reference. Medieval society was in many ways profoundly different from our own, and in these first three chapters we will look at some of the general features of the medieval world to help orient the modern reader in this alien territory. These features derive from common factors that gave the diverse manifestations

ILLUSTRATION FROM *LES TRÈS RICHES HEURES DU DUC DE BERRY, created between ca. 1412–1440, and one of the best surviving examples of a French Gothic illuminated manuscript. The foreground scene shows peasants sowing fields, with a scarecrow-like archer behind them. In the background stands the Palais du Louvre. At the top of the painting is a calendar for the month of October.*

of local life in the medieval world some measure of consistency. Shared historical circumstances and cultural background are the principal unifying factors in this chapter; shared human experiences give shape to Chapter 2; shared technological factors and material circumstances predominate in Chapter 3.

THE FEUDAL HIERARCHY

The Aristocracy

Crucial to any understanding of medieval society is the distinction between aristocrat and commoner, a distinction that reflects both the role of tradition in medieval daily life and the economic realities of medieval society. The Middle Ages inherited from premedieval Europe a cultural association between the free man and the warrior, as well as the tradition of a landowning aristocracy whose role was leadership in war and government. Toward the end of the early Middle Ages, the mounted knight emerged as the predominant force on the battlefield,

MOUNTED KNIGHTS DURING A CRUSADE. *Illustration from the Morgan Bible, a medieval picture Bible that dates to ca. 1244-1254, and is considered a masterpiece of Gothic art.*

and the class of arms-bearing free men was gradually redivided. Those who served as knights on horseback were assimilated into the aristocracy, often receiving land as a means of supporting their expensive military equipment, and the aristocracy itself came to be seen as society's warrior class. The rest, whose military service was now of minimal importance, lost status, and were increasingly assimilated into the category of the unfree.

The power and distinctive status of the warrior aristocracy were perpetuated by ongoing social realities. As the warrior class, the aristocracy had the power to acquire and hold wealth and its sources, while advances in military technology further concentrated power in their hands. Improved armor raised the cost of military equipment while widening the gulf between the effectiveness of a peasant spearman and a fully equipped warrior. Even more important was the introduction of the stirrup, which made possible a new form of warfare based on the power of the mounted knight. The knight was enormously expensive to train, maintain, and equip, but he was virtually unbeatable on the battlefield until the rise of the longbow and pike in the fourteenth century. The aristocracy had the resources to take advantage of the new technology, and their hold on those resources was reinforced by the technology itself.

Aristocratic status was inherited: again, this reflected the force of tradition as well as the natural inclination of parents to use their resources to benefit their children. Many of the medieval aristocracy had their ancestry among the Germanic warriors who had invaded the Roman Empire during its declining days, taking over the land as their own, and in some cases adopting the positions of the former Roman landlords. Others belonged to families that had entered the aristocracy more recently through some combination of military, political, and economic success. The line between aristocrat and commoner was never so firm that it could not be crossed through prosperity or decline, although the transition usually took more than a single generation.

There was enormous variation in wealth, power, and status among aristocrats. The wealthiest aristocrats in England in the thirteenth century might have an annual income of around £5,000, about five hundred times more than the poorest. At the top were the kings and upper nobility, whose extensive networks of patronage placed them in authority over large territories and populations, allowing them a major political role at the national and international level. Below them were aristocrats whose authority was more limited, some having only a few other aristocrats under their power, others at an even lower level having authority only over commoners; this last group corresponded to landowning knights. The very lowest tier of the aristocracy were those who had no governmental authority at all, professional warriors of aristocratic families who could only support themselves by taking military service with a greater aristocrat. Such men had significantly less wealth and power than the upper levels of commoners, and vastly less than the upper levels of their own class.

Within its own ranks, the aristocracy was highly stratified. A simple knight who rose through good fortune to join the titled nobility would be regarded as an upstart by other noblemen. Yet relative to society as a whole, the aristocracy shared a common culture and social image that associated the mighty duke with the landless knight rather than with the wealthy merchant. Both duke and knight were officially warriors, born to the role by right of inheritance, and claiming generations of ancestors who had been born to this status before them. Both maintained their elite status by participating in a courtly culture that became increasingly elaborate over the course of the Middle Ages. This culture involved not only the cultivation of martial skills such as swordsmanship and riding, but also an appreciation of arts such as poetry and music, familiarity with courtly pastimes such as hunting and chess, and command of an ever-changing code of fashion and etiquette. Wealthy commoners in search of social status, always latecomers to the world of privilege, were perpetually playing a game whose rules had already been set by the aristocracy.

All in all, the aristocracy of the High Middle Ages probably constituted about 1 percent of the population, but their power and influence were far greater than their actual numbers. In particular, the distinctively medieval institution of feudalism was dominated by the aristocracy, and as the framework of medieval law and government, it shaped the lives even of those who did not participate in it directly.

Feudalism

Feudalism took shape in the vacuum of authority left by the collapse of the Roman Empire in western Europe. The empire in its heyday furnished Europe with a highly developed political and economic infrastructure: roads, coinage, defense, governmental stability. As the empire withdrew from the West, the infrastructure withered, and each locality was obliged to look to its own resources. During the early Middle Ages, society rebuilt itself in response to the new political realities, and new systems of social organization evolved to replace those once provided by Rome. Feudalism emerged as a viable social framework that could function even in a relatively anarchic environment.

The most important factors in the feudal equation were land and military power. The two were closely interdependent, since those who had military power could assert and maintain control over land, while those who controlled land could amass the wealth needed to support military power. The emphasis on land reflected the low yield of agricultural produce to agricultural labor, which required nine-tenths of the population to be engaged in farming. It was also a natural result of the limited infrastructure for industry and trade. Although commerce came to play an increasingly important role in the economy of the High Middle Ages, land remained the greatest and most reliable source of wealth. The importance of military power in feudalism was a response to the weakness of governmental authority. After the collapse of the empire, western Europe could no longer look to the legions of Rome to ward off raids or invasions from without, or to keep the peace within. The advantage lay with those who could amass significant local military forces.

In the absence of centralized governmental authority, people look to personal relationships to bind society together. Feudalism evolved as a hierarchical system of personal relationships in which land and military power were the principal commodities exchanged. An individual with military power to offer gave his services to a feudal lord. The lord in turn secured his subordinate in the possession of the land that financed his military service. The feudal subordinate was called a vassal, and the vassal's land was termed a fee or fief (*feudum* in Latin, which is the source of the term "feudal"). A vassal who held a great deal

IN THIS SCENE FROM THE BAYEUX TAPESTRY, *Harold (right), future King of England, swears an oath to William (left), Duke of Normandy, in an act similar to a vassal swearing homage to his lord. Translated, the Latin text at the top reads "Where Harold made an oath to Duke William."*

of land might in turn grant fiefs to his own feudal tenants, who helped him fulfill his military obligations to his lord. Long-term stability was provided by the principle of heredity, as the feudal relationships between individuals were extended to apply to their heirs.

Feudal landholding lay somewhere between modern tenancy and ownership. The holder was considered the tenant rather than the owner of the holding. In principle, the lord might grant the fief at his will whenever it became empty. In practice, fiefs were treated as permanent and hereditary property, granted by the lord to the heir when the holder died, and only falling empty if there was no heir, or if the holder was forcefully dispossessed. Tenants regularly sold their tenancies, although the lord's permission had to be sought for the transaction. Heritability was advantageous for both lord and vassal, allowing the vassal to pass the property on to his heirs, and providing stability for the lord.

The feudal transaction was more than a bartering of land for military service. The feudal tenant held some measure of legal jurisdiction and political authority over his holding and subtenants. At the same time, his status as a vassal involved more than just military service. The vassal did homage to the lord, symbolizing his status as his lord's man *(homme* in French), owing him generalized loyalty and political support, while the lord in turn promised his patronage.

The king was the supreme feudal power in a kingdom. In theory, he was the owner and ruler of all the land, and delegated his authority to his tenants. In practice, his authority was often subject to challenge from his great lords, who together could wield military power comparable to his own. Not all land was held from a king or feudal lord. Some was held as inalienable property, called an *allod*. The holder of an allod might owe some form of allegiance to a suzerain (superior feudal lord). Suzerainty was a looser form of overlordship than sovereignty: the vassal owed homage to the lord, but because his feudal holding was not considered dependent on that relationship, homage was harder to enforce. Allods were not a feature of English feudalism, but they existed in France and were common in Germany.

Although historians sometimes speak of "the feudal system," feudalism was far from systematic. It evolved locally in response to local situations, and varied enormously from place to place. If a system can be perceived, it is because of shared circumstances, and because there was a degree of cultural contact and common cultural inheritance. Feudalism was complex, and the details varied greatly. Large landholdings were rarely solid blocks of territory, but scattered patchworks of feudal lands. Military service was commonly for forty days in the year, but it could be longer or shorter. The basic unit of feudal responsibility was the knight's service, the duty to provide a single mounted knight to serve one's lord. The exact number of services owed varied from fief to fief, depending partly on the value of the land, but also on the historical traditions associated with the holding. The distribution of power shifted over time, making new demands possible and old customs unenforceable, and in time these temporary shifts could themselves become established customs.

The Commoners

Feudal society was based on a fundamental distinction between the aristocracy, whose function was military and governmental, and the commoners, the 98 percent of the population whose role it was to labor. Like the aristocracy, commoners inherited their status from their parents. Most were rural workers, living under the manorial system that mirrored many of the structures of the feudal hierarchy. The manor was the smallest unit of feudal landholding, typically a few hundred acres. It was essentially a holding sufficient to support an aristocratic household, including its most important feudal element, the knight. The manor lord parceled out some portion of his land to peasant tenants, keeping the rest in his own hands as demesne land to be cultivated for his own benefit. Like feudal vassals, the peasants provided service in exchange for their land, in this case labor service that the lord used to cultivate his demesne.

In addition, the lord exercised legal and governmental authority over the manor peasants. The nature of this jurisdiction depended on each peasant's personal status. In general, the medieval commoner was classed as free or unfree. Like other forms of personal status in the Middle Ages, freedom and unfreedom were inherited. People born of unfree parents were unfree themselves. In mixed unions, the customs varied, but commonly, legitimate children inherited their father's status, illegitimate ones their mother's. Unfree peasants, also called serfs or villeins, were personally subject to their manor lord in a manner that served to guarantee him a stable supply of labor: the serf was obliged to provide certain labor services for the lord (see Chapter 4), and he had to have the lord's permission to move away from the manor.

The institution of serfdom had some of its roots in the older practice of slavery, and the serf's status was in some ways akin to that of a slave. By the High Middle Ages, it was no longer considered appropriate for Christians to own other Christians as slaves, and true slavery persisted only at the margins of Europe where Christians were in contact with non-Christian societies. Serfdom, meanwhile, had been shaped by centuries of customs that tended to ease some of the serf's disadvantages, so that it would be misleading to equate serfdom with slavery. Serfs owed services to their lord, but these were limited by custom. A serf could be bought and sold, but the buyer acquired only the lord's traditional rights over the serf, not complete ownership. A serf's personal property in theory belonged to the lord, but in practice lords only collected traditional rents, fees, and fines from their serfs.

The idea of freedom and unfreedom was part of the shared heritage of medieval European cultures, dating back to ancient times, but its local manifestations in the Middle Ages were complex. There was a wide variety of local traditions and a spectrum of degrees of servitude. Even a free peasant might owe labor services, while not all serfs were subject to the full obligations of serfdom. There was a gray area in the middle where the categories of free and unfree were hard to apply. In parts of Europe, there were even quasi-aristocratic serfs known to historians as *ministerials*. The ministerials were descended from serfs who had served their lords as soldiers or administrators. Because of their ancestors' prestigious and influential work, their heirs enjoyed a certain aristocratic status that entitled them to hold feudal fiefs and become knights, yet they remained technically unfree. Ministerials were unknown in England, but they existed in France and were common in Germany and the Low Countries; in some parts of Germany, a majority of the knights were of unfree origin.

Although serfs were not necessarily subject to the kinds of social or economic disadvantages that we might expect from their unfree status, they nonetheless perceived serfdom as an undesirable state. Numerous court cases of the period document the efforts of individual peasants to prove that they were not serfs, and resentment of serfdom was a factor in the Peasants' Revolt that erupted in England in 1381, since one of the principal demands of the rebels was the abolition of serfdom. The revolt was unsuccessful, but social and economic trends were already causing serfdom to decline. In the increasingly monetary economy of the High Middle Ages, many lords and serfs agreed to convert labor services into monetary payments. Some serfs were given their freedom outright, or purchased it from their lords. As a result, the unfree portion of the population declined over the course of the Middle Ages. In some places in the mid-eleventh century, serfs may have constituted 90 percent of the peasantry, but by the early fourteenth century, the figure may have been closer to one half.

The feudal and manorial hierarchy were defined by the aristocracy who were its principal beneficiaries. It is less clear how ordinary commoners perceived the social structure, since their perspective is generally missing from the written record. To some degree, they were participants in the feudal structure, yielding labor and taxes to their feudal lords, taking an active part in manorial institutions such as the manor court, and providing officers for the enforcement of the lord's manorial rights. It is far from certain, however, that the official distinctions between aristocrat and commoner or free and unfree were as important to the peasant as they were to his manor lord. Regardless of the serfs' resentment of their status, the distinction between serf and free commoner does not seem to have played a role in determining social status among commoners, and manorial records are full of small acts of resistance to the lord's authority. In the day-to-day life of the medieval commoner, relationships within the local community probably mattered more than the official feudal hierarchy.

Law and Government

The feudal and manorial structure went hand in hand with government and law. Political and judicial authority followed the contours of the feudal structure, with local manor lords exercising local jurisdiction, regional feudal lords wielding power over wider territories, and kings claiming a sovereign power that reached all levels of society. Generally speaking, law was seen as consisting of a community's traditional customs, and the function of a lord was to uphold those customs, consulting with his subordinates about their nature and applicability in any given situation. A lord also exercised political authority, but he was again expected to consult with his subordinates on matters that traditionally required their advice. In this way feudalism allowed, at least in principle, for the consent of the governed. The local manor lord presided over the manor court, but it was his peasant tenants who constituted the jury that actually ruled on legal disputes. The lord might exert his influence to sway their judgment, but contemporary advice recommended that he leave them to follow their own consciences. Feudal overlords and kings likewise consulted their vassals in their own courts and councils. A lord might invoke prerogative and override the will of his subordinates, but such a course could reap a bitter harvest. An overbearing manor lord might find his peasants recalcitrant and unproductive, and kings who gave no heed to the advice of their great lords ran the risk of an aristocratic rebellion.

On both sides, choices were heavily circumscribed by custom. In principle, a court only adjudicated on the basis of existing tradition, although there was leeway in the interpretation of tradition that allowed for a certain measure of de facto legislation. Similarly, a feudal lord, in principle, exercised only such authority as was traditionally assigned to him and his forebears, although the actual interpretation of how far that authority extended was susceptible to influence from current circumstances. If a lord was in a strong political position, he and his subordinates might take a generous interpretation of his traditional authority, but if his position was weak, he might find his powers eroded. The exercise of power could also be restricted from above. If a subordinate felt his lord had acted wrongly, he might appeal to the overlord, and kings in particular saw themselves as having a legitimate interest in justice at every level of society.

Punishment was generally determined by traditional expectations. Minor civil infractions commonly incurred a fine. Significant violations of morality, such as dishonesty or promiscuity, might entail some ritual of public humiliation, such as confinement in a pillory or walking in a procession in one's shirt through the streets. Criminal justice tended to be savage, reflecting in part the weakness of law enforcement. Criminals were hard to apprehend in a world with weak central governments and limited means of communication, and the legal system compensated for the rarity of punishment by handling convicted criminals severely: whipping for minor crimes, mutilation for more serious ones, and death for the most grave. Even a thief might be subject to capital punishment. Yet the very severity of the punishments often made it harder to secure convictions from courts that were well aware of the savage penalty a conviction might bring. Terms of imprisonment were not a prominent part of the medieval penal system. Accused criminals might languish in prison for some time awaiting trial, and the convicted might be confined in prison at the pleasure of the offended lord, but long-term incarceration was generally restricted to political prisoners.

The Church

Medieval political theory commonly divided society into three estates, consisting of the aristocracy, commoners, and clergy. The clergy, unlike the others, was not born into its class, but entered into it as a career, whether by choice or compulsion. Clerics were in large measure drawn from the aristocracy, particularly at the upper levels of church administration, but a clerical career was also one of the few avenues of advancement open to the lower levels of society. Like the aristocracy, the clergy constituted only a tiny fraction of the population, perhaps another 1 percent.

GERMAN ILLUSTRATION FROM *1492, depicting the three estates of medieval society standing before Christ for judgment. The pope of the Roman Catholic Church (left) and the emperor of the Holy Roman Empire (right) lead their respective estates, while two peasants represent the third.*

The clergy was divided into secular and regular clerics. The secular clergy ministered directly to the public at large (in Latin, *seculum,* the temporal world). The most common secular cleric was the parish priest who conducted religious services at the local church for the residents of the area, in some cases with the assistance of a staff of lesser clerics. Above the parish priest was a vast administrative hierarchy that covered all of Europe. The bishop administered a diocese that was composed of hundreds of parish churches. He was assisted in his duties by a substantial staff of church officers, notably a body of priests called canons who conducted religious services in the cathedral, or episcopal church, and took part in the administration of the diocese. Above the bishop was the archbishop, whose authority might extend over a half-dozen to a dozen dioceses, and at the head of the church as a whole was the pope. Both archbishops and the pope had large administrative staffs of their own, also drawn from the clergy.

The regular clergy was originally limited to monks, who sought spiritual perfection by withdrawing from the secular world and living communal lives according to a codified rule of organization and conduct (in Latin, *regula,* rule). In time, other clerics became regular clergy by taking on the communal mode of life under a rule, while continuing to interact with the secular world. Many groups of cathedral canons adopted rules, and eventually houses of regular canons were established independent of cathedrals. Regular canons enjoyed the strengths of monastic discipline and organization while still being permitted to interact with the world at large, a combination that made them extremely useful to both the church and secular society. During the High Middle Ages, there arose new regular orders called mendicants or friars, who also lived communally under a rule, but existed specifically to minister to the secular world. The regular clergy, like the secular, was ultimately subject to the authority of the pope.

The church wielded influence comparable to that of the aristocracy. The importance attached to so small a group reflects the status of religion in medieval society. There was no distinction between church and state, or even between church and community: to be a part of society was to be part of the church. This aspect of medieval society had roots in the premedieval world. The Roman Empire required its subjects to honor the state religion in addition to their own local deities, and among the barbarians religion was closely tied to a tribe's communal identity. Christianity was oriented more toward personal spirituality than were the older pagan religions of Europe, but in becoming the official religion in Europe it also took on the social roles once occupied by paganism.

The medieval church constituted a kind of second social system, sharing governmental authority with the feudal hierarchy, and occasionally coming in conflict with secular lords over disputed rights. Every community and neighborhood was under the auspices of a parish. The church had its own law code, called canon law, and a system of church courts to enforce it, exercising authority over many aspects of people's lives. Marriage and its legal ramifications fell under the jurisdiction of the church, and wills were also solemnized and enforced by church authority. The church was also responsible for what today would be termed moral legislation, including such matters as adultery, fornication, and blasphemy.

Overall, the administrative hierarchy of the church was more orderly than the jumble of feudal relationships. Unlike feudalism, the church was defined by a centralized and, to some degree, planned system of organization, and in many ways it was the heir in the West to the governmental structures of the Roman Empire. Many of the bishops' seats were still located in the administrative cities of the Empire, and the diocese was itself a unit of Roman civil administration.

In Western Europe, the Catholic Church was the only officially permitted form of Christianity. Various non-Catholic sects existed in the West, but lacking official sanction, they had to survive more or less underground. The most widespread of these sects were the Cathars, who believed that God and the Devil were two equal powers in eternal conflict. The Cathars were numerous in southern France, where they actually enjoyed a significant degree of unofficial support from some of the local lords, but their community was always at risk from official Catholicism. In the early thirteenth century, the church declared a crusade against them, with the support of the king of France, who saw an opportunity to strengthen his hold on the south. The independence of Catharism's aristocratic patrons was crushed, and over the next century Catharism declined swiftly in the face of ongoing persecution and conversion by the Catholic authorities. Outside of the West, the Eastern Orthodox Church was the officially established religion in most of eastern Europe. The Orthodox Church differed from Catholicism in many points of tradition, organization, and ceremony, but the doctrines of the two churches were close enough that many continued to hope for a reconciliation long after East and West went their separate ways in the early Middle Ages.

There were also a number of non-Christians in Europe. At the margins of Europe Christians came into contact with other religions: pagan Slavs in the east and Muslims in the south. Relations with non-Christian neighbors were unstable, often in a state of war, and those who were captured on either side were likely to be sold into slavery. Within Christian Europe, Jews were found in many European towns. There was a significant Muslim population in the south, particularly in Spain and southern Italy—parts of Spain remained in Muslim control until the end of the fifteenth century. In a society where church and community were one, these non-Christians were foreigners by definition, tolerated at best, but always at risk in a society where their legal status was precarious. Some medieval Europeans collaborated with non-Christians to make Jewish and Arabic learning accessible in Europe, but at times the same non-Christians were severely persecuted.

While the intermingling of religion and society allowed the church enormous influence over people's lives, their religious culture was not exclusively defined by the church. Most medieval people would have described themselves as Christians, but their actual interaction with Christian belief was not always orthodox. Popular participation in the official church was more limited than it is for many people today. Church attendance was sporadic, communion was taken only a few times during the year, and the quality of religious education was uneven in a world where even the priest was not necessarily well informed as to the nature of Christian doctrine. At the same time, popular religion reshaped Christianity to suit its own needs. The priest was called upon to provide blessings for salt, butter, and cheese, to bless eggs at Easter and seeds at planting time, to bless a child before its first haircut, to bless a boy before his first shave. People had their own rituals and superstitions that combined elements of Christian practice with traditional folk culture.

WOMEN IN THE MEDIEVAL WORLD

Far older, deeper, and in some ways more elusive than the medieval distinctions of class, was the division between the sexes. Modern scholars sometimes refer to women as the fourth estate of medieval society: the aristocracy, commoners, and clergy all included women, but to some degree these women had more in common with each other than with the men of their own estate. In every case, women were officially seen as standing in a position of subordination to men, and their powers of choice were always circumscribed to a greater or lesser degree by both official social structures and unofficial customs.

The official constraints on women were probably least restrictive among commoners. In a laboring household, women were generally assigned roles pertaining directly to the

ILLUSTRATION FROM *LES TRÈS RICHES HEURES DU DUC DE BERRY, created between ca. 1412–1440. In this scene, which takes places on the River Seine across from the palace in Paris, two women reap hay in the foreground while other peasants farm land in the background.*

home itself, while the man engaged in more external work. A woman's domestic responsibilities included maintaining the house, preparing food, mending clothes, and raising children. She also contributed directly to provisioning the household by raising poultry, dairying, and tending the garden; she might also engage in moneymaking labor within the home, such as spinning and brewing. Among the peasantry, it was quite common for women to take part in field labor during harvest time, and there is evidence that women were hired for a wide variety of agricultural work. In the towns, some trades were closed to women, others might be acquired by a woman from her father or husband, and some were principally occupied by female workers (see Chapter 7). An advocate of monastic life for women around the year 1200 offered this vivid, albeit biased, vignette of the pressures of a woman's domestic life:

> When she comes in the house, the wife hears her child screaming, sees the
> cat at the bacon, and the dog gnawing her hides; her biscuit is burning on
> the stone, and her calf is sucking up her milk; the crock is boiling over into
> the fire, and the husband is scolding.[1]

As one moves up the social scale, the pressure to earn a living decreases, and the preoccupation with proper social roles grows accordingly. An aristocratic woman might enjoy more power because of her social station, but she was at the same time more limited by the constraints of her class. An aristocratic wife, like her commoner counterpart, might have particular responsibility for running the household, and during her husband's absence might even administer the family estates. However, she would not normally participate in the aristocratic work of warfare or government. One of the standard courtly skills of the aristocratic woman was needlework, an extremely time-consuming activity whose prominence in the lady's routine suggests that she had an excess of idle hours to fill.

Women's participation in the clergy was the most restricted of all. Women could not become priests, so they were cut off from a large part of the activity of the church. The only clerical route open to women was in the regular clergy, living the monastic life as nuns, or, from the thirteenth century onward, joining one of the female orders associated with the mendicants. The life of such women, like that of the monks, was restricted by the rules of their order, which for women tended to be even more restrictive than for men. Yet women in the cloister might achieve a level of education not usually available to women at the time, and they were free from direct and constant male authority to a degree uncommon in medieval society in general.

Across the social spectrum, women were officially viewed as secondary people who were expected to be in a position of subordination: a girl to her father, a laboring woman to her employer, a wife to her husband. Even a widow, who in some parts of Europe enjoyed a certain measure of liberty, reverted in others to the authority of her original kinsmen. Yet the official view is not the whole story. As in later centuries, women who were restricted by the official order of things found unofficial alternatives. Aristocratic women, denied a role in government, manipulated the terms of their society by setting the tone of the aristocracy's cultural life. The twelfth-century German abbess Hildegard of Bingen, who could never perform the sacraments by which the priest mediated between man and God, became a mystic, and communed with God directly. Here, as in other aspects of medieval society, the version of history that finds its way into the written record is often created from the official point of view. The thirteenth-century regulations of the poulterers of Paris declare sententiously that "The man is not under the lordship of the woman, but the woman is under the lordship of the man"; but another hand has added in the margin, "Not always."[2]

2

THE LIFE CYCLE

CHILDHOOD

If we wish to see medieval life from the point of view of those who lived it, one of the best starting points is to enter the medieval world as they did, through the experience of childhood. At the moment of birth, medieval people were not very different from their descendants today—a millennium is not a long time for evolution—nor was the moment of birth very different from one medieval household to another. It was the years of childhood development that made medieval people distinctive as individuals of their time, place, and social setting.

Birth

The birth of a child in the Middle Ages normally took place in bed at the home of the mother. Hospital childbirth is a fairly recent innovation, and in fact the medieval world had no hospitals in the modern sense. Nor was it normal for a doctor to be involved, for childbirth was seen as a matter for women. The mother was assisted by her female relatives and friends, and if any sort of medical practitioner was present, it was usually a midwife. The midwife's professional status varied with the setting. In privileged households and towns, it was possible to call in a professional midwife, but in a small village the mother probably relied on the services of a neighbor or relative who had learned her skills through years of attendance at local childbirths. Only rarely were men involved in childbirth. A husband might assist if it was not possible to bring in any women, and a physician or surgeon might be called in if the delivery proved particularly difficult.

A WOMAN AND HER SUITOR *take a walk through the countryside in this Flemish miniature from an illuminated manuscript, ca. 1465.*

Yet it does seem that husbands were expected to play some sort of supportive role: Parisian guild regulations of the thirteenth century exempt men whose wives were in childbed from serving in the night watch.[1]

Birth was a moment of heightened danger both for the mother and child, although complications were the exception rather than the rule. Statistics on maternal mortality are rare for the Middle Ages, but in fifteenth-century Florence there were 14.4 maternal deaths for every 1,000 births. Such a figure suggests that death in childbirth was an unusual event, but still extremely high by modern standards—about twice the rate of the poorest countries of the Third World today.[2] If the mother died, the midwife or surgeon might perform a Caesarean section to deliver the child; if the child died, it might be necessary to extract it from the womb with a hook, an operation that could be quite dangerous to the mother.

Even if the delivery was successful, the child's prospects remained uncertain. Children have relatively weak immune systems, and the high incidence of disease and limited medical knowledge of the period meant that many children never reached adulthood. During the thirteenth century, about one child in six may have died in the first year, one in four by age five; perhaps two-thirds lived to age twenty.[3]

The arrival of the new child was marked by the ceremony of baptism. This sacrament was considered vitally important, since the church taught that the unbaptized could not enter heaven. Ideally, the baptism took place about a month after birth, but the peril of infant mortality sometimes required that the ceremony take place sooner. In an emergency, even a layperson might make the sign of the cross on the child and recite the baptismal formula, "*Ego baptizo te N. in nomine Patris et Filii et Spiritus Sancti Amen*" [I baptize you X, in the name of the Father and the Son and the Holy Spirit, Amen]. If the outcome of the delivery seemed in doubt, the midwife was enjoined to make the sign of the cross on the first limb that appeared.

If there were no complications, the baptism would be performed by a priest at the family's parish church, which had a baptismal font near the entrance for this purpose. By the High Middle Ages, it had become normal to sprinkle the child with the baptismal water, but some priests still adhered to the older practice of immersion as late as the thirteenth century. The priest also placed a pinch of salt in the child's mouth, and rubbed its chest and back with oil. Then the child was lifted from the font by its godparents, who promised on the child's behalf that it would abjure sin and undertook to educate the child in the Christian faith.

One of the most important elements of the baptismal ceremony was the assigning of a name. The child at baptism received only a single name—the term "Christian name" still survives today. In many cases, the parents would choose the name of a favorite saint, perhaps the saint on whose day the child was born. It was also common to choose a traditional name from the child's family, or perhaps the name of one of the child's godparents. Only when the child grew and began to enter the wider world would it have need of an additional name. For aristocratic children, family names were fairly well established by the High Middle Ages, but among ordinary people, surnames were more fluid. People might acquire an additional name indicating their parentage (Johnson), their dwelling or origin (Fleming, *le Flamand),* what they did (Smith, *le Fèvre)* or what they looked like (Small, *le Petit).* Some additional names could be quite colorful personal descriptions. Alice *Sans-Argent* (Lack-Money), a resident of Paris in the late thirteenth century, would appear to have had financial problems. Added names were still unstable in this period, and people might have several of them during the course of their lives. Sometimes these names stuck, and were passed on to the children, eventually becoming family names. Even elaborate personal descriptions might be passed on in the family. Robert *Qui-ne-ment,* who lived just outside the walls of Paris, might seem to have had a reputation for honesty— his name means "who does not lie"—but his neighbors also included Alain, Guillot, and Richard *Qui-ne-ment.*[4]

Baptism was not merely a religious occasion. In a society where church and community were so closely associated, religious observances inevitably became important social events. After the baptism, it was common to have some sort of celebration involving the child's family and their friends, and the occasion was often marked by gift giving.

The Family

The composition of the medieval family was not unlike that in Western countries today. It was common for couples to produce five children or more during their wedded life, but the high rate of child mortality meant that the typical couple had only two or three living children. On the average, family size reflected economic status: rich families tended to have more children, poorer families fewer. Yet the medieval household often extended beyond the nuclear family. A household might include unmarried relatives, or elderly parents who had reached the end of their working lives. Such an extended family was not necessarily very common, but even a fairly ordinary household might include dependent servants and employees. The presence of household members apart from the nuclear family again tended to reflect the family's social status, the more prosperous families supporting larger households.

The birth order of the children in a family might play a large part in shaping their future. Some regions of Europe adhered to the ancient principle of partible inheritance, in which all the male children of a family had a right to a part of the family's wealth (if there were no male heirs, the property was split among the daughters). Partible inheritance was particularly characteristic of peasant society in communities that relied heavily on animal husbandry rather than grain cultivation. The aristocracy of the early Middle Ages had meanwhile shifted toward the system of primogeniture, in which the principal inheritance, especially the family lands, went to the eldest son. Many peasant communities, particularly in grain-raising regions, also adopted this form of inheritance. Primogeniture helped keep the family's wealth and political power intact over the generations, but it severely limited the opportunities for younger siblings.

Child Care

Responsibilities within the household were generally distributed by gender, and childrearing fell within the female domain. During the first six years or so of life, the child was almost entirely in the hands of women. For the first two of these years, female care was more or less dictated by biological necessity. Breastfeeding was the only satisfactory means of nourishing an infant, since animals' milk

THE WIFE OF HASDRUBAL AND HER CHILDREN. *Ercole de' Roberti (Italian), ca. 1490–1493. Tempera on panel.*

was recognized as potentially hazardous (a problem that persisted until the discovery of pasteurization in the nineteenth century). Yet the milk was not always provided by the mother herself. Many wealthy families entrusted their children to the care of a wet nurse, and the practice was also followed in less-privileged households, whether for the sake of fashion, or because the income lost by nursing in person would be greater than the cost of hiring a wet nurse, or for some biological cause that impeded the mother's ability to nurse, for example, if she became pregnant again.

Wealthy families often had the wet nurse live in their home. A live-in nurse required space in the house, but it was much easier to oversee the quality of care she provided. Alternatively, the family could send the child away and visit from time to time to see that it was doing well. The wet nurse, of course, had to be lactating. In some cases, she was a mother whose infant had died—with the high rate of infant mortality, there were always more lactating women than nursing infants. In many instances, she was probably the mother of an older infant who weaned her child early in order to take on wet-nursing. The work paid well in comparison to other service employments: in 1350 the wages for wet nurses in France were fixed at 50 *sous* a year, or 100 *sous* if they were working at home, at a time when a chambermaid's income was only 30 *sous*.[5] In situations where breastfeeding was impossible, for example, if the woman was temporarily unable to nurse, the infant could be fed with a rudimentary feeding bottle made of a small cow's horn, with a hole at the point to which a sort of parchment nipple was attached.

During the first few months of its life, the baby would spend much of its time in swaddling clothes. Depending on local customs, the swaddled baby might be wrapped mummy-style in long bands of linen, with only its face showing, or in a large cloth with a few bands wrapped around it to hold it in place. Sometimes the wrapping left the arms or upper body free. Swaddling may have helped to keep the infant out of trouble, but its principal purpose was to keep it warm, a very real concern in the drafty living conditions of the time. The mummy-style swaddling bands were also intended to ensure that the limbs grew straight, a purpose based on medieval ideas of physiology, which held that a baby's body was so pliant that pulling or pushing on a body part determined how it grew.

The practice of swaddling cannot have made infant hygiene very easy. The linen swaddling cloths were washable, but keeping the baby clean was a challenge that was not always very satisfactorily met. Contemporary doctors emphasized the importance of regular bathing of the infant, and some recommended as many as three baths a day and changes of swaddling whenever the baby soiled itself, but such cleanliness was probably not very common, especially among poorer people. A fourteenth-century German clergyman noted that poor women, who had trouble providing cloth for swaddling bands, did not keep their children clean, but suggested that this uncleanliness was not harmful to the children of the poor.[6]

The swaddled infant spent much of its time in a cradle. As in more recent times, the cradle might have rockers, and some were equipped with straps across the top to keep the baby inside. Such precautions were especially necessary in the hazardous environment of the medieval home. Not only did the house have an open hearth, but in poorer families the cradle often had to be kept close to the fire to keep the baby warm. This put the baby at considerable risk both from the fire itself and from hot water, cooking implements, and other hazards of the hearth.

Most families lacked the facilities to provide much privacy, and throughout their early years children and parents shared the same living quarters. The homes of the wealthy might have been better equipped: the description of one thirteenth-century castle mentions a special heated room for infants. At night, many parents, particularly those in poorer families, had their infants sleep in bed with them. This helped keep the child warm and facilitated midnight nursing, since getting out of bed in the middle of the night in an unheated cottage was extremely uncomfortable for the mother and could bring illness on the child. But sleeping with parents was risky too, and medieval texts often lament the loss of children smothered in the night as the adults turned over in their sleep. Alternatively, baby and cradle spent the night at the foot of the bed. Then as now, lullabies were sung to soothe the baby to sleep.

Over the course of the baby's first few months, its swaddling was reduced, and eventually swaddling was dispensed with altogether. The toddler wore instead a shirt and gown, which must have greatly facilitated hygiene. While it was learning to walk, the child wore a padded bonnet to help protect its head against injury.

As it entered the second year of life, the baby was weaned from breastfeeding. A nursing baby might already have been introduced to other liquids like water, honey-water, or beer. Eventually it received soft solids such as mashed or premasticated food; bread soaked in honey-water, wine or soup; or a pap of flour and milk flavored with honey. Honey was often used to stimulate the child's appetite, although it may have been too expensive for a poor family. By age two the child had its milk teeth, and was fully ready for solid food.

Medieval authors generally reckoned that the first stage of human life lasted until about age seven. This division reflected numerological fascination with the number seven, but in practice the first half-dozen years did constitute a recognizable stage in the life of a medieval child. During this time, the child had virtually no responsibilities; life consisted of a daily round of food, sleep, and play. It was not common for a child to be sent to school before age seven, although basic tutoring might begin earlier. Of course, there was no education for most children, aside from elementary religious instruction, which consisted principally of memorizing the Lord's Prayer, the Creed, and the Ave Maria, all in Latin. People recognized that children of this age lacked the capacity to understand right and wrong, and responsibility for their actions was held to lie with the parents.

SEVEN CHILDREN AT PLAY. *Israhel van Meckenem (German), ca. 1490. Engraving.*

Medieval people also recognized that children had a natural inclination for play. Already as infants they were given simple toys like rattles, and as they grew, their repertoire of toys and games grew. Medieval toys included dolls, clay figurines, hobbyhorses, carts, tops, and whistles. Much of the play of medieval children, like children today, involved transforming the objects in the world around them: soil, wood, and scraps of fabric made dams, boats, mills, and ovens, a stick became a riding horse. The twelfth-century churchman Gerald of Wales recalled that his clerical vocation was evident even in childhood: while his brothers were building castles of sand, he chose to build churches and monasteries.[7]

The Older Child

Somewhere around age seven this period of relative idleness came to an end, as children began to be actively prepared for the expectations imposed by their assigned place in society. The sacrament of confirmation, which marked the child's admission into the church, was administered somewhere between the ages of five and seven, and by age seven or so, boys and girls began to split into their differentiated worlds. Girls remained under female tutelage, learning the skills appropriate to their class. For most girls this meant helping their mothers with tasks around the home, assisting with the care of younger children, and eventually learning the full range of a woman's household responsibilities. These included not only cooking, cleaning, and child care, but also tending the poultry and dairy animals, making butter and cheese, looking after the garden, preparing and spinning wool and flax to make thread, and basic home medicine.

For aristocratic girls, these physical labors were less important, and the emphasis was more on household management, needlework, and the various social graces expected of a lady of good breeding. If an aristocratic family had an excess of daughters, some might be sent to live in a nunnery, where eventually they were expected to profess the religious life when they came of age.

Boys, meanwhile, began the transition from the world of women to that of men. For the overwhelming majority, this meant beginning to participate in the work of agriculture. The physical demands of farm work meant that boys could take part in this work only incrementally, yet there was plenty that they could contribute even at the tender age of seven: removing stones from the fields, scaring away birds once the seed had been sown, and running small errands for the men. As they grew, they could learn more sophisticated tasks, such as herding animals, helping the plowman guide the oxen, and snaring small game.

Boys in the aristocracy headed in one of several directions. Many were prepared for a position in the warrior class by training for knighthood. A boy on this track was usually sent away from his family to the household of some greater lord. There he might live in the company of other boys in the same situation, depending on the status of the household he was entering: the more important the household, the more boys it was likely to have. He was expected to perform domestic services for the household, waiting on the householder at the table and in the chamber, and in exchange he received instruction in the skills appropriate to his class, including aristocratic etiquette, horsemanship, and eventually the arts of combat. He might also learn reading and writing, skills that were becoming increasingly common among the aristocracy, although still far from universal. This course was generally expected of the oldest son, who would in time come to inherit the family's feudal holding, and it was also followed by many younger sons as well.

The principal alternative, and one often followed in the case of younger sons, was a career in the church. This could take a number of forms. A boy might be earmarked for a position in the secular clergy, serving as a priest, with hopes of rising into a prestigious position in the church administration. Alternatively, he might be sent to a monastery, although by the thirteenth century the church had

AFTER A FIGHT, A YOUNG BOY SHOWS HIS WOUNDS TO A CLERIC. *From William of Tyre's* Histoire d'Outremer, *an illuminated French manuscript, ca. 1250–1259.*

decreed that boys who were sent to monasteries were not obliged to remain there once they came of age. A boy could become a tonsured cleric as early as seven years old. At this stage, he attended a church-sponsored school that taught him reading and writing, as well as the basics of the church liturgy. Even a poor villager's son, if he showed promise for a clerical career, might receive some schooling from the parish priest in exchange for helping him around the household or with his duties in the church. From the age of about ten or twelve years to sixteen, a boy on a clerical track attended a grammar school for further education, principally in Latin language and literature. Eventually he might be sent to a university for advanced education.

The choice of a clerical career was influenced by a number of factors. For younger sons, it offered a chance for significant social advancement, wealth, and power, which might otherwise be denied them by their lack of a substantial family inheritance. Many families considered it valuable to have well-educated and well-placed sons in the clergy to broaden the family's influence and resources. In some cases, a child might have been physically or temperamentally unsuited for a warrior's life. Aristocratic families sometimes placed physically or mentally handicapped children in monasteries, although the practice was officially forbidden. In other cases, the boy himself might have chosen a clerical career out of spiritual aspirations or a love of books and learning. Peter Abelard, one of the greatest scholars of the Middle Ages, was the eldest son of a minor nobleman and designated for training as a knight, but he was so fond of study that he convinced his father to let him pursue a career in the church.

The education of urban boys shared elements of both the peasant and aristocratic patterns. Some of them, particularly those from wealthy families, received at least a couple of years of formal schooling, learning to read, write, and handle numbers. After schooling or in lieu of it, they learned a trade. In some families this happened at home, the boy learning his father's livelihood by observation and incremental participation. Otherwise, he was apprenticed out of the house to learn from someone else, often living in the home of his master. While most apprentices were boys, girls might also go through apprenticeship in one of the trades that accepted women (see Chapter 7).

An apprentice stood in the position of a child in his new household. The master was expected to provide not only vocational training but moral guidance, and in some cases to arrange formal schooling as well. The apprentice in turn provided his master with labor and owed him the same obedience due his father. Like a father, the master could mete out physical punishment if the apprentice misbehaved. Apprenticeship was one of the most promising options available to urban boys, and a father had to pay the master to take his son. The cost varied: in thirteenth-century Paris an apprenticeship to a painter or saddler might cost as much as 8 *livres,* but 1 or 2 *livres* was more usual. The boy received no wages but was given room and board, and perhaps a bit of pocket money.

The age of the apprentice varied. Some apprentices were taken in as early as age seven, but eleven or twelve was more common, and some boys did not enter apprenticeship until they were almost twenty. The duration of the apprenticeship also varied. Low-skill jobs took less time to learn than high-skill ones, and a master in an attractive high-paying trade could drive a harder bargain to enjoy the cheap labor of his apprentice for a longer time. A cook's apprentice in thirteenth-century Paris was expected to serve for a mere two years, an apprentice goldsmith for ten. Seven years was a common term.

Most apprentices were in their teens, and predictably there were generational conflicts between apprentices and masters. Many guilds made provision for situations in which the apprentice ran off. Such occurrences seem to have been fairly commonplace, since several Parisian guilds required the masters to take back their apprentices if they returned within a year.[8] Among the makers of metal locks for coffers, if the apprentice left "on account of his recklessness," the master was required to seek him for one day, the father for another, and if the apprentice had not returned by the end of a year, the master was freed of the obligation to take him back.[9] Among the knife and scabbard makers, an apprentice who left his master three times without permission no longer had the right to be reaccepted,

> and the good men of the trade made this regulation to restrain the folly and recklessness of apprentices, because they do great damage to their masters and to themselves when they run off; for when the apprentice is engaged to learn, and he runs off for a month or two, he forgets everything he has learnt; and thus he loses his time and does harm to his master.[10]

The makers of iron buckles forbade members of their craft to sell the contract of their apprentice to another craftsman, for fear that apprentices would become "treacherous and prideful against their masters" when they wanted to transfer to another master.[11]

The urban poor, destined for work as servants or unskilled laborers, received neither schooling nor vocational training, but were put to work as soon as they had the physical and mental capacity, boys and girls alike. Many, perhaps most, began with household service, since it required very little strength or experience. As they grew older, they could find their way into the ranks of wage laborers.

Coming of Age

The point at which a child entered the adult world depends on the criteria used to define adulthood. The church generally considered the age of discretion as twelve for girls, fourteen for boys, reflecting the medieval awareness that girls reached physical maturity sooner than boys. These were the minimum ages required for assent to marriage, and were commonly the ages that churchmen thought appropriate for the child's first confession. Legal responsibilities also generally began at about this point. An English law of 1181 required militia service from boys beginning at age fifteen, and this was also the age of majority for the inheritance of property.[12] Yet although the law and church recognized teenagers as adults, in practice, it was uncommon for them to be in the position of independent members of society. Among boys who had been apprenticed, very few would have completed their apprenticeship by this age, while among the peasantry and laborers a boy of fourteen was still a bit young for the hardest physical labor. In the aristocracy, a boy might inherit at fourteen, yet remain under the care of a guardian until twenty-one.

Marriage

Across the social spectrum, full entry into adult society generally came with marriage and the establishment of a household of one's own. For men, this only became possible after acquiring the means to support a family, such as a landholding, a workshop, or a business. Since husbands had primary responsibility for supplying the family's livelihood, they were generally older than their wives. Reliable statistics are rare for the Middle Ages, but the evidence suggests that the typical age of marriage among the peasantry was the late twenties for men, the early twenties for women; similar ages probably applied for the urban laboring classes. The ages decline, particularly for women, further up the social scale. Among prosperous urban families, the marriage age for women was typically the late teens; the age varied widely for men. In the aristocracy, ages in the mid-teens for women and early twenties for men seem to have been common.

Marriage in the Middle Ages was a complex affair that combined economic, folkloric, and religious elements. At all levels of society, it involved a major economic commitment, and both parties were expected to consider carefully the likely economic consequences of the union. Since the man was usually the main source of household income, the woman needed to find a husband whose economic prospects met her expectations. The economic criteria for men depended in part on their class. Among commoners, the woman was often a significant contributor to the household finances, so a man wanted a wife who was skilled and industrious. In the upper classes, where the woman was less likely to contribute to household income directly, it was more important that the bride bring with her a substantial dowry of land or money from her family. Such considerations also played a role among ordinary people. A peasant might significantly enhance his economic status by marrying a woman who stood to inherit land in the village. The economics of the marriage were often settled beforehand through an agreement witnessed between the two sides, stipulating the property to be brought by the wife into the marriage, as well as the property bestowed by the groom on his wife to support her in case of his death.

The legal dimension of marriage fell under the jurisdiction of the church, which had its own requirements. The prospective couple were not permitted to be close relatives. The appropriate distance was debated for centuries, but as of the early thirteenth century, it was fixed at four degrees, meaning that a couple who shared a great-great grandfather could not marry. This relationship also included godparentage, which made the determination of kinship more complex. A preexisting marriage, or even a prior marriage agreement, also prevented marriage. To forestall prohibited marriages, the prospective match had to be announced in the parish church of both parties on three successive Sundays. These announcements, called banns, gave the local communities a chance to bring forward any possible impediments to the union.

The ceremony itself was celebrated at the door of the church, with the priest officiating and the community as witness. The wedding service of the Middle Ages included many of the same elements as mainstream Christian ceremonies of today, including the request that any impediments be brought forward and the mutual exchange of vows. The church emphasized the importance of the consent of both partners as essential to the validity of the marriage. There was only a single wedding ring, given by the man to the woman. After the ceremony, the company proceeded into the church for a nuptial Mass.

The wedding ceremony was followed by popular celebrations, depending on local folk customs. A feast was commonly held, and in some places a procession of neighbors accompanied the couple to their home. One thirteenth-century story mentions a French custom of casting grain over the couple as they crossed the threshold, shouting "Abundance, Abundance!" although the priestly author notes cynically that many wedded couples soon find themselves living in want and misery.[13]

Not every marriage followed these formalities. According to canon law, marriage could be contracted either by a vow of marriage expressed in the present tense or by a statement of future intent to marry followed by sexual consummation. The latter sort of marriage in particular could take place without the participation of church or community. Such marriages were illegal, but not invalid: although the couple might be prosecuted in the church courts, they

FRIEZE OF A MEDIEVAL WEDDING. Thomas Stothard (British), undated. Gray wash, graphite, pen, and black ink on textured paper.

remained legally married. Some couples took advantage of this as a means to elope without the approval of their families, clear evidence that love—or at least desire—could also play a part in the decision to marry.

Once the marriage took place, the couple were joined for life, and they were legally required to cohabit. Neither partner was permitted to enter a monastery, or even become celibate, without the consent of the other. Divorce as such was not permitted, although a marriage might be annulled in certain situations, especially if the marriage was invalid in the first place (for example, because of a prior contract or close kinship), or if it was never consummated by sexual union. It was also possible to secure an official separation in cases such as adultery or cruelty. In this situation, the couple was no longer required to cohabit, but they remained legally married. If one partner in a marriage died, remarriage was freely permitted. According to church doctrine, procreation was the sole purpose of marriage, and contraception and abortion were forbidden, as were all sexual acts that did not lead to conception. Of course, the very condemnation of these acts suggests that they were indeed practiced, and this is confirmed by records of legal actions against transgressors.[14]

The relationship between husband and wife was complex, reflecting both broad cultural patterns and customs specific to the time and place. In principle, a wife generally stood in a position similar to that of a servant or child, as a subordinate and dependent member of her husband's household. It was even considered appropriate for a husband to use corporal punishment to discipline his wife, just as he might use it with a child or servant. Actual brutality was not condoned, but the line between discipline and brutality is always problematic in corporal punishment.

Whether it was actually common for husbands to beat their wives is another matter. In practice, there were a number of factors that permitted her a measure of unofficial independence and influence. Unlike the servant or child, a wife had relatives of her own, comparable in social status to her husband, who might take an interest in her well-being. She might be capable of earning money in her own right, and many women among the working classes brought additional money into the household by hiring out their labor, or selling goods produced at home.

Most important of all, although hardest to perceive across the centuries, is the basic human dynamic of the marriage partnership. Then as now, every couple had to negotiate its own mode of interaction, and the most successful households were generally those in which each partner respected the other. An advocate of monastic life for women around the year 1200 suggests that many people saw marriage as a pleasant and desirable state:

> You say . . . man's vigor is worth much, and I need his help for maintenance and food; and of the companionship of woman and man arises well-being, and a family of fair children that greatly please the parents. . . . You say that a wife has much comfort of her husband when they are well matched, and that each is well pleased with the other."[15]

OLD AGE

Life expectancy at birth was relatively short, probably around forty years, but this figure is skewed by a very high incidence of mortality among children and teenagers, and generally reflects the effects of disease rather than the natural lifespan. Once a person reached twenty or thirty years of age, they had passed the period of highest susceptibility to disease and had a reasonable likelihood of reaching sixty or more. The bodies of medieval people were not much different from ours today, and presumably aged at about the same rate. This expectation is confirmed by medieval customs pertaining to old age. Legal requirements imposed on the able-bodied, such as military service and taxation, commonly remained in place until the age of sixty. Services of the mind rather than the body, such as the responsibility for serving on a manor court or providing political counsel to one's feudal lord, were often required up to age seventy. Such figures closely correspond with the modern practice of retirement somewhere around sixty to seventy years of age.

Old age was a time of heightened economic vulnerability. Most people supported themselves through some sort of physical work, and as their physical abilities declined, so did their earning power. Society provided no safety net for the elderly, who were obliged to find their own means of keeping body and soul together.

For people at the top of the social scale, security in old age was not a problem. Aristocrats who were supported by the profits from their lands and merchants who lived by commerce had the means to support themselves, and their families also had sufficient surpluses to look after their less-wealthy members as well. Important followers of wealthy men, such as the steward of a baronial estate, might also expect support from their patrons. Further down the scale, a more modest property holder might exchange his holding for financial support. Many villagers surrendered the use of their lands to their heirs, if there were any, in exchange for housing and a regular payment of cash or goods to support them. When Thomas Bird of Romsley in England took over a cottage holding from his mother in 1281, he promised to provide her with a suitable dwelling thirty feet long and fourteen feet wide, with three doors and two windows, with stipulated allowances of fuel and food.[16] The owner of an urban tenement sometimes donated or promised to bequeath his property to a church institution such as a monastery in exchange for support; in some cases, the donor took up residence on the property of the monastery, receiving food from the monastic kitchen.

Those with neither property nor connections were at greater risk. The income of a wage laborer was not enough to support investment in long-term sources of income such as property, and those who lacked family to support them, unless they died early, could expect only an impoverished old age. Many were doubtless obliged to beg for a living. Women were particularly at risk. Because it was common for wives to be significantly younger than their husbands, many experienced long periods of widowhood, and since the earning capacity of women was lower than that of men, a widow was particularly vulnerable to poverty.

Death

In a world with high rates of mortality at every age, death was a familiar occurrence, and although an object of fear, it was perhaps less a matter of mystery than it is today. Medieval people typically died as they were born and as they were conceived: at home in bed. The parish priest was summoned to administer

THE DANCE OF DEATH. *Michael Wolgemut (German), 1493. The Dance of Death is a medieval artistic genre that consists of images of the dead from all stations in life dancing to the grave, serving as a reminder of the fragility of life and that death unites everyone.*

to the dying person the rite of Extreme Unction, the last of the sacraments of the church. After death, the body was washed, wrapped in a cloth, and carried to the church for burial. Most people were buried in the churchyard, without a coffin or gravemarker. Traditionally, only priests were buried in the church itself, but by the thirteenth century some aristocrats were buried there as well. The very wealthiest might be laid in coffins of stone, and in the thirteenth century important graves were adorned with brass images of the deceased. The churchyard that served for burial was often an important public space in the community, serving not just as a repository for the dead, but as a place of public assembly, a marketplace, and even as a playing field. In this, as in so many aspects of medieval life, solemnity and secularity were closely intertwined, reminding us that medieval people saw the world in a manner often very different from our own.

3

MATERIAL CULTURE

A MODERN PERSON WHISKED BACK OVER THE CENTURIES INTO the Middle Ages would sooner or later realize that medieval society was profoundly different from that of the modern world, but the physical differences between the medieval and modern worlds would be evident at once. The simplest daily routines would become significant chores, readily available commodities would become valuable rarities, and commonplace interactions with one's own body and the physical environment would take on enormous significance. In this chapter, we will look at various material factors that shaped medieval life.

In today's industrialized world, it is hard to envision how much effort it takes to produce even the simplest of goods when each piece must be transformed by hand from raw materials to finished product. Medieval craftsmen made use of a wide range of tools, from the smith's simple hammer to the weaver's intricate loom, but in all cases the amount of human labor involved was enormous. There were only a few fully mechanized processes in the medieval economy; aside from the wind- or water-powered mills used for grinding flour, virtually every form of work was based primarily on human, or in some cases, animal, labor.

Materials

The production of ironwork illustrates the effort involved in medieval industry. Iron was a staple component in medieval material culture, and its use known in Europe since the first millennium B.C.E., yet its production remained a laborious task. The iron ore had to be extracted from the ground by miners. It then had to be heated to over two thousand degrees Fahrenheit (although there was no precise

FINELY DRESSED MEN AND WOMEN SOCIALIZE IN A COURTYARD *in this illustration from* The Romance of the Rose, *a very popular poem in thirteenth-century France.*

way to measure heat) to separate the iron from impurities in the ore, a process involving the consumption of large quantities of fuel in the form of charcoal, itself produced at the expenditure of considerable labor. The iron was then repeatedly heated and beaten to produce the desired carbon content before it could be shaped at the smith's forge by means of tools themselves made of iron. Because of the enormous amount of labor involved, ironwork was always expensive, and used as sparingly as possible. The same applied to a lesser degree to cheaper, more easily worked metals, such as lead, tin, and copper, and their alloys such as pewter, brass, and bronze. These did not involve as laborious a refining process as iron, and their lower melting temperatures made them easier to work, but they still had to be mined and the ore purified, so that these metals were also somewhat expensive.

Because of the expense of metals, the medieval household made greater use of less-costly materials like wood and clay. There was also incentive to make full use of natural objects and materials, particularly those available as by-products of other work. When cattle were slaughtered, the best meat was sold to the wealthy, the less-palatable portions like the head and feet to poorer buyers; the hide was sold to a tanner for leather, while the bones and horns were purchased by other craftsmen to make small household items. Bone, when highly polished, resembles ivory, and it was used for a variety of items such as knife handles and sheaths, gaming pieces, flutes, pins, and needles. Horn was in some ways the medieval precursor to plastic: it has a smooth surface, it is translucent, and when heated, it can be shaped. Items crafted of horn included combs and inkwells, and lanterns were fitted with panes of horn.

In a world where manufacturing was expensive, people were motivated to make the fullest possible use of manufactured wares. Old goods were not casually discarded. If they had reached the end of their usefulness to an owner but were still functional, they were sold to a dealer in used goods who mended them as necessary and resold them to someone further down the social scale. Resale of used items was always a significant part of the economy in medieval towns, and regulations had to be promulgated to ensure that refurbished secondhand wares were not passed off as new. Even those people at the top of the social scale did not waste used materials. When the king of England had the shingles on the royal kitchens at Marlborough Castle replaced with lead roofing in 1260, he ordered the constable to use the old shingles to reroof another building in the castle compound.[1] Old timbers were similarly reused when buildings were taken down, and Roman ruins were often treated as stone quarries for new construction.[2] Since shoe soles wore out much more quickly than the uppers, the uppers were often cut away from worn-out soles and used in new shoes.

Where an object was too worn or too damaged to serve, it might be recycled. Then as now, glass was one of the easiest materials to recycle, and it was also one that medieval technology had a limited ability to produce, particularly in colored varieties. Not only was old glass recycled, but a significant portion of the glass circulating in the Middle Ages actually dated to Roman times.[3] Metals were also regularly recycled: Parisian guild regulations of the thirteenth century make provision for the reuse of old copper, bronze, and brass for making buckles and prayer beads.[4]

The relative expense of manufactured commodities meant that the medieval household had a far smaller inventory of such items than is the case today. The ordinary household might have bedding, cooking and eating utensils, a table, stools, a set or two of clothing for each person, a chest or two for storage, and such tools as were needed for the livelihood of the household, but very little else. Even an aristocrat's household furnishings were no more extensive than those of a middle-income person today: many of the visitors to the household of Thomas à Becket, archbishop of Canterbury in the twelfth century, had to sit on the floor, and to provide for their comfort the archbishop had his hall strewn with straw or hay in the winter and fresh rushes or green boughs in the summer.[5]

Clothing

Fabric

The distinctive character of medieval material culture is especially evident in the production of clothing, which was one of the principal industrial activities of the Middle Ages. Medieval fabrics were made of natural fibers, principally linen—derived from the fibers of the flax plant—and sheep's wool. Cotton was sometimes imported into Europe, and some even grew in the Mediterranean areas, but the short fibers of cotton were difficult to spin into thread using medieval spinning technology, and cotton was more likely to be used as stuffing, or spun in combination with flax. Linen was generally used for inner garments, wool for outer garments, reflecting the respective properties of the two fibers. Linen is soft and absorbent; it soaks up sweat and oils and can be cleaned, properties that make it comfortable and serviceable to wear against the skin. Wool does not clean readily or absorb water well, and it tends to be scratchy, so it is less suitable for wearing against the skin, but it resists water and can be quite warm, both useful qualities in an outer garment. Wool also holds dye better than linen, making woolen cloth well suited for the visible outer layers of an outfit. Linen was nonetheless sometimes used for outer garments, particularly those worn in hot weather.

The preparation of clothing was an extremely labor-intensive process that illustrates both the limitations and creativity of medieval material culture. First, the fiber was harvested, in the case of flax, or shorn in the case of wool. It was then cleaned, purified of unusable fibers, and dressed by combing or carding so that the fibers all ran parallel to each other. The fibers were then spun by hand into thread. The traditional instrument for spinning was the drop spindle, a stick approximately a foot long with a weighted disk at the bottom. The spinner attached the fiber to the spindle and gave it a twist that set it spinning: the spindle twisted the fibers together while its weight drew them out into thread. A more recent invention was the spinning wheel, which was essentially a spindle connected by a drive band to a large drive wheel. This arrangement put more power and momentum behind the spindle, significantly increasing the spinner's speed, although she had to turn the wheel by hand and pull her fiber away from the immobile spindle—the treadle-wheel that both twists and pulls did not appear until the fifteenth century.

Once sufficient thread was spun, it could be woven into cloth. The threads were tied one by one onto a loom, then woven into fabric one cross-thread at a time. This process was facilitated in the Middle Ages by the introduction of the horizontal loom. On the vertical loom, which still dominated in the early Middle Ages, the lengthwise threads hung downward, and were pulled tight by weights

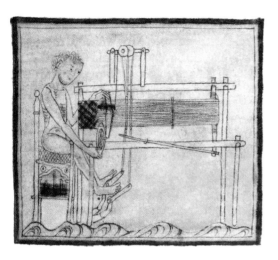

MAN AT A LOOM. *From the twelfth-century illuminated French manuscript* The Romance of Alexander.

tied to the ends. On the new horizontal loom, the threads were wound around rollers at each end, and kept tight by a ratchet on the roller. The horizontal loom speeded the weaver's work, although the actual weaving was still done by hand.

The woven fabric still had to be finished and dyed. The finishing of wool in particular was a complex process, involving cleaning, stretching, and felting: the fibers on the surface would be teased up, then shorn and washed, giving the surface a smooth appearance and increasing the fabric's resistance to wind and rain. The colors available were limited to those obtainable from natural dyes. These dyes tended to yield muted colors that faded with exposure to the sun, so the clothing of most people was probably rather faded in appearance; only the wealthy were likely to overdye or replace faded garments.

Tailoring

The construction of medieval clothing differed significantly from modern practices. Because cloth was so laborious to produce, garments were assembled from many small pieces to keep waste to a minimum. Before 1300, clothes were constructed with straight seams, rather than the curved seams that allow a garment to be tailored to the contours of the body. In fact, tailoring was impossible, since garments were pulled over the head and had to be loose-fitting. Buttons were used as decorations in the thirteenth century, but they began to be used as fasteners only toward the end of the century, principally to close sleeves and neck openings. Not until the fourteenth century, when buttons came to be used as closures for open-fronted garments, did a tailored fit become possible. Medieval ingenuity did find alternative ways of achieving a tighter fit for the fashion-conscious. Certain styles of women's garments in the twelfth century used lacing, and in the latter part of the thirteenth century some garments were cut with sleeves so tight that the wearer had to be stitched into them. Medieval clothes lacked not only buttons but most of the other fasteners we rely on today; medieval people made extensive use of straight pins to hold their clothing together.

The absence of contour tailoring somewhat restricted the variety of clothing in use, and overall the styles of the twelfth and thirteenth centuries were less diverse and slower to change than was the case in later periods. Change was particularly slow among the lower classes, and more rapid among the social elite who followed the trends of fashion, although the fundamental elements of attire were fairly consistent across the classes.

Male Clothing

As in other periods, there was a certain degree of differentiation between male and female garments. A man's first item of clothing was his linen breech, or *braies*. Roughly speaking, braies are comparable to a large and loose fitting pair of boxer shorts or pajama trousers. There was no elastic to hold them up at the waist: after pulling them on, the man would secure them in place with a *braiel*, which was either a leather belt or a lace comparable to a long shoelace. The braiel was fastened around the waist, gathering the loose upper edge of the braies with it. It might pass through a casing or eyelets in the braies, or the edge of the braies might be wrapped around it to hold them in place. The braies reached to the knees or even lower, and illustrations often show another lace at the bottom that could be used to fasten the braies at the bottom, or tie the loose cuff of the longer braies back up to the braiel when they were being worn without overgarments because of the heat. The braiel might also support a purse, since this was a reasonably secure place to keep money.

The next layer of a man's clothing was a pair of hose. These were two long stockings of woolen cloth, each covering the entire leg. The hose pulled up over the bottom of the braies and came to a point at the top, with a lace attached to tie it to the braiel. Hose were cut on the diagonal for extra stretch, but even so they were loose and given to bunching—a far cry from the tights we usually see in period films. A poor man's hose might not have feet, or have only a strap under the arch of the foot.

Over the braies and hose the man wore a linen shirt, which reached to the thighs or knees. The shirt had a gusset from hem to crotch to allow greater mobility for the legs. On top, the man wore a longer tunic of similar design. The tunic was usually made of wool, and possibly was adorned with decorative trim or embroidery around the collar, cuffs, and hem. Its length depended on the intended use. Labor and other physical activities required a shorter hemline, typically to the knee or so, while high-status men in more formal settings might wear long tunics reaching to the feet. Like the shirt, the tunic might have a gusset from hem to crotch, or might simply be left open, particularly if the tunic was worn while riding. Since the tunic pulled on over the head, it required a fairly large neck opening, which might be round, square, or triangular. Some had a slit in the middle of the front, fastened at the top with a brooch.

Female Clothing

A woman's undergarments were somewhat different from those of a man. Medieval references indicate that she did not wear braies, which were considered a specifically masculine garment. There are occasional references to a "breast-band," perhaps a piece of linen fabric bound around the torso as the equivalent of a bra, although it may refer to some sort of sash worn outside the garments.[6] One subject on which contemporary sources are predictably reticent is the handling of menstruation—a significant matter that was as much a part of a woman's life then as now. The menstrual flow was particularly inconvenient in an age when women wore no underwear other than a relatively valuable white linen shirt. Medieval medical treatises, however, have much to say about the treatment of menstrual pathology, and several recipes recommend the insertion of medication wrapped in a linen cloth; perhaps a similar arrangement was used to absorb ordinary menstrual flow.[7] The woman's principal undergarment was her shirt, similar to a man's, but longer, and possibly constructed with triangular inserts in the side seams instead of in front and back. Since her torso garments were longer than a man's, her hose could be shorter, reaching only to the knees, where they were fastened in place with a lace or a buckled leather garter. Her tunic was similar in design to a man's, but it too might have gores instead of gussets and was always long, reaching to the ankles or feet.

Outer Wear

Outside their tunics, men and women alike wore a narrow leather belt, useful for suspending a purse, knife, or other necessities. A variety of overgarments were in use. One of the most common was the overtunic, perhaps somewhat shorter-skirted and of finer material than the tunic underneath. Some thirteenth-century overtunics had a vertical slit at the front where the sleeve met the body, allowing the arm to be slipped through while the sleeve was left dangling behind.

Overtunics might also have a pocket slit at the waist to allow access to items worn on the belt underneath. The layering of tunics allowed for a fashionable look, and also served the practical need for extra warmth. There were also looser outer garments of various styles. Some had long sleeves gathered at the top into the shoulder seam, again sometimes with slits for the arms, while others had shorter, bell-shaped sleeves. These loose overgarments sometimes had hoods attached to them. Most were principally male garments, but the plain mantle, the simplest form of overgarment, was worn by men and women alike. In its early form, the mantle was a semicircular garment, fastened with a brooch at the breast or shoulder. Later mantles were nearly full circles, and were closed with a cord or chain anchored to either side of the opening, by either an eyelet hole or an attached metal knob or

ILLUSTRATION OF TWO BURGESSES
wearing typical medieval men's clothing.

stud. The very end of the thirteenth century saw the appearance of the sleeveless surcoat, a loose overgarment that became very popular in the fourteenth century. Outer garments were sometimes lined with fur for extra warmth; linings available to ordinary people included rabbit, cat, fox, or fleece. Gloves and mittens were also worn, either for warmth or to protect the hands when working.

Footwear

For footwear, men and women both wore similar styles of leather shoes and low boots; the latter were particularly favored by working folk. The dominant style of the twelfth century relied on drawstring thongs laced around the ankle to keep the shoe on the foot; surviving thirteenth-century shoes are sometimes fastened with lacings up the inner side or with toggles. The sole was flat, with no additional heel. As the sole wore out, it might be patched with another piece of leather, or even removed entirely and a new sole attached to the upper. Medieval shoes were simple in design and did not last long. Monastic rules allowed monks a new pair each year, and most monks did not walk beyond the confines of their cloister. Shoes were periodically washed and greased to preserve the leather and keep it watertight.

Shoes were sometimes worn with "pattens," wooden overshoes resembling sandals that helped keep the shoes out of the mud. Poorer folk sometimes went without hose, wearing their shoes directly against the skin, and the very poor might go entirely barefoot.

Headgear

Headgear was the single most obvious distinction between male and female attire, and it was also especially subject to the currents of fashion. Men of this period are often depicted bareheaded. The simplest form of male headgear was the coif, a linen bonnet that covered the hair and tied under the chin. The coif kept a man's head warm and his hair clean, and was particularly favored by laboring men. Men also wore a variety of caps and hats made of cloth or felt, or perhaps knitted. Agricultural laborers of the period are often shown wearing straw hats in the summer. Ordinary men sometimes wore hoods, usually made of wool, but sometimes made of leather. The hood might have a small cape attached to it that draped onto the shoulders.

Young aristocrats in the thirteenth century might wear chaplets (wreaths) of flowers, a style also affected by young aristocratic women.

Women were more likely to keep their heads covered. Like the male coif, the various elements of a woman's head covering were typically made of linen. Ordinary women of the period are often shown wearing a simple head wrap, probably consisting only of a long rectangle of fabric, either tucked into itself, or secured in place with a band wrapped twice around the head. Women of slightly higher status wore the veil, an oval or rectangular piece of fabric that lay atop the wearer's hair. This was secured in place with a fillet, also made of fabric, either worn on top of the veil, or, more usually, serving as an anchor underneath to which the veil could be pinned. In the mid-twelfth century some women began to wear a "barbette," a strap that passed under the chin and was pinned together at the top of the crown; this too helped anchor the veil. The late twelfth century saw the appearance of the wimple, a larger piece of fabric that was draped under the chin, covering the front of the neck; it was probably secured with pins to the fillet or barbette.

A NOBLE LADY (RIGHT) AND HER MAID OF HONOR (LEFT) *wear medieval clothing common to their respective classes.*

Women's hair was not always covered. Fashionable women in the twelfth century often wore their hair in two long braids, or wrapped the two tresses in ribbons or fabric. In some cases they even extended the wrapped tresses to the ground by weaving false hair into them. In the mid-thirteenth century fashionable women began encasing their hair in nets. Younger women sometimes wore their hair uncovered, either loose or in a single braid down the back. Such styles were somewhat coquettish, appropriate for marriageable girls, but generally not for married women, widows, and others from whom a greater degree of modesty was expected. As in modern times, a woman's appearance was often treated as an important personal asset, and many wore makeup or dyed their hair.

Fashion

Headgear was one of the aspects of medieval clothing that was most used to proclaim the individual's social identity, but fashion played a role in the rest of the outfit as well. The clothing of the wealthy was similar to that of ordinary people in general cut, but might differ in material, detailing, and decoration. For workaday wear, aristocrats wore wool and linen like commoners, but they could afford higher-quality versions of both types of cloth. They could also afford silk, which was used for both outer and inner garments. The furs they used to edge or line their garments were finer than those available to ordinary people, taken from rare and imported animals like ermine, sable, and certain kinds of squirrel. Their clothes also tended to be more brightly colored, made with superior dyes and redyed as they faded. Young aristocrats of the period began to cultivate a fashion for parti-colored outfits, with each side of the tunic or each of the two hose made of a different colored cloth; this style first appeared in southern Europe, particularly Spain, in the twelfth century, then gained favor in the north during the thirteenth century. The south also led the way in the fashion for fabrics woven in striped or checkered patterns.

PORTRAIT OF A MAN. Pisanello (Italian), ca. 1433. Tempura and silver on wood. The unknown man in this painting must have had considerable means, indicated by his ornate headgear and the elaborate embroidery on his outer garment, as well as his financial ability to commission a portrait.

The actual cut of the garment might also vary according to the latest styles. Fashionable women in the twelfth century wore tunics that were tight-fitting around the torso, an effect that was made possible by lacings, usually up the back of the garment. Tunic cuffs in the same period were often worn with a sudden flare at the wrist, sometimes so extreme that the cuffs extended to the ground; they might even be knotted to shorten them. In the late twelfth century in German-speaking areas, it became fashionable for young men to have the bottom edges of their tunics cut into long strips; this style, called dagging, caught on in other parts of Europe during the following century. A fashionable look could also be achieved by extensive use of decoration such as embroidery. The wealthy also displayed their status by the use of fashionable accessories, including rings, brooches, decorative belts, and gloves.

The Use of Clothing

The protocol of clothing differed markedly from modern customs. Medieval people did not leave much skin uncovered in public. Usually only the face and hands were visible, and demure women covered their hair as well. To be seen in one's underwear was equated with nakedness. Medieval rituals of punishment often required the victim to be naked, meaning that they were dressed only in their shirts. Laboring men and women sometimes stripped down to their shirts for very hot work such as harvesting, and men might even work in just their braies.

Medieval people lived in their clothes much more than we do today. Many people slept naked—this seems to have been the case for the peasants of the southern French village of Montaillou—but others in colder climates slept in the underclothes they wore during the day, only removing them on Saturday to wash and replace them with a fresh set. Laundry appears to have been done on a weekly basis, at least among those who could afford a second set of undergarments. Linens were washed with water and lye, then laid out in the sun to dry and bleach. Woolen garments were not necessarily washed at all: medieval references generally describe brushing wool clothing to remove the dirt. Wrinkles were smoothed with hemispheres of glass or polished stone that were heated prior to use.

Because cloth was expensive, even a single garment represented a substantial personal investment. An ordinary person probably owned no more than two of each undergarment, perhaps only one outer garment, while the wardrobe of a rich person was no larger, albeit more sumptuous, than that of a middle-income person today. Each garment was treated as a valuable item of property. As felted wool aged, it began to look threadbare—the felting was lost and the individual threads became visible. At this point, the garment might be refelted to restore the look of the cloth and its resistance to weather. Holes were mended promptly to prevent further deterioration, and when the condition of the garment was too disreputable for its owner to be seen wearing it, the piece was sold to a used-clothes dealer for resale to a less fashion-conscious buyer. Ordinary people probably did not often buy new clothes. The thriving trade in used clothes reflected the relative durability of the cloth. Linen clothing might wear out before being resold, since it was in constant contact with human skin and was regularly washed. Wool, however, is an outstandingly durable fiber, and a fair number of medieval woolen garments have survived to this day in archeological contexts. Many garments outlived their owners, and medieval wills commonly make special reference to the disposition of these along with other property of value.

HOUSEHOLD AMENITIES

Light

A modern observer in a medieval household would quickly become aware of the dearth of what we consider fundamental comforts, a lack that was as much a feature of the nobleman's castle as the peasant's cottage. Even light was more limited. The only really effective light source was the sun, and people relied heavily on daylight, adjusting their schedules throughout the year to take full advantage of every daylight hour. Indoors, the need for light conflicted with the desire to keep out the cold. In an ordinary household, the windows might be covered with oiled linen cloths that let in some light while cutting down on the draft. A wealthy home might have glass window panes, but even these were cloudy and uneven—the process by which early glass was handblown produced a rippled surface that has contributed to the myth that glass "flows" over time. At night, windows could be shuttered for better insulation.

Windows were larger and more numerous in wealthy households, where the inhabitants could afford more fuel for heating. Even so, the window surface in any given room was significantly less than is usually the case today and even the wealthy home would look slightly dim to the modern eye. In poorer households, windows were few and small. The interior of an ordinary person's house would be so dark that even in the daytime a person entering from outdoors needed a moment to adjust to the substantially reduced level of light.

At night, people had to rely on fire for light. There was usually a fire on the hearth, which provided a low general level of light, but this was unevenly distributed. Various sorts of portable lights provided specific illumination. Candles, a medieval invention, came in two types: wax—made from the honeycombs of bees, and tallow—derived from sheep fat. Both provided a comparable level of light, although wax candles, with their higher melting point, were easier to use—they were also about three times as expensive. Poorer households also used rushlights, made of lengths of rush dipped in fat; these were fairly cheap, but offered less light than candles. Various sorts of oil lamps were also used. The illumination afforded by all of these lights was weak compared to modern electric lighting. The lack of artificial light was evident outdoors as well as indoors. A moonlit night was fairly bright, but when the moon was new, there was a deep pitch blackness that today is seen only in the remotest areas.

Heat

The medieval living environment also tended to be cold. Even where windows had glass panes, they still admitted drafts (double-glazing is a modern invention), and buildings were poorly insulated. The only artificial source of heat was fire. Every house had at least one hearth, and wealthy households had hearths in several rooms. Even so, the warmth in any room was unevenly distributed: near the fire it was quite warm, even uncomfortably hot, but farther away the drafts asserted themselves. The hearth fire constituted a significant hazard to people and property, and in the evening, to reduce risk while the household slept, it was allowed to die down. The poorly insulated buildings of the Middle Ages soon became extremely cold once the fire was out. No one who has spent a winter's night in an unheated cottage will wonder why medieval people preferred to have heavy curtains around their beds.

At night, the fire might be covered with ashes to allow the coals to smolder slowly without actually burning themselves out. Some households made

A WINTER SCENE *from* Les Très Riches Heures du Duc de Berry*, created between ca. 1412–1440. Inside a prosperous farm men and women warm their legs by the fire.*

use of perforated ceramic lids that performed the same function.[8] This simplified the task of restarting the fire in the morning. Starting a fire from scratch was not as easy. It required striking a piece of hardened steel against the sharp edge of a piece of flint. The flint sliced tiny pieces off the steel, heating them red-hot in the process; these sparks were caught in a piece of charred cloth that began to smolder. Step by step, this weak combustion was built up: the cloth would be held against some highly flammable tow (fibers of flax unsuitable for spinning), and blown to produce a small flame; this would be used to ignite small pieces of wooden tinder that in turn ignited larger pieces of wood.

Although every house had a hearth, chimneys were still uncommon. In most homes, the hearth was built in the center of the room; the smoke escaped through the roof, perhaps assisted by a louver at the top. Such an arrangement precluded any upper floors above the hearth, although there might be upper levels above other parts of the building. The smoke did not always escape well, and even with a chimney, adverse drafts might prevent effective evacuation of smoke. The smell of smoke was a familiar feature of the medieval home.

The domestic fire was used for multiple purposes, since it served for cooking, heating water, and providing light as well as warmth. The fire may well have been kept burning for most or all of the household's waking hours, and even a small household might consume a substantial amount of fuel in a day. Yet wood was not a limitless commodity. Town dwellers had to purchase their firewood from vendors. Villagers might have access to wood supplies locally, but since much of the agricultural land was highly developed, the supply was limited, and firewood supplies were managed to ensure that they were not depleted. Country folk relied heavily on fallen wood, which might be supplemented by the practice called "coppicing, " in which individual branches were cut from the upper part of the tree while leaving the trunk intact, allowing the tree to produce more branches. Since windfall and coppiced wood tended to consist of thin sticks that could not sustain a substantial flame, they were often bound into bundles to provide a better fire.

Water

Running water was extremely rare in the medieval home; it was found only in monasteries and some of the wealthiest aristocratic households. Everywhere else, water had to be fetched by hand, usually from a well or a stream. To ensure a constant supply, the household might have a cistern or barrel to store water for domestic use. Hot running water was entirely unknown. When the household needed hot water, it had to be heated in a cauldron over the fire. It was probably common to keep a constant supply of water on the hearth to minimize delay when hot water was needed—the monastic custumal of Cluny emphasized the importance of putting a new cauldron on the kitchen fire as soon as the old one was removed.[9]

Hygiene

Given the cold surroundings and the difficulties involved in obtaining a large quantity of hot water, it is hardly surprising that bathing in the Middle Ages was less frequent than today. Monasteries commonly allowed (but did not require) two to three baths a year. Baths were more frequent among wealthy laypeople, but were still not an everyday occurrence. The bather sat in a wooden tub–resembling the bottom half of a barrel-filled with water. It helped to be waited on by someone who provided a supply of fresh hot water to pour over the bather's body. In larger towns there were commercial bathhouses that provided these services. Ordinary people lacked these sorts of facilities, and would not have bathed very often—perhaps only outdoors in good weather; the peasants of Montaillou do not seem to have bathed at all.

Partial washing was more frequent. It was common to wash one's face and hands first thing in the morning; hands were also washed several times during the course of the day, particularly before and after a meal. Mealtime washing was especially important since food was handled with the fingers. Such washing usually involved rinsing the hands and drying them on a towel, but soap was used at other times. Hair was washed separately from the rest of the body, using a lye solution. Information on medieval oral hygiene is rare, but there are indications that some effort was made to clean one's teeth. A twelfth-century description of Wales indicates that the Welsh used green hazel twigs and woolen cloths to clean their teeth; this was in keeping with European customs of later centuries.[10]

Shaving was significantly more difficult than it is today. Mirrors were available, whether of polished metal or glass with lead backing, but the image was neither large nor clear, so it made sense to rely on the services of a professional barber. One text of the period suggests that a weekly shave may have been typical, at least among the well-to-do, who had the leisure and resources to devote to personal grooming.[11]

There was one aspect of daily hygiene that no one could escape. Without running water there were no flush toilets: the closest equivalent were the latrines built over water conduits in many monasteries and in a few of the best-appointed castles. The usual facility was an outhouse built over a cesspit. Some homes also used chamber pots, which spared the user a visit to an outdoor privy; after use, the pot was emptied into a cesspit. To wipe themselves after defecating, people made use of a clump of hay, grass, or straw.

One easily overlooked aspect of home hygiene was the omnipresence of vermin. Fleas and lice were a constant problem: among the peasants of Montaillou, delousing was an important social activity. Mice and rats were also common in the medieval household. To combat the rodent population, it was common for people to keep cats: they may have been companions to some extent, but they functioned primarily as working members of the household.

Privacy and Personal Space

The biology of the human body was less embarrassing to medieval people than it is for us today, since the realities of nature were always visible and inescapable. The basic facts of birth and death were constantly in evidence: babies and corpses alike were much more familiar to medieval people. Houses did not necessarily have private rooms and beds were often shared. A lack of privacy raised the threshold of embarrassment when it came to the natural functions of the body. Children living in a single room with their parents could hardly have grown up innocent of the reality of sex, and in a society in which no baby could be raised without mother's milk, the sight of a woman breastfeeding her child could scarcely have been a source of serious discomfort—indeed, this was a favored scene in medieval paintings of the infant Jesus with the Virgin Mary. Even defecation found its way into humorous scenes painted into the borders of medieval manuscripts. Medieval people were not very squeamish about urine: not only was it an essential element in tanning leather and fulling cloth, but the medieval physician's analysis of a patient's urine was expected to take into account taste as well as appearance.

Food

The limitations of medieval material culture were especially evident in the matter of nutrition. The food supply was erratic. Food production per capita and per acre was relatively low (the latter about one-tenth of modern rates), and the means of preservation and transpor-

MADONNA AND CHILD. *Andrea di Bartolo (Italian), ca. 1415. Tempera on panel.*

tation were limited. The result was a subsistence style of agriculture that easily came up short in years of poor harvests. Successive bad harvests, by no means an uncommon occurrence, easily led to famine.

Seasonality and Preservation

The diet of medieval people varied among the classes, and although rich and poor alike were subject to the limitations of medieval technology. One aspect of the medieval diet that would be most striking to the modern observer is its strict seasonality. The availability of any given foodstuff depended on the time of year and on its amenability to preservation. Fresh vegetables and fruits were generally available only between late spring and autumn, depending on the maturation schedule of each plant. Only a few could be kept in cool storage for any length of time: root vegetables such as carrots, turnips, and parsnips, and apples and pears among the fruits. Some fruits, such as grapes, were dried for long-term storage.

Cereals could be kept year-round, although there was always the risk of rot or mice damaging the stores. Once they had been ground into flour their shelf life dropped significantly, so cereals were usually stored as grain and ground only as needed. Legumes such as beans and peas could be dried and were therefore also available at all times of the year. Because of their ready amenability to storage, grains and legumes were perennial staples in the medieval diet.

Milk was available principally in the spring and summer, once the calves were weaned and when fodder was plentiful. Since it did not keep well, especially in an age before refrigeration, most milk was made into butter and cheese. The butter could be kept year-round by packing it in salt, while the reduced water content of cheese similarly helped to preserve it. Eggs were most plentiful in the principal laying seasons of spring and summer. Meats could generally be had year-round, for those who could afford them, although during the winter much meat was salted rather than fresh, which spared the cost of hay during the months when no grazing was available and allowed large animals to be eaten over a longer period of time. The salt removed the water content of the meat to prevent decay, allowing the meat to be preserved for a long period of time. Prior to cooking, the salt meat was soaked in water several times to remove the excess salt.

Poultry was always eaten fresh, since the birds were small, and did not depend on seasonal grazing for their food.

Some seafood was also seasonal, particularly migratory fish that were accessible for fishing only part of the year. Salt fish was available all year, and it was the only seafood available to many inland dwellers. Seafood played a much larger part in the diet than it does for people today because of religious fasts. Wednesdays, Fridays, and Saturdays were officially fast days, during which the eating of meat was not permitted, including poultry and eggs. The fast also applied to the evenings before major religious holy days, and to the period of Lent, from Ash Wednesday to the evening before Easter. In all, fast days accounted for over half the year. The prohibition of meat was probably not very important to ordinary people in cereal-growing regions, whose diet included little meat to begin with, but the wealthy, who could afford meat regularly, do appear from medieval household accounts to have been fairly conscientious in their observation of fast days.

Two meals a day were the usual norm. Breakfast was not a feature of medieval life. Some people ate a quick bite of food in the morning, but many waited until late morning or midday before breaking their fast. The main meals were dinner, served in the late morning or in the middle of the day, somewhere between ten and noon, and supper in the evening; dinner was usually the larger meal of the two.

Food Production

Food production and preparation absorbed most of the labor of the medieval population. Bread, the staple

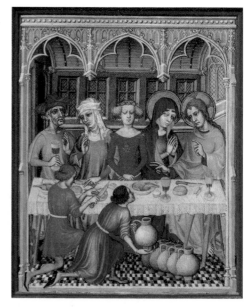

ILLUSTRATION OF A MEDIEVAL MEAL, *including two saints seated on the right.*

foodstuff in most of Europe, required a significant amount of preparation even after the grain had been harvested. The grinding of flour was one of the few mechanized processes in the medieval economy: hand mills were still in use, but most grain was ground in large mills powered by wind or water. Baking was an involved process. The oven was typically a chamber of brick or clay, several feet across and rounded on top. It was filled with fuel, lit, and allowed to burn until it reached a sufficiently high temperature. At this point, the coals were raked out, the hot baking surface cleaned with a wet rag, the bread inserted, and the aperture sealed. The bread was baked by the oven's residual heat. The yeast by which the bread was leavened was usually taken from a batch of ale or from a previous batch of bread, after the fashion of sourdough.

Other forms of food preparation were similarly labor intensive. Butter involved a long period of churning to make the cream solidify. To make cheese, the milk had to be curdled with rennet and the curds drained and pressed to remove the water; the cheese might then be packed in salt to form a rind, which would allow it to keep longer. Meats were roasted at the side of a fire, and had to be turned constantly to ensure that they cooked evenly; a pan was laid underneath to catch the drippings, useful both in cooking and as a source of grease for various domestic uses, such as oiling shoes.

Drinks

The production of drinks was also a major part of the medieval economy. In northern Europe, ale was the staple drink. It was brewed from barley, sometimes mixed with other grains. First, the seeds were artificially sprouted, then heated to stop growth, and roasted. This process, called "malting, "caused the seeds to convert their starch content into soluble starches and helped flavor the ale. The sprouted grain was then ground, boiled in water to extract its contents, and strained to remove the solid matter. Herbal flavorings were added, and the liquid was fermented with yeast, usually from a previous batch of ale. Ale did not keep well, but later in the Middle Ages hops were added to ale to make beer: the hops not only gave beer its characteristic bitter edge, but had preservative properties that increased the drink's shelf life.

Further south, wine, both red and white, was the dominant drink, and it was also consumed by the aristocracy throughout Europe. Its production was a simpler matter: the grapes were pressed to extract the juice, and the resulting liquid was flavored and fermented. Medieval wine was generally consumed young, since it did not keep as well as modern wines. It was often mixed with water, spices, or sweeteners such as honey or sugar. In some areas, similar alcoholic drinks were made with other fruits, including perry from pears and cider from apples. In some places poor in fruits and grains, mead, made from a fermented mixture of honey and water flavored with herbs or spices, was the usual drink.

All of these alcoholic drinks were dietary staples, consumed at every meal by children as well as adults. They were not necessarily very strong, and they had nutritive properties lacking in the principal "soft" alternative, water. Milk was not a staple drink. It was only available during the dairying season, and was usually reserved for cheese and butter-making. Whey, the watery by-product pressed out of curds in cheese-making, was sometimes consumed, especially by children and peasants.

Nutrition

The medieval diet, like other aspects of medieval life, was heavily determined by class. The diet of ordinary people was plain, although it was in some respects better than that of the medieval aristocracy, or of the average North American today. A very large portion of their daily carbohydrates came from grains, often boiled whole in a soup or stew (the most nutritive option), or ground into flour for bread (slightly less nutritive), or sometimes malted and brewed into ale (the least nutritive). They consumed a variety of grains beyond plain wheat, such as oats, rye, barley, and spelt. Even when the grains came in the form of wheaten bread, the flour was relatively unrefined, making for a higher nutritional content. Legumes such as beans, peas, and lentils were also prominent. The proteins provided by the combination of grains with legumes were supplemented by eggs and dairy products; in some areas fresh- and saltwater fish were also included. Meats were relatively rare. The most common was poultry; red meat was not common in the peasant diet except in regions ill suited to raising grain. Additional nutrients were provided by garden vegetables and fruits. Flavoring was mostly provided by domestically available plants such as onions, garlic, and mustard. Salt was used for flavoring, but probably not to excess, since it had to be purchased from meager cash resources. Alcoholic consumption among ordinary people was common but probably moderate. Figures from the later Middle Ages suggest that a gallon of ale a day was not unusual, but the actual alcoholic strength of the drink was probably quite low. All in all, the peasant's diet rated high by modern nutritional standards. The specifics of their diet varied with local conditions: people in grain-raising areas derived most of their calories from cereals, while those who lived more by animal husbandry relied more heavily on meat and dairy products.

The chief weakness of this diet was its unevenness. The availability of fruits and vegetables depended on the season. Substantial fluctuations in the harvest could significantly affect prices, especially since there were limited means for storing and transporting foodstuffs to help deal with temporary and local problems. A poor harvest meant shortages of food, especially in the summer, as the previous year's supplies were used up and the next year's were not yet gathered. Successive years of bad harvests led to famine. Few people actually died of starvation, but a protracted period of poor nutrition left individuals susceptible to disease.

The wealthy, like ordinary folk, were limited by what the seasons provided, but were limited less by cost. They could generally afford fresh meat at all times of the year. Meat constituted a very high portion of their diet, at the cost of grains, legumes, and vegetables. They also consumed more seafood, and in greater variety, including both fresh- and saltwater fish as well as shellfish. Their bread was made of refined wheat flour. Their food was seasoned with costly spices imported from the Near East and Asia. Ironically, this diet was in many ways less healthy than the poor man's diet in many respects, due to an excess of fat, and relatively little fiber, vitamin A, and vitamin C. The principal dietary advantage for aristocrats was constant supply. Even in times of scarcity, they were able to afford to maintain their usual level of food consumption, even if the cost was several times higher than in other years.

Health and Disease

Unevenness in the diet, poor sanitation, infrequent bathing, and the general hardship of life had health consequences. The lack of fresh fruit and vegetables for much of the year contributed to a high incidence of scurvy. Poor sanitation led directly to the proliferation of disease, as well as fostering vermin that carried disease. The heavy physical work required of urban and rural laborers probably contributed to the arthritis that has been found in many skeletons from medieval burials. Infrequent bathing contributed to a high rate of skin disease. Leprosy was recognized as a major problem in the eleventh to thirteenth centuries. In medieval usage, leprosy covered a range of diseases that manifested themselves on the skin, rather than the restricted modern use of the word to designate Hansen's disease. In general, diagnosis was hampered by a very limited understanding of the nature of disease.

Personal injury was also a very common health risk in the medieval world. The open fire was a feature of every household; many people lived by extremely hard labor under rough conditions; and violence and warfare permeated society more broadly than is the case in the West today. Even recreation was hazardous: the aristocracy was addicted to combat sports, and even the commoner's football game was an extremely rough pastime that often resulted in injury and sometimes even death.

Medicine

The level of health was affected by the limitations of medieval science. Medieval science was far from primitive; in fact, it was a highly sophisticated system based on the accumulated writings of theorists since the first millennium B.C.E. The weakness of medieval science was its theoretical and bookish orientation, which emphasized the authority of accepted authors. The duty of the scholar was to interpret and reconcile these ancient authorities, rather than to test their theories against observed realities.

In medicine, the fundamental authority was the Greek physiologist Galen (ca.130–200), who believed that the body was composed of four humors: Choler, Phlegm, Melancholy, and Blood. These humors corresponded to the four elements of which all matter was believed to be composed. According to Galenic medicine, illness was principally a result of imbalances in the humors, and could best be

ANATOMICAL MAN, FROM *LES TRÈS RICHES HEURES DU DUC DE BERRY*, *created ca. 1412–1440. In medieval medicine, the signs of the zodiac corresponded with parts of the body, starting with Pisces at the feet and traveling up to Aries at the head. Other various beliefs pertaining to the four complexions (hot, cold, wet, or dry), the four humors, and the four cardinal points are illustrated around the body.*

addressed by medicines that redressed the balance. Astrological influences were also invoked, and incorporated into an intricate but orderly system of correspondences among the elements, zodiacal signs, planets, humors, and parts of the body. Medieval scholars produced an enormous body of medical literature detailing ailments, symptoms, and cures according to this system, which made the course of study to become a doctor long and demanding.

The physician himself was a respected figure in society, educated at a university, and therefore semiclerical in status. His work was principally diagnosis and prescription. The actual preparation of medicine was the work of the apothecary, while physical work on the body itself was left to the surgeon. Both apothecary and surgeon were tradesmen rather than scholars, who learned their craft through apprenticeship rather than university schooling, but their positions, though less lofty than that of the physician, were prestigious and well paid; and they were likely to be literate, and even quite well-read.

Most people did not have access to the expensive services of the physician or surgeon. Surgical procedures might be performed instead by a barber, who also extracted bad teeth, in addition to his work trimming hair and shaving beards. For curing diseases, most people likely turned to a practitioner of folk medicine, who might be a professional or a semiprofessional, or in some cases was no more than a neighbor or family member. Women in particular learned traditional medical practices as part of their training for running a household. Some of these folk remedies were largely based on superstitions, but others had an element of demonstrable medical value: people knew that it was beneficial to cleanse a wound with wine, even though they did not understand the antiseptic properties of alcohol.

In spite of dietary problems and the shortcomings of medieval medicine, medieval people were not the stunted grotesques we sometimes imagine them to be. A survey of medieval English graves found mean heights of about 5 feet 7 inches for men, 5 feet 2 inches for women; the figures for a similar survey in Denmark were 5 feet 7 inches for men and 5 feet 4 inches for women. Dental cavities are rare in medieval skeletons, reflecting a diet low in sugar, although tooth loss from other causes was high: one surveyed sample found an average rate of 7.6 percent of teeth missing.[12]

MONEY

The money of the Middle Ages was in many ways profoundly different from what we think of as money today. A cash transaction always involved a precious metal, usually silver, although gold coinage was introduced in the course of the thirteenth century. In this sense, the use of cash was also a form of barter. The distinctive feature of the precious metal was that a small quantity was enormously valuable—a single ounce was worth a week's wages for even a skilled worker-and its value was relatively stable, in contrast with agricultural goods, which were subject to spoilage, or manufactured goods, which varied in quality. The actual value of the coin depended on its precious metal content, which in turn reflected the coin's physical size and the purity of the precious metal, since it was always alloyed to some degree with a cheaper metal. Minted coin provided a relatively stable medium of exchange by providing standardized quantities and purity of silver, backed by the reputation of the issuing authority whose name and symbol were imprinted on the coin. The imprinted image also helped verify whether the coin had been tampered with by removing metal from any of its surfaces.

Where modern money is almost invariably issued only by national governments, the right to coin money in the Middle Ages was widely dispersed. In France, there were two major royal coinages, the *denier* of Paris and the *denier* of Tours, in addition to a dozen or so important regional coinages, and a multitude of local mints under the authority of minor feudal lords. Only in England was the monarchy successful in establishing an exclusive right to mint coin, and from the thirteenth century onward it had a unique reputation for the quality of its coinage, still reflected in the term "sterling. " Whereas today foreign exchange is only a matter for international travelers, in the Middle Ages even a homebody might encounter a range of different moneys and would need to know their relative values.

Then as now, exchange rates were not stable. Today, the value of a currency represents a complex market reaction to economic circumstances in the country that issues the money. In the Middle Ages, fluctuation was in a large measure a result of changes in the coinage itself. From time to time, medieval rulers succumbed to the temptation to debase their coinage. By melting down old coins and reissuing them in a smaller size or with a higher alloy content, they could increase the amount of money they had at their disposal. Of course, this quickly caused the market to set a lower value on the coin, sometimes with serious economic consequences. People needed to keep an eye on any change in the coinage, as it directly affected the value of the money they used. Fluctuations in the availability of silver itself also affected the value of money.

Overall, the tendency, then as now, was inflationary. The actual rate of inflation was extremely low by modem standards. Over the course of the thirteenth century, the average rate was something like 0.5 percent per year, well below the 2 to 4 percent that many economists consider healthy in western economies today. For contemporaries, the actual rate of inflation was obscured by dramatic short-term fluctuations from one year to the next. These fluctuations were the result of the instability of agricultural production in a subsistence economy highly sensitive to the cost of produce. A good summer might bring a bountiful harvest, lowering the price of produce, while a rainy growing season, crop blight, or disease among the livestock could decimate output, making produce significantly more expensive. A twofold rise or fall in the price of grain from one year to the next was not uncommon. Most of the population was obliged to spend an enormous proportion of their annual income on food, particularly grains and derivative products like bread, and as food prices rose, they needed to demand proportionally more money for their work, leading to a domino effect that affected prices throughout the economy.

Currencies

The predominant monetary system of the Middle Ages was that of pounds, shillings, and pence, known by various names in different languages. The pound (in French, *livre*) consisted in principle of a pound of silver coin. It was equivalent to 20 shillings (in French, *sou*), and the shilling was equal to 12 pennies (in French, *denier*). The pound was purely a money of account, since no coins were actually issued of such enormous value. Even the shilling had no coin equivalent in northern Europe until Saint Louis issued the *gros tournois,* valued at 1 *sou tournois,* in the mid-thirteenth century. The penny was the principal form of coin in most ordinary transactions. In principle, a penny weighed about a thirtieth of an ounce, but its value differed from mint to mint due to variations in actual weight and purity. The English penny was one of the more stable currencies of the Middle Ages, weighing generally about 1.4 grams (about .05 oz.), with a very high purity of silver at about 92 percent. In

BOTH SIDES OF A SILVER PENNY *minted in Bath, England from 1016–1035. The profile featured on the coin depicts King Canute the Great.*

France, there were several prominent monetary standards. The royal Parisian penny, or *denier parisis,* was lighter and less pure than the English penny, generally weighing less than a gram and containing around 38 percent silver; it was also more subject to fluctuations in both size and purity. In the middle of the thirteenth century, Florence and Genoa began issuing medieval Europe's first gold coins, and France followed soon after. These coins, worth about ten times their equivalent in silver, greatly facilitated the handling of large sums of cash. There was also a shortage of smaller coin, particularly in England, where the penny was the lowest denomination minted until the appearance of the halfpenny and farthing (1/4 penny) in about 1280.

The following table offers a quick guide to the relative value of these coins in the latter half of the thirteenth century. The last column offers rough modem equivalents, but these figures must be taken as a general guide to magnitude rather than a precise exchange rate. The actual structure of medieval prices was fundamentally different from that of the modem economy. Labor was much less valuable, while manufactured goods were much more so—the low wage of the manufacturing laborer was overbalanced by the vastly greater time required to produce any given item. An English penny did not have the same purchasing power across the board as a modern $10 bill, but it is more comparable to $10 than to a U.S. penny or $100 bill.

Currency	Approximate Exchange Rate	Approximate Purchasing Value	Modern U.S. $ Equivalent
English pound (£) = 20s.	65–70 sous parisis	1 good carthorse	$2,500
English shilling (s.) = 12d.	39 deniers parisis	1 day's wages for a knight	$100
English penny (d.) contains about 1.3 grams fine silver	3 ¼ deniers parisis	1 day's cheap labor	$10
Livre parisiss = 20 sou	6s.	1 month's rent for a small house in Paris	$1,000
Sou parisis = 12 deniers	3 ¾ d.	1 day's wages for a craftsman	$50
Denier parisis contains about 0.39 grams fine silver	¼ d.	1 1-lb. loaf of bread	$3

Other French currencies varied in value. Twenty *sous parisis* were equivalent to 21 *sous* of Chartres, 25 *sous* of Tours, 27 *sous* of Provins, 30 *sous* of Noyon, and 40 *sous* of Tournai. Countless other currencies were in circulation across Europe; one of the few to have substantial international standing was the florin, minted in Florence, and worth about 8 *sous parisis* or 2s. 6d. sterling.

Prices

The best way to get a more accurate idea of the value of medieval money is to look at its actual purchasing power. The following table offers some common sample goods, with typical prices for each in English currency of the latter part of the thirteenth century. The actual price could vary substantially depending on current economic circumstances, local supply, quality of the item, and of course the skill of the negotiator, since medieval financial transactions were rarely based on a fixed sticker price.

ITEM	PRICE	ITEM	PRICE
2-lb. loaf of bread	¼d.	Dried dates, raisins, figs	1½–2d. per lb.
Eggs	½d. per dozen	Cheese or butter	½d. per lb.
Wine	2–3d. per gallon	Ale	½d. per gallon
Sugar	1–2s. per lb.	Salt	3–5d. per bushel
Pepper	10d. per lb.	Cinnamon	1s. per lb.
Ginger	10d.–2s.6d. per lb.	Book	6s.
Sword	2s.	Pickaxe	4d.
Tallow candles	2d. per lb.	Wax candles	6d. per lb.
Canvas	2d. per ell	Linen	3d. per ell
Fine wool cloth	3s.6d. per yd.	Ordinary wool cloth	1s. 4d. per yd.
Hose	10d.	Shoes	2½d.
Shirt	5 ¾d.	Traveler's costs for a day, with horse	4½d.

Wages and Income

These prices can be compared to some sample incomes of the period, again all in English currency for the sake of simplicity:

Duke	£4000–5000/year	Earl	£1500/year
Baron	£100–200 year	Knight	£10–20/year or 1–2s./day
Royal official	3s./day	Priest	£2–10/year
Educated tradesman	8–9d./day	Tradesman	3–4d./day
Ordinary soldier	2–3d./day	Laborer	£l/year or 1 ½–2 ½ d./day
Servant	1 ½d./day	Woman or child	1d./day

As with other aspects of the medieval economy, actual income levels were complex. Wages not only varied with the skill of the worker and the current economic climate, but with the time of year: in 1222, masons working on Winchester castle were paid 4d. a day in September, 3½d. a day in October, and 2½d. a day in November. These variations were due in part to changes in the work schedule according to available daylight. Laborers in the fifteenth century began the working day at dawn; they ended at about 7 P.M. in the summer, or at dusk in the winter. Their work days therefore varied from about ten and a half hours in the summer to seven or eight hours in the winter. Pay was also higher in August because of the enormous demand for harvest labor. Laborers involved in industrial work could find relatively high-paid harvesting jobs during this month, and their employers had to offer more to keep their services. Methods of pay also varied. As in the modern world, some positions were paid by the year, others were waged—which in the Middle Ages meant the day rather than the hour, since clocks were not yet in general use. Income might also be paid in kind as well as in cash. Long-term employees were especially likely to receive food and lodging as well as money, and perhaps seasonal perquisites such as an annual outfit of clothing. Even daily workers might receive at least one meal from their employer, and perhaps also lodging if the laborer was an itinerant seasonal worker.

Credit and Banking

Not all transactions involved cash. Credit was a well-established feature of local life, heavily used by villagers and townsfolk to compensate for the chronic lack of coinage. Such credit transactions relied on the network of local connections to ensure repayment. During the thirteenth century, credit also began to enter the world of long-distance trade. The Italians led the way by establishing networks of financial houses across the European map, so that a letter of credit from a financier in Florence could be redeemed with his agent in Paris.[13]

Weights and Measures

The complexities of medieval money were in part one manifestation of the intricacy of medieval systems of weights and measures generally. We can still see a vestige of this intricacy in the system

TWO BANKERS OR MONEYLENDERS *count their money in this engraving by Quentin Matsys, a sixteenth-century Flemish artist.*

of inches, feet, yards, and miles, or ounces, pounds, and tons still predominant in America today. In the Middle Ages, weights and measures were even more complex because different objects were measured by different standards, and the standards themselves varied from place to place.[14] The following table gives some idea of the range of standards in common use:

Measure	Use	Equivalent
Ounce	Weight	Apothecary or Troy oz. = 31.103g. Avoirdupois oz. = 28.35g.
Pound	Weight	Apothecary or Troy lb. = 12 oz. London lb. = 15 oz. Avoirdupois lb. = 16 oz.
Stone	Weight	Stone of wax, spices, almonds = 8 lbs. Stone of glass = 5 lbs. Stone of lead = 12 lbs.
Gallon	Liquids, grain	8 lbs.
Barrel	Liquids	Ale barrel = 32 gallons Beer barrel = 36 gallons Wine barrel = 31.5 gallons (⅛ tun)
Tun	Wine	Usually 252 gallons, but sometimes as low as 208 gallons.
Peck	Grain	2 gallons
Bushel	Grain	8 gallons
Quarter	Grain	8 bushels (64 gallons)
Foot	Length	12 inches
Yard	Length	3 feet

Ell	Length, especially linen cloth	45 inches, but sometimes equated with 1 yard.
Fathom	Length	6 feet
Mile	Length (English)	5,000 feet (1,000 paces)
League	Length (French)	10,000 feet (2,000 paces)
Perch	Length of agricultural land	Usually 16.5 feet, but local variants range from 10 to 25 feet.
Rood	Area of agricultural land	40 square perches (¼ acre)
Furlong or acre	Area of agricultural land	4 perches x 40 perches
Virgate	Area of agricultural land	Commonly 20 to 30 acres, but local variants ranged from 15 to 60.

4

VILLAGE LIFE

FOR THE OVERWHELMING MAJORITY OF PEOPLE IN THE MIDDLE Ages, daily life meant village life. Agricultural techniques had advanced significantly since Roman times, yet crop yields were still only a fraction of their modern equivalents, and mechanization of agricultural processes was virtually nonexistent, so that a very high proportion of the population—probably around 90 percent—was needed to raise food. The medieval rural community could take many forms, depending on local traditions, geography, and economy. In areas of northwestern Europe that relied on cereal crops, the community was commonly what historians term an "open-field" or "champion" village, consisting of a cluster of dwellings lying in the center of a large area of cultivated fields, the land being farmed by the villagers on a semicommunal basis. In less-fertile regions, where animal husbandry played a larger role, communities tended to be smaller and less collaborative, in some places consisting only of isolated homesteads.

On land suitable for agriculture, grain cultivation produces more calories per acre than the grazing of livestock, making it the most efficient mode of food production. In Europe's feudal heartland, grain was the main dietary staple, and since grain cultivation was the single most important rural activity in medieval Europe, we will focus here on the open-field village as representative of a characteristic medieval form of cereal-growing community. In particular, we will use the small English village of Cuxham as an example of the type. Substantial manorial records survive from which to reconstruct life in Cuxham at the end of the thirteenth century, and by comparing the material in these documents with information from other sources, we can see common features in village society, and something of the diversity among individual villages.[1]

SCENE OF A GRAIN HARVEST, *with a monk praying in a church. Fresco.*

The Rural Settlement

There is documentary evidence of inhabitation in Cuxham as early as the ninth century, and pottery from the Roman period has been found nearby. A history of habitation stretching back to Roman times would not be surprising for a medieval village. Wharram Percy in Yorkshire, which has been more thoroughly excavated than any other village of the period, was already occupied in Roman and even Iron Age times, and has even yielded archeological finds from the Neolithic and Bronze Ages. Not all rural settlements were so old. The population of Europe was growing rapidly during the Middle Ages, reaching a peak around 1300, so there was always pressure to bring new territory under the plow, and many feudal lords actively encouraged agricultural development of their lands.

Cuxham had many features that encouraged early development. Its soil is good, and low-lying land like Cuxham was generally more populous and more highly developed than upland regions. The village had ready access to transportation, lying near the road from London to Oxford, less than fifty miles from London itself, and only four miles from the river Thames. Perhaps most important of all, the village had an ample supply of water. Water availability was crucial in determining the location of vill-ages, which were generally sited near springs or streams. Cuxham had both: the village lay along a stream that flowed into Cuxham from the neighboring village of Watlington, and near its center another brook rose from springs within the grounds of the manor house. Where suitable surface water was lacking, the village relied on wells instead.

SCENE OF DAILY LIFE *in a medieval country village.*

In the center of an open-field village was the living space of the inhabitants, consisting of a cluster of homes, often gathered around a village green or a dirt street, and in many cases with a church and manor house in the same area. The homesteads in Cuxham lay along a street consisting of about two dozen households, with a total population of perhaps 125 to 150 people. Other settlements were smaller, some larger. Wharram Percy seems to have had about twice the population of Cuxham, while the largest villages had more than five hundred inhabitants, making them larger than the smallest towns. The following list of the principal householders in Cuxham in 1298 gives some idea of the shape of the peasant community, although it does not take account of subtenants, laborers, servants, family, or residents of the manor house complex:

Rector of the Parish Church:
>   Master Adam of Watlington

Free Tenants:
>   Robert at Green. Held some of his land by right of his
>   wife Alice, daughter of William Newman.
>   Richard Cook

Millers:
>   Adam the Miller. Leased the Prior of Watlington's mill.
>   Robert Waldridge. See Villein Landholders below.

Reeve:
>   Robert Bennet

Villein Landholders:
>   Gilbert Almoner
>   Roger Wallace
>   Robert White
>   Henry Weylond
>   Richard East. His cottage lay in the east end of the village.
>   Richard Bovechurch. His cottage lay just uphill from the parish
>   church.
>   Robert in the Hurne ("at the Corner"; formerly Robert Shepherd).
>   His home lay at a bend in the village street. Held land by
>   marriage to Aline, widow of Adam in the Hurne.
>   Adam at Heath

William at Heycroft. Held land by marriage to Christina, daughter of Adam at Heath.

Widow Cecily. Already a widow by ca. 1280.

Robert Waldridge. Father of Robert Oldman. Also leased the lord of Cuxham's mill, which was subsequently leased by Robert Oldman.

Robert Oldman (formerly Robert Waldridge). Son of Robert Waldridge. Held land by right of his wife Agnes, widow of Robert Oldman. Later took over the lord's mill and became the manorial reeve.

Adam Brian. Apparently a relative of Thomas Brian.

Emma, widow of Thomas Brian. Later married Adam son of Robert, who became known as Adam Brian.

Villein Cottagers:

Richard of Turweston

Matilda English

Clarissa, daughter of Evelot

Agnes Stoyleap. Apparently the widow of William Stoyleap.

Walter Luteprec

Matilda Jolif. Apparently the widow of William Jolif.

Alice Jordan. Apparently the widow of Jordan, son of Reginald.

Nicholas Sawyer

The Village Lands

Surrounding the nucleus of the settlement were the village fields. In an open-field village, a villager's landholding was not a compact block, but a scattering of individual strips lying here and there in the village fields. This form of landholding had existed since the early Middle Ages, and by the High Middle Ages it was largely a matter of custom, although it did fulfill a practical purpose by ensuring that each landholder had a reasonably fair share of superior and inferior land. The arable land at Cuxham was divided into three large fields of about 125 acres each. Each field was subdivided into about fifteen parcels

A VIEW OF THE MEDIEVAL TOWN *of Dortmund, Germany.*

called furlongs. The furlong was in theory a furlong in length, or 660 feet. At Cuxham the furlongs averaged about twelve acres, but the size and shape varied enormously. The furlongs at Cuxham bore such names as "Stir Furlong," "Fox's Hole," "Burrow Halfacre," and "Fifty Acre."

The furlongs were further divided into selions, narrow strips belonging to the individual landholders. In principle, a selion covered about an acre and corresponded roughly to a day's plowing, but the actual dimensions varied. The boundary between one villager's selion and that of his neighbor was indicated by the ridges and furrows made in plowing. To prevent encroachment, the villagers at Cuxham used boundary stones as permanent markers.

Every furlong was surrounded by a narrow strip of unplowed land, termed a balk. Balks served as a network of pathways among the cultivated areas of the field. There were no fences within the fields, which is why such settlements are known as open-field villages. Each of the three main fields as a whole was enclosed by hedges and fences, which served principally as a barrier to livestock. The hedges required regular maintenance to keep them thick and strong enough to prevent animals passing through—they were not simply allowed to grow wild, but were carefully arranged and guided as they grew to make them effective barriers. Fences also required maintenance, and they cost more to construct, so they were used primarily where hedges were not an option, particularly at the gates giving access to the fields.

Although wheat was the principal source of sustenance and income in villages like Cuxham, there were various forces that encouraged diversified land use. In the early Middle Ages, when the village system was taking shape, commerce was at a minimum, and the local community needed to be largely self-sufficient. By 1100 self-sufficiency was less crucial, yet the village still retained the economic diversity dictated by its needs in an earlier period. Diversity was also encouraged by contemporary factors. Crop yields were unreliable, since poor weather or blight could lead to a disastrous harvest. It was advantageous to grow a combination of crops as a hedge against a bad year for anyone of them, and to have other resources to supplement the crops.

Diversity in the village economy was facilitated by the three-field system of agriculture, one of the principal agricultural innovations of the Middle Ages. In earlier times, it had been the custom either to farm land repeatedly until its fertility was exhausted, or to divide the land into two fields, each of which was alternately farmed and allowed to lie fallow (unfarmed). In the early Middle Ages, farmers began to use a three-part cycle in which each field was planted one year with a winter crop (wheat, rye, spelt, or barley, planted some time around October), the next with a spring crop (barley, oats, or legumes such as beans and peas, planted some time around February), and left fallow the third year. The spring crop actually helped to revitalize the soil, while allowing each field to be idle only one year in three. This system was still not universal in the High Middle Ages, but it was well established in Cuxham, as reflected in the division of the arable land into three fields. Each year all the land in a field was used either for winter crops, for spring crops, or for fallow.

Three-field agriculture worked particularly well in conjunction with animal husbandry. When a field was lying fallow or had been harvested, animals could graze on it. At such times, the hedges or fences around the field kept the livestock in rather than out. While the field provided the animals with sustenance, they in turn fertilized it with their manure. The livestock not only provided produce and income for the farm, but also played an important role in village agriculture, some as draft animals, and all as sources of manure. To support the animals when they could not graze in the fields, the village lands included pasture for grazing and meadows to provide hay for winter fodder. Meadows and pastures were generally located in lands less suitable for raising crops. At Cuxham, this was the valley area lying along the stream, which was marshy and given to flooding.

At Cuxham, each landholding came with the right to harvest a stipulated number of acres of hay in the meadows; the actual strips to be harvested may have been reallocated each year. A villager's landholding might also include some pasture land, and even those villagers who had no pasturage of their own had access to the large common pasture, as well as the right to graze animals in the village fields at those times of the year when they were opened for grazing. Since animals on the common pasture and fields were intermingled, the villagers pooled their resources to hire common herdsmen to look after them. Overgrazing could be a problem, so in many cases the terms of the landholding also stipulated the number of horses, cattle, and sheep that the landholder was permitted to keep on the village commons. Like the fields and furlongs, individual meadows and pastures were known by name. Cuxham meadows included "Newmead" and "Northmead." The names of the Cuxham pastures reflected their location in the wet floodlands near the stream: the main common pasture was called "the Moor," and the smaller pastures included "Oldpond," and "Waterland."

The last major component in village topography was the "waste," undeveloped land often in the form of forest, marsh, or rugged land at the outskirts of the village fields. The waste also played an important part in the economic life of the village. It provided necessary raw materials, such as stone or timber for building, reeds for thatching, and wood or peat for fires. Cattle could be grazed in marshy land, and pigs fattened in forests. Access to the resources of the waste land was a common right of the villagers, like access to the common pasture, again subject to some restrictions. Cuxham was already intensely developed in the Middle Ages, and had no waste land at all. As a result, the resources that in other villages came from the waste had to be purchased from outside Cuxham, although some firewood was harvested from trees in the village pastures.

THE MANOR

Coexisting with the geographically based community of the village was the legal and administrative community of the manor. The manor was the basic unit of aristocratic landholding, and constituted the point of contact between the peasantry and the feudal hierarchy. Roughly speaking, the manor can be thought of as equivalent in size to a village, although the two did not always coincide. At Cuxham, the manor and the village covered the same territory, but some manors included more than one village, while some villages were divided among more than one manor.

The manor of Cuxham was in the hands of the Foliot family for much of the High Middle Ages. In the thirteenth century, when the manor lord Walter Foliot died without a male heir, Cuxham passed into the hands of his son-in-law, Ralph Chenduit. The manor lord of Cuxham was a tenant of the lord of Wallingford, who was a direct tenant of the king. Like many other manors, Cuxham constituted a knight's fee, for which the manor lord owed the lord of Wallingford the service of one knight.

The Foliots may have found some alternative to service in person. They held at least one other manor from the lord of Wallingford, that of Chenies, about twenty miles away in Buckinghamshire. Theirs was an extensive family, with complex feudal relationships; the Foliots of Cuxham may even have held land from other feudal lords as well. The lordship of Wallingford was itself an extensive fief, including dozens of other manors, mostly scattered about Oxfordshire and adjacent Buckinghamshire and Berkshire.

Manors were the principal source of reliable and substantial annual income. In modern terms, a manor might be compared to an investment portfolio consisting of perhaps a million dollars in reliable bonds, enough to generate a handsome annual income for the holder. Even the greatest lords, including the king, kept some manors in their own hands to provide them with supplies and cash. Many church institutions derived income from manors that had been donated by lay patrons. In 1268, Ralph Chenduit's son Stephen sold Cuxham to Walter de Merton, chancellor of England, who bestowed the manor on his newly founded Merton College at Oxford. The money and produce from the manor helped to support the scholars who lived at the college—the medieval equivalent of the modern university's cash endowment. Other manors were held by monasteries, cathedrals, and important church officeholders.

Like other manor lords, the lords of Cuxham farmed out a portion of their manor to their peasant tenants, and kept the rest, called the *demesne*, directly under their own control. The demesne at Cuxham seems to have constituted about eighty to one hundred acres in each of the three fields, amounting to 70–80 percent of the total land available for agriculture. This was fairly high—a demesne of 35–40 percent would have been more usual. The demesne lands were administered by hired servants, and worked by a combination of paid workers and labor services owed by the manor serfs.

Serfs

Like others in the feudal hierarchy, peasants did not generally own their land; rather, they held it as tenants of the manor lord. The size and terms of the holding depended largely on custom, and could vary greatly from one holding to the next. At Cuxham, as elsewhere, there were two general classes of peasants, corresponding to two forms of land tenure, free and unfree. Unfree tenants, known in Cuxham by the English term "villein," were more common. The obligations placed on villeins depended on local tradition, but most of them were designed to ensure that the manor lord had control over his labor supply. Villeins were forbidden to depart from the manor without the lord's permission; this permission could usually be acquired by payment of chevage, an annual fee exacted for permission to dwell outside of the manor. Fees also had to be paid for a girl to marry someone not belonging to the manor, or for a boy to enter the clergy. Such fees varied with the wealth of the people involved: in 1279, John North paid 20s. for permission to wed Eve Black, then died, and Richard Bovechurch paid 40s. to marry the same woman. Local custom might place additional impositions on villeins. In Cuxham, manorial custom stated that a villein could not "give his son or daughter in marriage or sell a cow that has calved nor a plucked male pullet . . . without permission of his lord. And whenever he brews he must pay one penny."[2] As in other manors, the villeins of Cuxham were also required to grind their grain at the lord's mill. The peasant might come to an arrangement with the manor lord to commute his labor services: by 1288, at least four of the villeins in Cuxham were regularly paying 15d. each to be released from their manorial labors.

The lord exercised civil jurisdiction over his villeins through a manor court. A villein might bring an action against another villager in the court, but he had no recourse against the lord himself. In theory, all the villein's possessions belonged to the manor lord, although in practice the lord generally restricted himself to collecting the villein's best beast at the time of his death, a payment called "heriot" in England. Villeins also rendered fines, rents, and other payments to their lord, clear indication that in practice their goods were treated as their own property.

Cuxham is typical of medieval villages in having three identifiable types of villeins: landholders, cottagers, and the landless. Holdings, like people, were classed as free or unfree, and had traditional obligations associated with them according to their status. Landholding villeins had a fair degree of economic security by medieval peasant standards. At Cuxham the terms of their holdings were determined by general customs of the manor regarding such holdings. The standard villein landholding in Cuxham was a half-virgate, amounting to about twelve acres, divided more or less evenly among the three village fields. Such a holding yielded enough produce to support a family. In other places, the usual holding might be a full virgate, and some villeins held even more. Roughly half of the two dozen or so households in Cuxham belonged to landholding villeins.

In principle, a villein held his land at his lord's pleasure and might be turned out at will, but over the centuries it had become customary to treat the landholding as heritable property. A token of the lord's right to bestow the land at will was retained in the entry fine, a sum paid by the heir to the landholding in order to be allowed to take possession. Entry fines at Cuxham were generally between 20 and 30s.

The rent for a villein's land was principally in the form of labor services owed to the lord, which the lord used to farm the demesne lands. The services owed depended on the customs associated with the landholding. The duties of the Cuxham villeins were fairly typical. According to the customs recorded for Richard East in 1298:

He will plow and harrow at his own expense a fourth of an acre. And throughout the year he will work every second day, either carrying or mowing or reaping or carting, or doing some other work according as the lord or his bailiff commands him, except on Saturdays and major church holidays. And at harvest time he will find two men to reap for two days for the customary additional work at his own cost, that is two men on each day. And at the end of harvest time he will reap with one man for the whole day at his own cost.[3]

The ordinary weekly work requirement came out to approximately two days. The villein did not necessarily perform his service in person—he might instead send a member of his household or a hired laborer to fulfill his obligation. In 1299, Robert Waldridge was fined 2 pence "because he sent for the lord's work a laborer who was too weak and inadequate."[4] This labor also entailed obligations on the lord's part:

All the aforesaid villeins at the end of mowing will have sixpence for beer and a loaf of bread apiece. And he must provide three bushels of wheat for the aforesaid bread. And each of the aforementioned mowers will have one small bundle of hay each evening, as much as he can mow with his scythe.[5]

The villeins at Cuxham also owed a small amount of material rent:

Richard East . . . pays half a penny at Martinmas for "salt-silver," and at Michaelmas eight bushels of pure wheat for seed; and at Martinmas one peck of wheat and four bushels of oats and three hens; and at Christmas one rooster and two hens and two loaves of bread worth a penny [called "present-bread"], or two pence.[6]

The living of the villein cottager was more precarious. A cottage holding consisted of a house with its attached plot of land, but little or no land in the village fields. The cottager's principal source of income was the sale of his own labor. Cottager households constituted about a third of the households in

Cuxham. The cottagers paid lower entry fees than landholders, and they did not owe heriot, but their holdings were based on individual contracts and were therefore less stable. The lord leased out the holding for a certain number of lifetimes: some covered just the lessee, some the lessee and his wife, some the lessee, wife, and son. At the end of the lease, the land reverted to the lord, who could add it to the demesne, or lease it to a new holder at a new rate. In the inflationary period of the High Middle Ages, the new rate generally meant higher rents for the next tenant. The terms of cottage holdings at Cuxham varied, but those of Richard of Turweston are fairly typical:

> Richard of Turweston . . . . pays 3s. annually in two instalments. And he will assist in mowing hay with one man when it is to be mown, and he will stack hay for one day with one man, and will have half a penny for all the aforesaid labors. And he will reap at harvest time for two days with one man, with food provided by the lord.[7]

Those children of villein families who did not inherit land entered the ranks of the landless villeins, a group whose number is hard to determine because they do not often enter the written records. A few may eventually have been able to establish households of their own by negotiating with the lord for a holding or by marrying a landholder. Others were obliged to live in the households of others, working for one of the other villagers, for the manor lord, or for the rector of the parish. If there was insufficient work for them in the village, they might seek their fortunes elsewhere, although they were required to obtain their lord's permission to leave the manor. Some emigrated to a town, others found work elsewhere in the country. A few were allowed to enter the clergy, where even if they never rose above the status of a parish priest, they at least enjoyed a degree of comfort and security unknown to the casual laborer.

The Free Peasantry

Free peasants were less numerous than villeins, although Cuxham is an extreme case in this regard: toward the end of the thirteenth century there were only two freeholding households among the two dozen in Cuxham, but once there had been more. The free peasant was not subject to the various obligations and restrictions imposed on the villein, but his economic status was not necessarily better. Some free peasants were tenants of freehold land. The freeholding was fully heritable: when the holder died or chose to relinquish the holding, the right to occupy it passed on to his heirs. The tenant of a freehold might even sell the holding, transferring the tenancy to the buyer, provided he had the lord's consent. The tenant paid a fixed rent, generally in cash or in kind, although some freeholdings had minor labor services attached to them. The rent varied substantially: some tenants paid under a shilling an acre, others over two shillings. Robert at Green was one of the principal freeholders in Cuxham:

> Robert at Green holds a homestead and three and three-quarters acres of land which he received when he married Alice, the daughter of William Newman, paying for it each year three shillings in four instalments. . . . And he holds a homestead and nine acres, paying for it one pound of pepper at the feast of St. Thomas the Apostle.[8]

The freeholding had many advantages over unfree land, but it was not necessarily more valuable. Freeholdings tended to be polarized between larger holdings that offered significant prospects for financial advancement and small ones that were insufficient to support a family. Small freeholders, like villein cottagers, had to hire themselves out as laborers to make up the shortfall; such free peasants were generally at an economic disadvantage relative to the substantial villein landholder.

Not every free peasant had land. Those who did not inherit a holding were faced with a similar range of choices as those of the landless villein, although it was easier for them to leave the manor, since no permission was required. If they wanted land, they might arrange to lease it from a manor lord or from another peasant. However, if they leased a holding that traditionally had been a villein tenement, they ran the risk of being reclassified as villeins themselves.

Landholdings, Status, and Wealth

The position of a peasant in the community had more to do with his economic status than with his standing as a villein or freeman. One of the principal determinants was the size of the landholding. The landholding required to support a household depended on the quality of the land and the size of the family. Roughly speaking, a holding of about ten to fifteen acres was sufficient to support a household. It might produce a surplus in good years, but could fall short if the harvest was bad. Such subsistence farmers may have constituted about a quarter to a half of agricultural landholders, and a higher proportion among landholding villeins. Peasants who held around twenty acres or more could regularly produce a surplus and achieve a fairly high standard of living relative to their neighbors, with prospects of economic advancement if they invested their earnings well. Perhaps a fifth of landholding peasants fell into this category, with a tiny proportion holding over forty, or even over sixty acres of land. Most of these very prosperous peasants tended to be freeholders, who had greater flexibility in making their investments. At the bottom end of the scale, a holding of about five acres or less was insufficient to support a family, and peasants in this position worked as part- or full-time laborers. Both free peasants and villeins were in this class.

Subletting

Peasants' access to land was not entirely limited to inherited holdings and leases from their manor lords. Some tenants sublet land to tenants of their own, and by this arrangement even a villein might hold land in multiple manors. At Cuxham in the early fourteenth century, three villein householders, Robert Oldman, Alice, widow of Robert Bennet, and William at Haycroft, were leasing between one and three acres of free land outside the manor. In 1299, Robert at Green had at least five cottagers on his lands. In the early thirteenth century, one of the freeholdings in Cuxham was held by Ascelin from the nearby village of Pyrton. Ascelin's son Robert sublet this holding to Robert Sergeant, and after the manor lord bought back the freehold, it was regranted directly to Sergeant. Ascelin also held land in Warpsgrove and Golder, several miles north of Cuxham. Clearly, such peasants were no strangers to enterprise.

Tradesmen and Laborers

Not every villager's livelihood and status depended on possession of agricultural land. The village economy also supported tradesmen who were able to command high prices for their services and maintain a steady income. One of the most universal figures in the medieval village was the local miller. Some peasants still ground their grain by hand, but villeins were generally required to take their grain to the lord's mill, which was powered by wind or water. At Cuxham, there were two mills. The one at the east end of the village street had been donated by the Foliots to the prior of Wallingford. The name of the other mill, Cutt Mill, suggests that its watercourse was specifically cut for the purpose. Cutt Mill lay at the western edge of Cuxham beyond the pastures and meadows, and it belonged to the lord of the manor. Both mills were powered by water. Like most other buildings in the village, they were apparently timber-framed structures with wattle-and-daub walls and a thatched roof. Operation of a water mill required a millpond and dam to allow the miller to control the flow of water, and many millers added to their income by stocking the pond with fish.

A MILLER POURS GRAIN INTO HIS MILL *as a villager looks on.*

The miller was a high-status figure in the community, enjoying a steady income and a relatively attractive job. Both Cuxham mills were operated in the late thirteenth century by leaseholding tenants. The prior of Wallingford's mill was leased by Adam the Miller for about £1 a year. Robert Waldridge leased Cutt Mill for a rent of about £2 a year; it later passed to his son Robert Oldman.

At Cuxham, as elsewhere, the miller was something of a local entrepreneur, and it is hardly surprising that he was sometimes the object of distrust among his neighbors. Popular tales of the Middle Ages portray millers as unscrupulous, always looking for ways to misappropriate their customers' flour. This was a very real problem, since the farmer could never know exactly how much flour his grain should yield, and unless he closely supervised the entire process in person, he could not be sure that he had not been cheated. One manor court case from Cuxham reveals some of the tensions between the villagers and the miller:

> Richard Bovechurch complained against Robert the Miller [i.e., Robert Waldridge], alleging that when this Robert was ordered to grind Richard's grain as he was legally required, the same Robert ground and stored Richard's grain poorly, to the serious harm of the same Richard. And furthermore, when Robert was asked to make amends for this harm, he cursed Richard and his wife. And all these things are understood to be true by the whole court. . . . Robert the Miller is to be fined because he brought action against Richard Bovechurch and Richard White and Richard East, complaining that they failed to grind at the lord's mill. And it is concluded by the whole court that it was Robert's fault that they ground elsewhere.[9]

The other most common trade in the village was that of the blacksmith. Ironwork was expensive and used sparingly in the peasant community, but no villager could do without it. A typical example is the medieval digging spade: to conserve iron, the blade as well as the haft was made of wood, but a plate of iron had to be attached to the cutting edge of the blade in order to make the tool strong enough to penetrate the ground. Much the same held true for many of the tools of medieval agriculture, which were built principally of wood, but with working surfaces of iron. There was an ongoing demand for the services of a blacksmith to make, repair, and replace iron fittings, although not always enough to allow the smith to live exclusively by his craft—the smiths in Cuxham were also farmers. Metalsmithing required a fairly high degree of training and a substantial inventory of tools, so the craft was often passed from father to son.

No other crafts are represented in Cuxham before 1300, but there were other sorts of craftsmen living in the countryside. The improved building techniques of the thirteenth century fueled the demand for craftsmen specializing in building construction, such as carpenters, masons, thatchers, and tilers. Cuxham imported such specialists from the surrounding area as needed. The presence of numerous livestock also provided work for butchers and tanners in some villages. As with the smith, the practitioners of these trades were not necessarily full-time craftsmen.

There was a certain amount of export industry in the countryside, fostered by ready access to raw materials and energy sources. Cloth production in particular was as much a rural as an urban activity. Cuxham had a water-powered fulling mill, used for finishing cloth, in the early fourteenth century, and such mills were not particularly rare in the country. Quarrying, mining, and lumber harvesting were distinctively rural industries, as was smelting: the purification of iron ore required a great deal of fuel, so it was most efficient to smelt the iron in forested areas. For similar reasons, charcoal production was another woodland activity.

Laborers

Industrial activities furnished work for laborers as well as craftsmen. The demand for hired labor provided employment opportunities for those peasants who were not supported by their own family landholding, such as noninheriting siblings of landholders and excess children whose labor was not needed for the household land. Laborers were employed for farm work as well. The village economy had an ongoing need of carters, herdsmen, and threshers, and at harvest time opportunities and wages improved in response to the increased demand for labor.

Agricultural laborers might be hired by peasant householders, either to work their landholdings or to fulfill labor services on the demesne. Others found work with the manor lord. Laborers were commonly taken in as temporary members of their employer's household, receiving food and lodging in addition to their wages. Their terms of employment varied. Some were short-term workers hired for specific purposes, others were long-term servants supplying general labor for the household. At Cuxham in 1295, five villein landholders, one villein cottager, and one freehold cottager were fined in the manor court for having lodged outsiders during the harvest. Such practices were quite common, and as is often the case with manor courts, the fine probably should be understood as a fee rather than as

ILLUSTRATION DEPICTING THE DIFFERENT FARM WORK REQUIRED *for each month of the calendar. From a 1459 French edition of the fourteenth-century Bolognese manuscript* The Treaty of Agriculture.

a penalty. In 1299, the villeins Robert Oldman and Gilbert Almoner sent servants from their household to fulfill their winnowing service, and were fined "because their servants, when they were winnowing the lord's barley, hid a large part of the barley in the chaff, until they were caught by the barn-warden."[10]

WOMEN

Women and Land

For peasant women as for men, social status often depended on access to land. A woman could come into a holding by marrying a landholder, with whom she might be a joint tenant, depending on local custom, or she might inherit land in her own right. A daughter inherited land only if there were no sons, but this was not an especially rare situation in families where the average number of children was only two or three. There was enormous pressure on an inheriting daughter to marry so that there would be a man to work the holding, but marriage was expected of landholding men as well. A married couple was generally considered joint tenants of the landholding, with the husband as the official head of the household, but an heiress's holding continued to be recognized as her inheritance. Such had been the case in Cuxham for Robert Waldridge's father William, whose holding, according to the manor court, "was the right of his wife, and not his own inheritance," and we have already seen that the freeholder Robert at Green held some of his land by marriage.[11]

If a woman's husband died, the holding remained in her hands. If the marriage had produced children, this reduced the pressure to remarry for the sake of producing an heir. She still required someone to perform the male work of the household, but this could be fulfilled by a male relative—the son if he were old enough—or by a hired hand. If a widow remarried, her new husband again became a joint tenant, but as with an inheritance, the holding continued to be recognized as her right rather than his. If he outlived her, he might continue to hold the land during his life, but it would pass to the heir of the first marriage after his death.

In all, two of the landholding villein households in Cuxham in the late thirteenth century belonged to women, as did five of the cottage holdings. Most or all of these women were widows. Such women might enjoy a fairly prominent status in the community. When the younger Robert Waldridge married Agnes, widow of Robert Oldman, Waldridge acquired not only the land but the surname of her first husband. The same happened to Robert Shepherd, who came to be known as Robert in the Hume after he married Aline, the landholding widow of Adam in the Hume.

Women's Work

The labor of the peasant family was segregated by sex, but the woman was still very much an active partner in the economics of the household. Broadly speaking, the man was responsible for work that took place in the village fields, while the woman presided over activities in the home and on the land attached to it. Some of her responsibilities provided domestic support for male labor, for example,

LABOR OF THE MONTH OF APRIL: WOMEN PLANTING A GARDEN IN QUADRANTS. Anonymous Flemish artist, ca. 1510. Ink and paint on parchment. Medieval gardens were very organized, with the herbs and flowers planted in a grid by type. For example, fragrant and medicinal herbs went in one section, with flowering plants in another.

cooking meals, looking after the house, and raising children. Other parts of her work contributed materially to the household economy. She was in charge of the home garden, where she raised vegetables, fruits, and herbs for cooking and medicine. She was also responsible for the household poultry, an important source of protein in the peasant diet, occasionally as meat, but most importantly as providers of eggs. Part of the garden and poultry produce was consumed by the household itself, and the remainder could be taken to market and sold to bring cash into the family coffers.

Sustenance and income were also provided by the woman's dairying work during the milking season. Dairy animals included cows, sheep, and goats, depending on local dairying customs. This milk was a valuable source of nutrients for the peasant family, but since milk goes sour quickly in the absence of refrigeration, the woman had the task of making it into butter and cheese, both of which could be kept for a significant period of time. This labor-intensive work must have occupied a significant part of the peasant woman's time during the dairying season. Brewing was another predominantly female activity that provided both nutrition and income for the household. Medieval ale was made without hops, and did not keep very well—one of the principal advantages of hops is its preservative quality. Since a single household was not necessarily able to consume a full batch of ale before it went sour, there was usually a surplus to sell.

Finally, the female householder often generated additional income by spinning. The production of thread to make cloth involved an enormous amount of labor, since each thread had to be spun by hand, but the work itself was not difficult and could be carried out with the simplest equipment. A woman using a drop-spindle could produce thread while she was busy doing her other household chores. This thread would be sold to agents who purchased it to send to the weaver. In the early Middle Ages, when weaving was done on the simple upright loom, this too was a domestic activity for women, but in the High Middle Ages the craft was taken over by the more expensive and efficient horizontal loom, and was transformed from a domestic activity for women into an industrial craft dominated by men.

Not every peasant woman was a householder. Like the men, many women ended up as laborers, and their role in the hired workforce was scarcely less important than that of the men. One thirteenth-century tract on estate management recommends hiring women as they can be paid lower wages.[12] and later sources indicate that women were hired for such tasks as road repair, manuring, thatching, sheep-shearing, weeding, mowing, transporting grain, and even plowing, which was normally thought of as man's work.[13] The demesne household at Cuxham provided work for several women, and the manor court records of 1294 show that the villagers also hired female servants: the villein widows Agnes Oldman and Aline in the Hurne each had at least one maidservant, and the freeman Robert at Green had two.

The Peasant Home

Some idea of the material resources of a peasant household is offered by the Cuxham tax assessment of 1304. The goods listed for Richard Bovechurch were typical:

> 1 horse, value 2s.;
>
> 1 cow, value 4s.;
>
> 1 piglet, value 6d.;
>
> 3 hens, value 3d.;
>
> Also 1 bushel of beans, value 3d.;
>
> Also 2 acres sown with grain, value 4s.;
>
> Also 2 acres sown with vetch, value 2s.;
>
> Also 1 cottage, value 18d.;

Also 1 brass pot, value 12d.;

1 pan, value 3d.;

1 cart, value 8d.;

Also miscellaneous gear, value 18d. Sum: 17s. 6d.[14]

Richard's assets fell near the middle of the range of wealth among Cuxham's landholding villeins, who were assessed at sums ranging from 8s. to 34s. The cottageholders were poorer: the only one with sufficient assets to warrant assessment was valued at under 3s.

The House

The typical peasant house of the High Middle Ages was a fairly simple structure, built by the peasants themselves and limited by their resources and skills. Such houses tended to be rather impermanent. Archeological excavations of village sites have found succeeding layers of rebuilt peasant houses, and in many cases the later structures are aligned quite differently from their predecessors, indicating a complete rebuilding.

The building materials varied, depending on locally available materials. Wood was especially common, since a simple wood structure required little in the way of specialized tools. The peasant builders erected a frame of timber. Sometimes the vertical timbers were set into postholes in the ground, which improved the building's stability but reduced its lifespan by allowing moisture from the ground to soak up into the timbers, causing them to rot over time. Slightly more durable was a frame set on padstones, large flat stones distributed at key weight-bearing points that helped keep the wood dry. Best of all was a true foundation of stones that kept the timbers from touching the ground at all. Stone houses were rare among the medieval peasantry, but in some places they were coming into use in the thirteenth century. Building standards seem to have been improving in many areas at this time, probably reflecting an increased reliance on specialized builders, facilitated by the growth of a market economy.

The materials used to fill in the walls depended on local resources. Wood was generally too valuable for this purpose, except in heavily forested areas like northeastern Europe. In some areas, clay was used as wall filling, in others, slabs of turf. Peasant houses in Cuxham made use of the common technique known as "wattle and daub": a row of vertical stakes was secured in place along the line of the wall, and pliant wands were woven horizontally through them, making a basket-like surface (wattle) that was covered with daub, a mixture of clay, dung, and straw. The walls of the peasant cottage were coated with limewash, which helped brighten the interior while making the exterior resistant to rain.

The roof was the most crucial element in the whole structure. It needed to be fully waterproof, but not so heavy as to collapse the structure underneath, nor too expensive to be beyond the peasant's means. One of the most common solutions was to thatch the roof with a thick layer of reeds, straw, broom, or heather. These materials were all extremely cheap, and a thatched roof was fairly light and quite waterproof. Such a roof was also reasonably durable: depending on the materials, a thatched roof could last anywhere from ten to seventy years.[15]

The peasant house was one story high, without a cellar, although some of the space under the roof might be used as a loft. The ground plan depended on the building's use. In some areas, the typical form of peasant home was the "long house," measuring perhaps 15 feet by 50 feet or more, with human living space at one end, and an area for animals at the other. The long house had a central hearth in the middle of the living space, and one end might be sectioned off to make a smaller bedchamber. There might also be a cross-passage separating the human and animal ends of the building. Various forms of peasant houses built to accommodate both people and animals occurred across Europe, since it was a particularly economical design. In other areas, including Cuxham, the custom was to build a cottage for the humans, with animal accommodations in a separate building. A poor cottager might have just one or two rooms, each measuring about 15 feet by 15 feet—in timber-frame houses, the size of the rooms was determined by the spacing between the upright timbers, which generally had to be kept to 15 feet or less to avoid overburdening the horizontal beams. Most houses at Cuxham appear to have had two rooms or more.

The house typically was home to a married couple and a few children, and perhaps a hired worker or two. If the householder had any surviving parents, they might also live in the house, although retirement agreements often stipulate that the heirs will furnish the retirees with a small cottage of their own. Sometimes the householder had one or more unmarried siblings living there as well, essentially in the role of hired help. However, this does not seem to have been particularly common, and we should generally imagine the peasant household less as an extended kin group than as something comparable to the modern nuclear family. The household might also keep a dog and a cat. These were not domestic pets so much as working animals: the dog was helpful for herding and keeping watch over the homestead, while the cat preyed on the mice and rats that would otherwise infest the home and granary.

A RECONSTRUCTION DRAWING OF A THIRTEENTH–FIFTEENTH CENTURY PEASANT HOUSE *in Wharram Percy, a deserted medieval village in North Yorkshire, England.*

The Interior

The interior of the peasant house was quite spartan. The floor was no more than packed dirt or clay, perhaps covered with fresh straw from time to time. The house would have a wooden door with iron fittings, and possibly even some form of lock. The windows were small to minimize heat loss, with no glass to cover the opening, but with simple wooden shutters to close it at night. The discovery of candleholders in the peasant cottages of Wharram Percy offers evidence that peasants did not always retire to bed when daylight failed. Light also was provided by the fire on the hearth, lying in the center of the room.

The furnishings of a peasant home were simple and few. Stools and benches provided seating and there may have been some sort of trestle table, although one text of the period describes the typical peasant eating his meal not at a table but holding his bowl in his lap. For bedding the peasant used straw, which provided good insulation and a reasonable degree of comfort, although the surface was much harder than a modern bed. The straw might be stuffed inside a sack to make a kind of rough mattress. Bedding straw was a notorious harborer of lice and bedbugs; these unwelcome pests were discouraged by including an herb like wormwood in the bedding, but the straw still needed to be changed from time to time. Late thirteenth-century commoners from the English town of Colchester, assessed at a similar value to Richard Bovechurch of Cuxham, owned wooden bedsteads, linen sheets, and coverlets.[16] Woolen blankets would also have been within the peasant's means.

Cooking and eating utensils were few, and because metal was costly, they were more likely made of clay or wood. Clay pots served for cooking food and could also be used for baking after the manner of a Dutch oven, with the dough inside and the pot covered with hot coals. Bowls and drinking vessels were made of clay or wood, and spoons made of wood as well. Forks were not used at any level of society, but a knife was part of everyone's personal equipment, and served as an eating utensil as well as a working tool. Many of the peasants of Cuxham are known to have had brass cauldrons, useful for heating water, and Richard Bovechurch's contemporaries from Colchester had gridirons and cooking tripods, as well as jugs, basins, and hand towels. An English manorial custumal of the thirteenth century envisioned peasant tenants bringing a plate, mug, and napkin to a meal.[17]

Storage was provided by simple wooden chests, caskets, cupboards, straw baskets, and coarse fabric sacks; not many were needed to contain the peasant's limited personal possessions. Excavations at Wharram Percy have turned up keys, suggesting some peasants had valuables to protect, perhaps money, brooches, or silver spoons like some of the Colchester residents kept in their caskets. The largest part of the household equipment consisted of various sorts of tools for agriculture, dairying, sewing, and spinning. The household probably also had a broom: the cottage floors at Wharram Percy show signs of frequent sweeping.

Toft and Croft

Outside the human living quarters, the homestead included other facilities necessary to the farming household. The cattle were kept in a cow house, either built into the main house or as a separate building. If there were other livestock, they too needed shelter: a stable for horses, a sty for pigs, a henhouse for poultry. Many of the villagers of Cuxham owned horses, cows, sheep, pigs, hens, or geese. If the family had farmland, they also needed a barn to store their grain, and perhaps other sheds for their agricultural equipment, especially large items such as the plow, harrow, and cart, although in some cases these may have been borrowed. A craftsman such as a smith would have a workshop. Well-to-do peasants might have other buildings as well. If the wife did any brewing, additional buildings were needed for this purpose: a malt kiln to sprout and dry the grain, and a brewhouse to boil the water and wash it through the malt. She might also have a bakehouse to hold an oven. If there were a number of buildings, they might be grouped together to form something of a yard, providing a degree of shelter against the wind.

One indispensable facility was the household privy. This took the form of a small shed near the house, similar to the outhouses used in some places today. Since the journey to the privy was cold and inconvenient at night, the household probably used a ceramic chamber pot that was emptied later into the privy. The privy was built over a cesspit and used not only for human waste, but for disposal of all sorts of household rubbish. As the cesspit filled up, it needed to be emptied. The waste was then dumped on the fields as fertilizer, which might be a factor in the lack of raw vegetables in the medieval diet, since plants fertilized with human feces are not very healthful when eaten uncooked. Some households probably had only a cesspit, with no shed for privacy.

Behind the land on which the house and its outbuildings stood—termed the toft—the peasant had a plot for agricultural use, called the croft. The crofts of cottagers in Cuxham were small: the total area of toft and croft was generally around half an acre, and some were even smaller. The homestead plots of landholding villeins at Cuxham were nearly twice this size, and in some villages a croft might cover several acres. The croft provided space for a garden where the housewife grew vegetables and fruit to supplement the family diet, herbs for cooking and medicinal use, or flax to spin into linen thread, to bring some extra income into the household. The croft could provide grazing for the household livestock, and it might also include an orchard for fruit trees or even a small plot of arable land for grains. At Wharram Percy, the boundary between the toft and the street was marked by a stone wall, while the crofts were surrounded by earthen banks topped by a hedge or fence, which kept animals from straying in or out.

THE MANOR HOUSE

The largest household in the village was that of the manor lord. In contrast with the modern world, where rich and poor tend to live apart from one another, the manor lord's extensive residence stood amidst the humble cottages of his tenants—at Cuxham, the village's smallest cottage tenements were carved right out of the grounds of the manor house. These grounds covered nearly fifteen acres in all, and were enclosed by a wall. The sections of the wall near the manor house were made of stone, while the more remote parts consisted of an earthen bank, apparently covered with thatch to protect it from the rain. The main entrance to the enclosure, near the village church, was through a stone gatehouse, a substantial building with a gate of oak fitted with two locks. Above the gate was a room that may have served as a porter's lodge, itself fitted with a lock and reached by wooden stairs. There was at least one smaller pedestrian gate on the far side of the complex leading into the grounds of the rectory; this too was fitted with a lock.

The wall around the Cuxham manor grounds could keep livestock

PRESENT-DAY PHOTOGRAPH OF IGHTHAM MOTE, *a fourteenth-century medieval moated manor house in Kent, England.*

in or out, but it would not have been very effective against a determined human intruder, and offered only minimal protection for a military force. Probably its most important function was to emphasize the lord's prestige and distinguish him from his peasant neighbors. Some manorial complexes were more fortified than Cuxham, but in general, such places served civilian rather than military purposes, as residences for the lord, bases for farming the demesne, and centers for manorial administration.

The Hall and Solar

The main gate of the manor grounds led into a courtyard surrounded by a complex of buildings, including the manor house itself, which served as the lord's home. By the twelfth century it was becoming fashionable to build the manor house of stone, but this was extremely expensive, and many aristocrats had to be content with cheaper materials. The manor house at Cuxham does not survive, but records suggest that it was a two-part building consisting of a timber-framed great hall in front of an attached "solar" of stone, comparable to the twelfth-century manor house that has been excavated at Wharram Percy.

The great hall at Wharram Percy was a more sophisticated version of the timber-framed dwellings of the peasantry, with pillars supporting a high roof to create a large open room. Here the manorial household ate meals and transacted public business. At the back of the hall there was probably a raised dais for the table of the lord, his family, and his most privileged guests. At night, the hall might serve as sleeping quarters for some of the household staff. The room would have had a central hearth, with the smoke escaping through the roof, possibly with the assistance of a louver. As in the peasant cottage, this arrangement limited the possibility of having an upper floor. The more modern stone halls generally had fireplaces and two floors, with the main room above (accessed via an external staircase) and a cellar underneath. The hall at Cuxham was evidently a well-made timber-frame building, with stone foundations, whitewashed and plastered walls, and a tiled roof.

At the top or dais end of the hall at Cuxham was a doorway leading into the upper floor of an attached structure termed a solar. At the entrance to the solar there seems to have been a lobby and a door fitted with a lock. At both Cuxham and Wharram Percy the solar was a stone building of two floors. The lower floor at Cuxham, which may have been partly underground, appears to have been fitted with a lock and used as a cellar for storage, possibly with a dairy in the same area. The upper level was used by the lord's family as a private area away from the more public space of the hall. Here would be beds for the family, and perhaps also for favored guests. The servants who waited directly on the family might also sleep in the area, to be at hand if they were needed. The solar at Wharram Percy had a fireplace and chimney, and the same was probably true at Cuxham. At Cuxham there were external stairs giving direct access to the solar from outside, possibly through the lobby behind the hall. Such an arrangement cut down on drafts when the outside door was opened. There might also have been additional partitions subdividing the rest of the solar into smaller chambers for additional privacy. Interior partitioning could be in the form of wooden or stone walls, or perhaps just curtains.

The solar at Cuxham was lit by several windows, including a "great window" fitted with iron bars, and smaller windows in the gable end. These windows were equipped with shutters, but it is uncertain whether they were filled in with glass. The building was roofed with shingles; other manor houses had thatched solars.

Cuxham had a privy attached to the solar, also roofed with shingles and fitted with a window. Where the solar lacked an adjoining privy, the family may have used chamber pots, which the servants emptied into a detached privy at some distance from the manor house.

Ancillary Buildings

Surrounding the manor house were the service buildings of the manor. Closest were those that served the manor house itself. Primary among these was the kitchen, which was usually located near the front of the hall, and sometimes attached to it, to facilitate the serving of food to the table. The kitchen at Cuxham had a tiled roof, a common precaution in such buildings where fire was a serious hazard. Cuxham also had a bakehouse: here the fire risk was even greater, and the building was made of stone, again with a tiled roof. There were also a window,

TWO WOMEN COOK IN THE KITCHEN *in this illustration from* Tacuinum Sanitatis, *a medieval handbook on health and well-being.*

fitted with shutters. With both the kitchen and bakehouse, the use of separate buildings reduced the likelihood of damage if a fire broke out. The same was true of the malting kiln and brewhouse built on many manors to provide the household with ale. Cuxham certainly had a malting kiln, and probably a brewhouse to accompany it. Some manor complexes also included kennels for the lord's hunting hounds and a mews for his falcons. There certainly were dogs at Cuxham in the late thirteenth century, since in 1288–1289 four bushels of vetch were used for their food, but by this time there was no longer a resident lord at the manor, and the dogs were probably working farm animals.

Other buildings in the manor complex served the demesne farm, and were less fine in construction than the household buildings. Cuxham had at least two barns. Like most of the farm buildings, these were timber-framed structures with thatched roofs, used to store the sheaves of grain when they were carted back from the fields. The wheat barn had two doors: a small pedestrian door, and a large one to admit carts to facilitate unloading. There were also a granary, a strawhouse, and a carthouse. The demesne kept only a single cart, but the carthouse may also have housed the lord's two plows.

Several of the buildings in the manor complex were used for the demesne livestock. There were a henhouse and a pigsty: the demesne stocked several dozen chickens, and over a dozen pigs. Some manors even had peacocks, for both decoration and eating. The manorial buildings at Cuxham certainly included a stable. The demesne had a half-dozen horses, two of which were specifically for the cart, the others used for the plow and miscellaneous purposes. When the horses were let out to graze, they were sometimes fitted with fetterlocks, a sort of locked shackle for their legs that served to keep them from straying and as an antitheft device. There were also several dozen sheep, but these hardy animals may have spent all their time outdoors. There was a byre used for cattle, of which the Cuxham demesne usually had two to three dozen. These animals served various purposes: the cows were milked, steers (young gelded males) were sold or trained, and oxen (trained gelded males) were used for plowing. A bull was also kept for breeding. The demesne had a dairy where the milk was made into cheese and butter. This room was fitted with a lock, and may have been in the cellar under the solar, which was a cool room suitable for keeping milk from going sour too quickly. From the mid-fourteenth century there is evidence of beekeeping at Cuxham. The bees would have been kept in hives made of straw, yielding honey and wax, both of which were valuable commodities.

There was also a dovecote among Cuxham's manorial buildings. This was a round structure with small openings around the outside to attract nesting doves. Shortly before the chicks were ready to begin flying—an age at which they had maximum meat and minimum muscle—they could be fetched down with a ladder and eaten or sold. The dovecote at Cuxham was a substantial building, built of stone with a tiled roof. The doves themselves were too numerous to be counted: the demesne collected several hundred chicks each year. In 1276, the dovecote was being farmed out for £1 a year, half the yield of the lord's mill.

The buildings covered only a corner of the extensive manor house grounds at Cuxham. The rest was given over to the garden, which was used for a variety of purposes. There were plots for herbs and vegetables—those planted at Cuxham included leeks, onions, beans, and hemp—and there also may have been decorative plants as well. There were trees that provided apples, pears, cherries, nuts, and timber. Grapevines were planted in 1288. The grounds included a fishpond that could be stocked as needed to ensure a supply of fresh fish for the lord's table. Several dozen ducks and geese also made use of the pond, sometimes in conflict with the fish: the Cuxham manorial accounts occasionally note that some of the ducklings were eaten by pike. The garden may also have been used as a recreational area for the family. There was probably also pasturage on the grounds of the manor house for the manorial horses and cattle.

The manor complex served as home to both the household of the lord himself and the full-time workers of the demesne. The lord's immediate family may have been larger than those of his tenants, since aristocrats tended to have more children than commoners, and they were more likely to have nonnuclear family members living with them. The family would also have personal servants and kitchen staff. The demesne's fulltime farm workers at Cuxham in the late thirteenth century included four plowmen (two working each plow), a carter, a dairy worker, a cowman, a shepherd, and a gardener. Each of these workers did a variety of tasks: one of the plowmen was assigned to sow the seed, the carter harrowed the fields, the dairy worker winnowed the grain. The manor complex also hosted part-time workers, especially seasonal farmhands hired at harvest and threshing times, and craftsmen employed to work on the buildings of the manor complex. In all, there were probably between a dozen and two dozen people residing in the complex at any given time.

A PREACHER AND HIS FOLLOWERS. *Miniature from* Decretum Gratiani, *a twelfth-century collection of Canon law.*

THE PARISH

Much less wealthy than the manor lord, but nonetheless important in the life of the village, was the parish priest. The parish was the fundamental local division of the church. At Cuxham, the village and parish covered the same area, although this was not always the case, since some parishes extended over two or more villages. The parish had its own church, tiny and plain in comparison with the great cathedrals, yet still an impressive building relative to other structures in the village. The church at Cuxham, the only building from the period still standing today, is built of stone and measures about thirty-five feet long and twenty-four feet wide, with a bell tower over the entrance measuring about twelve feet by twelve feet. The church stands some thirty-five feet tall, and its overall volume is probably about four times that of the more substantial peasant cottages that once stood near it. The building was distinguished by its materials and decoration as well. Apart from the manor lord's solar, it was the only large stone building in the village. It would have been fitted with glass windows, and the interior would have been limewashed. The interiors of many parish churches were brightly decorated with murals depicting biblical stories and other religious themes, and they were richly furnished relative to the simplicity of the peasant cottage. As was customary, Cuxham's church was built with its entry facing west and its altar at the east—the origin of our term "orientation."

The parish priest celebrated Mass for the villagers on Sundays and holy days. Attendance was probably uneven, but the whole village was most likely present on major feasts such as Christmas and Easter. The church was an important focal point in the community: the children of the parish were baptized in the font, couples were married at the door, and the dead were buried in the yard. The building also served as a meeting place, since it was the only public building in the village large enough to hold a significant number of people.

The parish of Cuxham lay under the jurisdiction of the bishop of Lincoln, but as in many other villages, the right to appoint the priest belonged to the manor lord, whose predecessors had probably built the church. The Foliots, like many others, seem to have regarded the appointment as a suitable position for their relatives, since in the early thirteenth century the position was given to a priest named Walter Foliot. In other cases, the village priest was of peasant origins like his neighbors. Poor and remote parishes were unappealing to many priests, and they were often served by those whose learning was quite limited, although it was still well beyond that of their neighbors, since the priest could at least read and write and had some knowledge of Latin.

The priest's income was not great, but it was reasonably comfortable by village standards, ranging in England from £4 upward, with £10 as a common figure. The whole of the property and income rights associated with the parish church were called the rectory. At Cuxham, the rectory was probably worth substantially over £7 a year in the thirteenth century. A large part of this derived from tithes on the villagers—a tax of one-tenth of their proceeds each year, whether in cash, crops, livestock born during the year, or any other form of income. The rectory also included lands in the village fields, called the *glebe*. Detailed information on the glebe is lacking for medieval Cuxham, but in the early seventeenth century it consisted of about thirty acres, scattered about the fields as other holdings were.

In many cases, the rectory was in the hands of someone other than the parish priest, such as a local lord, a monastery, or a cathedral, who used part of the rectory income to hire a parish priest and kept the rest as profit. This was sometimes the case at Cuxham after the manor and rectory came into the hands of Merton College: a scholar at the college was appointed rector at Cuxham and received the income from the rectory, then used a portion of the money to hire a priest for the parish, and kept the rest to support himself at Oxford.

The rectory also included the priest's house. The priest's house was located on grounds of its own, covering about two acres at Cuxham, much smaller than the manorial grounds, but over twice the size of the more substantial peasant homestead plots. The priest's home at Cuxham was probably a superior version of those of his peasant neighbors, timber-framed and thatched. The homestead would also include farm buildings to serve the glebe and to accommodate the variety of produce received as tithes. From the early fourteenth century, there is evidence that the priest owned cows, oxen, and a cart, and employed various laborers under the supervision of a bailiff to attend to the glebe. There is also evidence of a fishpond on the rectory land, and in the early sixteenth century there was a dovecote.

Aside from the hired hands and probably a servant, the priest's household was small. Married clergy were relatively common in the early Middle Ages, a time when the parish priest belonged as much to his village community as to the external community of the church. From the eleventh century onward, there was a movement of reform in the church that sought to draw a sharper distinction between clergy and laypeople, in part by forbidding priests to marry. The subject was still somewhat controversial in the twelfth century, but opponents of clerical marriage had the upper hand, and the parish priest at Cuxham in the High Middle Ages was almost certainly not married.

LABOR AND LEISURE

Village life was heavily shaped by the annual cycle of nature. Different seasons required different work, and the intensity of labor varied greatly over the course of the year. The following description applies for a three-field village in England like Cuxham, but the schedule in other places depended on the local climate and system of planting.

Winter

The peasant's year began after Michaelmas, September 30, at which point the last of the previous year's harvest had been gathered. The season from Michaelmas to Christmas was reckoned as winter in England, and the peasant's first task at this time of year was to plant the winter crops in the fields that had lain fallow the previous season. The main winter crop was wheat, but sometimes barley was included. Spelt was also a winter crop in some parts of Europe, and rye was an important winter grain in northern Europe, since it is hardier than wheat and ripens quickly. At Cuxham, wheat was the normal winter crop and occupied about half the land cultivated every year. The winter crop germinated before winter weather set in, but its real growing season came during the following spring and summer; by planting it before the ground froze, the farmer spread out his plowing work over the year, and had all his planting finished early enough in the spring to take maximum advantage of the growing season.

Planting a field involved several stages of work. First, the ground had to be broken up to provide the seed a good bed in which to grow. To do this, the farmer guided his plow up and down the fields, pulled by a team commonly consisting of four oxen. A plow team generally included two people, one to handle the plow, the other to control the oxen. The plow had a vertical blade called a coulter that sliced through the ground, with a blade behind it called a plowshare, that cut the soil horizontally; behind the plowshare an angled surface called a moldboard cast the soil off to the side, leaving in the plow's wake a trench with a ridge of soil beside it.

Once the plow had done its work, the farmer could sow his seed. The quickest and most usual method with grains was "broadcast": the sower walked up and down the fields with his seed, casting handfuls in an arc before him as he went. Once the seed was in, the ground was harrowed. The harrow was a large wooden frame with spikes protruding beneath it, which the farmer had his team of oxen or horses drag through the fields to even out the surface, leveling the ridges back into the furrows and covering up the seed. The harrowing of the winter crop was supposed to be complete by the end of October or early November.

Planting the winter crop was the most demanding work on the farmer's schedule in the months before Christmas. October was also the season for gathering various types of fruit. Tree fruits such as apples and pears ripened in this season, and it was also the time for grape harvesting in those parts of Europe where grapes were grown. The months after Michaelmas were also a time for threshing and winnowing. The sheaves of harvested grain included stalks and husks as well as the edible seed: to extract the seed, the grain was beaten with flails (or in some cases, trampled by oxen), and then shaken in baskets or blown with fans to separate the seed from the inedible chaff.

In early November, the livestock were brought in from pasture, and foddered with hay while the cold season lasted. The frugal householder conserved his hay by slaughtering any animals he planned to eat during the winter and preserving the meat for future use. Martinmas, November 11, was traditionally the occasion for slaughtering excess livestock.

CHILDREN EXCITEDLY INDULGE IN A SNOWBALL FIGHT *in this whimsical winter scene from a Book of Hours, ca. 1510. Work goes on, though, as a man toils in the background. Ink and paint on parchment.*

As winter approached, with snow and frozen ground, agricultural work became less feasible. This was a good season for tending to the maintenance of the farm and its equipment: repairing buildings and tools, gathering firewood, and cleaning out the privy. The Christmas season itself brought a holiday from work for the full twelve days from Christmas Eve to Epiphany. This was a time when the need and opportunity for farm work was at a low ebb, and villagers took the opportunity for a rare holiday. During the Christmas season, many peasants owed some part of their annual rent to the lord, but they also might receive some of his obligations to them. The customs of one English manor in the early fourteenth century stipulated that at Christmas the lord was to provide one of his tenants with

> his laborer's-feast at Christmas, along with two men, namely two white loaves, as much ale as they will drink in the day, a platter of beef and of bacon with mustard, one of chicken-stew, and a cheese; fuel to cook his food and that of the other tenants . . . and to burn from dinner time until evening and afterwards; and two statute candles to burn out one after the other while they sit and drink, if they will sit so long; . . . and the next day after noon his "gift-ale" with one man, as much ale as he will drink until evening.[18]

Spring

As soon as the ground was sufficiently thawed, the spring crop was planted—spring was reckoned among English farmers as extending from Epiphany to Easter. The spring crop was typically a combination of grains, such as barley and oats, with legumes, such as beans, peas, and vetch; lentils were also grown in southern Europe. The spring crop was planted in the fields used for the winter crop in the previous season; it needed to be in the ground by the end of March or so. Spring was also the season in which the women began to prepare the household garden, and because it was the time when lambs and calves were weaned, it marked the beginning of their dairying work as well.

Summer

Easter, like Christmas, brought a respite in the cycle of labor, lasting through the week following Easter and into Hocktide, the Monday, Tuesday, and Wednesday of the subsequent week. When work resumed, it was at an easier pace. The main responsibilities of the farmer in April and May were weeding the planted fields and plowing the fallow fields one or more times in preparation for the next season of planting. This relatively easy pace continued into June, when the farmer's most substantial task was to shear his sheep. Many villages held a summer festival in Mayor June. There was often another major festival at Midsummer, June 24, a last chance to celebrate before the rigors of the harvest. The Midsummer festival commonly featured a bonfire, and this is one of the few folk customs to have left a trace in the Cuxham records: in 1340, Robert Oldman's son John took a penny's worth of brushwood from within the grounds of the manor house on Midsummer's Eve, evidently collecting it for the fire.

Harvest

The hay harvest began at the end of June and the pace of work picked up again. The grass in the meadows had grown quite high by this time and was ready to be turned into hay. The farmers mowed it down as close to the ground as possible with scythes, then spread it out to dry. Once dry, it was gathered into stacks, pitched onto carts, and carried home for storage. Wet weather was the farmer's bane during haymaking season, since improperly dried hay rotted into uselessness.

By the beginning of August, haymaking was over, and livestock were sent into the meadows to graze on the leavings. Now began the hardest season of the farmer's year, as all the field crops had to be harvested and transported home within the next two months. The first priority was to reap the grains. First their upper ends were cut, handful by handful, using a sickle. These were bound into sheaves, loaded onto a cart, and brought home to the barn. Again, rainy weather could be disastrous, as harvested grain was susceptible to rot if it got wet. Once the grain was cut, the rest of the stalk was mowed as the hay had been, providing straw for countless domestic uses such as thatching, bedding, basket-making, and floor covering.

The demand for rural labor was at its peak during the harvest, as every farm needed to get its crops in promptly. It was a particularly difficult time for the villein, since he not only needed to attend to his own crops but also owed extra labor services to the manor lord at harvest time. Because of the heightened need for labor during this season, women commonly took part in the harvest, and many farms also hired day laborers.

Grain yields were significantly lower than they are today. The actual ratio of seed harvested to seed sown in any given year fluctuated wildly, depending mostly on the weather, but the average figure for wheat was probably in the vicinity of five to one. Of this, one part had to be kept back for planting the fields the following year, giving a net yield of four to one, which is about a fifth of the typical modern yield.

Once the fields were harvested, it was customary in many places to allow the landless peasants to search them for leftover bits of grain dropped by the harvesters, a process known as "gleaning. " After human hands had gleaned the fields, villagers turned out their geese to fatten themselves on what was left. The end of the harvest season was also a time for celebration, with a harvest festival around Michaelmas. After Michaelmas, the next year's planting began: the spring fields became the fallows, the winter fields became the next year's spring fields, and the previous year's fallows became the new winter fields.

Leisure Time

In addition to the major festivals of the rural year, there were numerous minor holy days, each bringing a break from labor. One thirteenth-century tract on estate management estimated that eight weeks of work every year were lost to holy days and other impediments to work—considerably more than the vacation time allowed most North Americans today.[19] Saturday evenings were a favorite occasion for merrymaking, since even those conscientious villagers who attended Mass on Sunday morning still had a less demanding day than during the working week. Sunday afternoons were also free.

A variety of entertainments occupied the peasant's leisure hours. Dancing was popular and probably took the form of circle and chain dances, as well as

SET OF ILLUSTRATIONS FROM A BOOK OF HOURS, *ca. 1300. On the right a man plays a stringed instrument, probably a vielle (an early form of the fiddle), while on the left a woman looks at him while she dances. Music and dancing were important in medieval society and allowed opportunities for men and women to mingle. Ink, paint, and gold on parchment.*

less-structured cavorting and capering to music. These dances might be performed to instrumental music or accompanied by the voices of the participants. Certain instruments were especially characteristic of the peasantry. Bagpipes provided a loud and continuous sound that was ideal for outdoor dancing. Flutes of various sorts were simple and cheap and within the means of even the poorest; bone flutes have been found in the peasant houses at Wharram Percy. The pipe and tabor, combining a three-holed flute played with the left hand with a small drum beaten with the right hand, provided melody and rhythm together, and was also well suited to dancing. No actual instances of peasant songs from this period survive, but various contemporary allusions mention popular balladry.

Games were another common form of peasant entertainment. Excavated peasant houses at Wharram Percy have yielded dice and a stone with a board for Nine Men's Morris scratched on it. Wrestling, football, and field hockey were also popular in the countryside. Medieval football was an outstandingly rough sport that often resulted in personal injury; no rules survive, but the evidence suggests that it was a simple game in which each team tried to bring the ball to a predetermined goal, with local custom determining whether the ball could be held or touched. Hockey seems to have originated among shepherds, who in the Middle Ages carried short bent staffs resembling modern field hockey sticks.

The peasant's life was also enlivened by at least a modest amount of travel. There was not much of a market in the village for the peasant's surplus produce, nor was there a supply of many of the crafted items that a household needed to purchase from time to time such as pottery, furnishings, clothes, or utensils. To buy and sell, the peasant resorted to one of the network of small towns that provided local access to services not supported in the smaller economy of the village. These towns supported a variety of full-time craftsmen and typically hosted a market each week where peasants could sell their produce. Most villages had at least one market within six or seven miles, which corresponded to the distance of a day's roundtrip travel on foot, with time allowed for marketing in between. At Cuxham, there were two markets at about this distance, Wallingford and Ibstone. For less-frequent purchases, the villager might wait for a fair, which offered a wider range of merchants competing for business, with correspondingly better opportunities for the buyer. Fairs were generally held on an annual basis, and fewer places had them, so they involved a longer journey. Usually there was one within a day's travel, involving one or two night's lodging at the fair. Cuxham's closest fairs were at Oxford and Henley, each about a dozen miles distant.

PEASANT PERSONALITIES

Although the peasantry constituted the largest part of the medieval population, they remain its most elusive component. Unlike the aristocrat or clergyman, they never wrote about themselves or their world. In medieval writings, peasants are usually portrayed through the eyes of the upper classes, who often preferred to reduce them to stereotypes:

> He had broad shoulders and was big in the chest, his arms were thick, his limbs quite robust. A hand's breadth lay between his eyes . . . his hair was bristly, his face black as coal; he had not washed in six months—he made no use of water except that which fell from the sky.[20]

PEASANT FAMILY GOING TO MARKET. Martin Schongauer (German), ca. 1470–1475. Engraving on laid paper.

Even sympathetic authors like Peter the Venerable, abbot of Cluny in the twelfth century, tended to emphasize the peasant's passivity:

> Everyone knows how secular lords rule over peasants, bondsmen, and bonds-women. For they are not content with the customary and proper servitude owed to them, but mercilessly claim for themselves things along with people and people along with things. Accordingly they not only demand the usual taxes, but plunder their goods three or four times a year or as often as they like. They afflict them with countless services and impose heavy and unbearable burdens on them. In this they often oblige them to leave their own soil and to flee to distant parts. And what is even worse, they do not hesitate to sell these people for a worthless price, that is for money, when Christ redeemed them with a price so precious.[21]

Certainly the life of the peasant was difficult. Most led a precarious existence, working for minimal wages, with little employment security. A slump in agriculture might leave them without income or resources, and a long life could simply mean a destitute old age. Even the landholding peasant had a hard existence. His work was demanding; he was burdened by services and rents due to his lord; a tenth of his own produce was owed to the parish church; and his diet, clothing, and accommodations were little more than adequate.

Yet the burdens of peasant life did not crush the peasant's humanity. We have already seen that amidst the work of the agricultural year the villagers found time for a cultural life. We have also seen evidence of economic enterprise. An ambitious peasant might invest in additional land within or outside the village, leasing it from the manor lord or subletting it from another villager. Some improved their prospects by renting profitable facilities like mills, or by practicing trades in addition to farming. Perhaps most surprising is the role of moneylending in the village economy. Cash flow was a problem in an environment where access to coin was limited and much of people's income was in the form of agricultural produce. Villagers extended credit among themselves to make up for this lack—an approach facilitated by the stability of the population and the frequency of manor courts at which debts could be enforced. In most cases, credit was simply a means of compensating for the lack of coin, but some villagers used it as a source of income: in the Yorkshire village of Holme during the famine of 1316, one villager was lending at 50 percent per year, a rate that pales in comparison to that of one of his neighbors who took 200 percent.[22]

Villagers also played an active role in local administration and law enforcement. The lord's manor court consisted primarily of a sworn jury of manor peasants. The court at Cuxham usually met once or twice a year. The jurors of a manor court were called on to investigate and adjudicate matters ranging from petty breaches of the peace to disputes over property, and even to legislate manorial bylaws. The manor itself was usually administered by a *reeve*, an officer drawn from among the manorial serfs. The reeve was assisted by a clerk who actually wrote up the manorial accounts. At Cuxham this position was for a time held by Robert the Clerk, son of Adam, the prior of Wallingford's miller, evidence that not every peasant at Cuxham was unlettered. The peasants supplied other manorial officers as well. Many manors had a beadle who was responsible for collecting rents, and as in other villages, the villagers of Cuxham chose a hayward to supervise the harvest.

Villagers also had a role in defense and law enforcement. Various laws restricted the bearing of arms among peasants, but some form of weaponry was common in the peasant home. When a crime was committed, a cry was raised, and the villagers were expected to pursue and apprehend the criminal. In England, a royal order of 1242 required villages to maintain a nightly watch of four or six men. To make this possible, the villagers were required to own arms according to their wealth, and each village was to have one or two constables to supervise local preparedness. In times of war, peasants might be temporarily impressed into the army.[23]

The military potential of the medieval peasant was limited, restricting their willingness to use violence against the aristocracy, but villagers found alternative means of resisting their manor lords. In the English village of Broughton in 1314, three villeins were fined for playing Halfpenny-Prick, a knife throwing game, when they were supposed to be doing labor service for the manor lord. One villager in Shillington "lay at the head of a selion in harvest and obstructed the work of the lord."[24] On one occasion, the villeins of Broughton "went away from the great harvest work, leaving their labor from noon till night . . . giving the malicious and false cause that they did not have their loaves [i.e., the bread customarily allotted to them for their work] as large as they were accustomed formerly and ought to have them."[25]

Even individual personalities among medieval villagers can occasionally be glimpsed through the impersonal medium of manorial records. At Cuxham, one of the villein cottagers, Matilda English, featured in two related cases in the manorial court in 1294:

> Richard of Turweston is fined for a transgression against English in striking her. . . . It is declared by the whole Court that a certain English destroyed a hedge that lay between her and Richard Turweston, valued at 2d., a hedge that Richard was required to support and maintain . . . and because it is declared by the whole Court that this English has been cursing her neighbors beyond measure, and for her transgression, she is to be fined.[26]

In the following year, Matilda was fined by the court again for having complained against her neighbors to the king's bailiff, who had subjected them to a fine. Her assertiveness may have had something to do with age and experience: Matilda was already a widow in 1279, and she may well have been forty years old or older by 1294. Perhaps she also resented the apparent decline in her family fortunes. Although she had only a cottage holding, her deceased husband Gilbert was probably a descendant of the William English who held a half-virgate in the early thirteenth century, and her father's name, Thomas Clerk, suggests that he was literate. Matilda usually appears in the records just as "English," a peculiarity that might be related to her distinctive personality. A short fuse seems to have been something of a family trait, to judge by complaints made at about the same period against others who appear to have been relatives:

Geoffrey English is distrained to respond to the Bailiff for having cursed
him in the full court.[27]
Agnes English is fined because she threw a stone at the barnwarden of the
lord and struck him in the chest, to the great harm of him and the contempt
of the lord.[28]

Notwithstanding the stereotypes placed on medieval peasants then and
now, theirs was clearly a complex and intensely human society.

5

CASTLE LIFE

THE MANOR HAD EVOLVED AS AN EFFECTIVE RESPONSE TO THE economic disruption of post-Roman Europe, but the military dangers of the medieval world required solutions on a larger scale. Although the manor lord might be able to turn out a levy of his tenants in an emergency, they were poorly equipped, unused to combat, and not necessarily very useful in a fight. His own household probably included a few better equipped soldiers, he himself might well have had the training and equipment of a knight, and his manor might have been protected by some light fortifications, but none of this would do much good in the face of a serious military force.

The military threat was always very real. Raiding was common in border regions, and even in the heart of a fairly stable kingdom, civil strife could arise at any time in an age when central government was weak, the political structure founded on fluctuating personal relationships, and society ruled by a class whose avowed function in life was warfare. War was still an exceptional event in most people's lives, but it was common enough that local military preparedness was essential. Effective response to the military challenges of the medieval world required the power of a great lord able to command a substantial following of local knights, and by the High Middle Ages, the castle had arisen as the distinctive seat of a great feudal lord's power.

This chapter will explore the castle as it represents the world of the feudal aristocracy, using the example of Dover Castle, at the southeastern tip of England. Dover was in many ways exceptional, for it was among the most important castles belonging to the king of England, and one of the most powerful fortresses in Europe in its day. However, because of its very size, it incorporates a full range of features that were found only piecemeal in less important castles. It is also

CONSTRUCTION OF A CASTLE *in a medieval English village. From a fifteenth-century Psalter.*

PRESENT-DAY PHOTOGRAPH OF DOVER CASTLE. *Founded in the twelfth century, its defensive importance earned it the nickname the "Key to England."*

particularly well documented in surviving records, including a substantial series of household accounts kept on behalf of Eleanor de Montfort, countess of Leicester, during her stay at the castle in the summer of 1265. Since the facilities at the castle were entirely rebuilt over the course of the twelfth and thirteenth centuries, this chapter will focus in particular on Dover as it appeared at the time of Eleanor's visit.[1]

Functions of the Castle

As the manor supported the knight economically, the castle evolved to support him militarily. It provided a base from which a force of knights could strike an opposing force when they saw an opportunity, and to which they could retire for safety when they were at a disadvantage. The earliest castles were built of earthworks and timber, and some of these were still in use in the thirteenth century, but from the twelfth century onward, castles were generally built of stone, and the technology of castle construction was becoming increasingly sophisticated. As castles became more powerful, they grew in importance as strategic centers, and by the twelfth and thirteenth centuries much of medieval warfare focused on the control of castles.

The castle as a military center was also important to civilian life. It could serve as refuge for local civilian populations, particularly in border regions where raiding was endemic. In the late fourteenth century, the inhabitants of the area around Dover were ordered to withdraw to Dover Castle in the face of a threatened invasion.[2] Many castles were constructed within or adjacent to towns by their feudal overlords, serving at once as protection and as a reminder of the lord's authority.

The castle's functions were not purely military. Many of them doubled as manor houses, and the more important ones were often administrative centers for major feudal lords. At times, the castle served as a residence for the lord himself; when he was away, it was entrusted to one of the lord's officials, who administered the castle and perhaps the feudal domain attached to it. Both administrative and residential uses can be seen at Dover. This castle was one of the most important residences of the kings of England, who stayed there frequently during the twelfth and thirteenth centuries. The ongoing administration of Dover, like that of many castles, was in the hands of a constable. The constable was responsible not only for the castle itself, but also for royal government in the surrounding region, overseeing sea traffic in the port of Dover, collecting customs, and supervising the defense of the southeastern coast of England. He was also assigned the wardenship of the Cinque Ports, the administrative association of the chief ports on the southeastern coast. The constableship of Dover was a position of considerable importance in England and was always occupied by a well-connected aristocrat.

The castle was also an important logistical center. The king kept a substantial store of military supplies at Dover, not just for the castle itself, but to arm his troops in case of war. Other sorts of supplies were also stored there: in 1251 King Henry III had a large shipment of lead delivered from the castle for one of his building projects, and in 1262 he stored some of his valuables in the castle's royal chapel.[3] A few years later, an elephant that had been given to Henry by Louis IX, the king of France (later canonized as Saint Louis), was lodged at the castle for a time.[4] The security offered by a castle made it a suitable place for keeping prisoners, and Dover served as a royal jail.[5] The castle also hosted important guests. Baldwin II, the deposed emperor of Byzantium, was lodged there on his way to the Continent in 1247,[6] and many members of the English royal family and important visitors from overseas used Dover as a stopping place on trips across the English Channel. The castle served not only as accommodations for the king's guests, but as a testimony to his royal grandeur: in 1247 Henry sent word to the constable of Dover that one guest was to be shown around the castle "in a courteous manner, so that the nobility of the castle may be demonstrated to him, and so that he shall see no shortcomings in it."[7]

The Castle Environment

The design of castles varied enormously, depending on local topography, the lord's resources, the function of the castle, and the current state of military technology. The design of Dover reflected its status as one of the most important military and administrative centers belonging to the kingdom's greatest feudal lord. The castle's strategic location is unmistakable. It lies atop the chalk seaside cliffs at the narrowest stretch of the English Channel, within sight of France. To the west, the ground drops sharply to the town of Dover, at the mouth of the River Dour. The river constitutes the only break in thirteen miles of high coastal cliffs, and the shelter it offers from the sea at Britain's closest point to the Continent made Dover an important port even before the Middle Ages. Already in the Iron Age, there was an earthwork hill fort on the future site of the castle, and the remains of a Roman lighthouse still stand within the castle precincts.

Many castles were built on a high point in the local terrain, the height improving the garrison's ability to keep watch on the surrounding area, as well as conferring an advantage for the defenders in combat. If built on flat ground, a portion of the castle might be raised on an artificial mound. At Dover, the military advantage of the hill outweighed certain drawbacks, notably access to water. A secure water supply was crucial to any castle, as it could not long withstand a siege if it had no internal water source. Dover's water supply was secure, but it had to be drawn laboriously from wells dug deep into the chalky soil. During Eleanor de Montfort's stay at the castle, she regularly paid to have water carried up to the castle from the town below. Some castles were deliberately constructed on a rocky base as a means of preventing a besieging force from digging tunnels to bring down the walls. The chalk subsoil at Dover was particularly prone to mining in this way, although it also facilitated the construction of defensive tunnels. Some castles stood in the countryside, others, like Dover, stood in or next to a town; sometimes the presence of a castle stimulated the growth of a town where none had previously existed.

During the century after William the Conqueror made himself king of England in 1066, he and his Norman successors did some work on the fortifications at Dover, but the main period of development began in 1179, during the reign of

Henry II. Henry hired Maurice the Engineer, one of Europe's leading military architects, to design a completely new set of fortifications. Maurice's plan was to be a trendsetting innovation. Most earlier castles had consisted of two adjacent enclosures, called baileys, with a single point of access from outside that led into the outer bailey, which itself then gave access to the inner bailey. At Dover Castle, the inner bailey was entirely surrounded by the outer bailey, with a large fortified tower, or keep, standing in the center of the inner bailey.

The rebuilding of Dover's defenses was a protracted project that spanned some seventy-five years in all. By the time of Henry's death in 1189, he had completed the keep, the wall of the inner bailey, and a section of the wall of the outer bailey. The development of the castle was neglected during the reign of Henry's son Richard I: the completion of the inner bailey was left to the reign of Henry's youngest son John. The castle reached its fullest state of development by about 1265, during the reign of John's son Henry III. When the work was completed, the castle covered an area of about thirty acres within an outer wall three-quarters of a mile long, with multiple additional walled enclosures within. This was an unusually large castle: Richard I's magnificent Castle Gaillard covered only about two acres, and the formidable Crusader fortress of Crac des Chevaliers in Palestine covered only about six.

Such major fortifications as Dover did not come cheaply. During the years 1179–1188 Henry II spent over £6,500 on the castle, an enormous sum at a time when the crown's normal annual income was probably around £10,000. Richard I spent something under £1,000, John an additional £2,000, and Henry III over £6,000. The central keep was the greatest single expense, perhaps amounting to some £4,000. The keep took about ten years to build, which was fairly typical for such a building—a keep generally could be raised about ten to twelve feet in the course of a year. The expense of Dover reflected the rising costs of keeping up with the latest military technology in the twelfth and thirteenth centuries. By the late thirteenth century, a castle could cost £10,000 or more, a price that put it out of the range of all but the wealthiest aristocrats. Even once the castle was built, there was still the ongoing cost of operations and maintenance.[8]

The Walls

Visitors to Dover Castle in the mid-thirteenth century approached the outer wall from the western side, winding their way up the hill on the road leading to the great gate. Even from a distance, the castle was an outstanding presence in its surroundings, commanding the skyline for miles around. Dover Castle sprawls across Castle Hill above the town of Dover and is visible even across the Channel in France. The final approach to the castle ran parallel to the outer wall, along a causeway paved with stone and lime and bordered by a deep ditch on either side.[9] The ditch next to the castle ran all the way around the outer wall, cutting deep into the ground to impede access to the walls as well as to discourage any attempt to mine under them. This ditch, or moat, was dry, since Dover lay on high and well-drained ground. In many low-lying castles, the moat was filled with water as an additional impediment to attack.

From the base of the moat, the castle wall towered inaccessibly high above. In a less-sophisticated castle, this wall might be no more than a wooden palisade standing on top of the ridge thrown up by the excavation of the moat, with a wooden fighting platform behind it to allow the garrison to defend the perimeter. Wooden palisades were a relatively quick and cheap form of defense, but stone provided greater strength and resistance to fire, and during the High Middle Ages stone walls were becoming increasingly common for those who could support the expense. The king of England could certainly afford stone for so important a castle as Dover. The walls have since been lowered, but they probably stood some thirty feet high, with a walkway built into them and battlements to protect the defenders.

Towers were built into the walls at intervals of about 200 feet or less, roughly the range of a bow, ensuring that every point along the perimeter was covered by two towers. The towers rose higher than the wall itself, providing maximum visibility for the defenders, who normally used the towers as their principal bases for defense. Additional defense was furnished by arrow-slits in the tower walls. The towers also provided shelter against the weather, an important consideration since rain lessened the effectiveness of the defenders' bows. The towers in the oldest section of the wall were square, but the later ones were round, eliminating the dead space at the corners of the square towers where defenders inside the tower could neither see nor shoot. These towers also served as living spaces for the defenders. There is evidence of privies in some of the mural towers at Dover, and there may also have been wooden residential buildings adjoining them for the use of the garrison.

Gates

The weak point in a castle's perimeter wall was the gate, since it was by definition a point of access. By the twelfth century, the gate was usually protected by some form of gatehouse. In older castles, this was often just a mural tower through which the entryway passed. Dover was among the first castles to defend its gates with pairs of towers flanking either side of the opening. The main gate on Dover's western wall was especially well defended. It was a massive structure of no less than five turrets. As with other towers, the gate had both loopholes and battlements to allow bowmen to defend the entry against attack. A small exit, or sally port, issued from the gatehouse directly into the moat, allowing the defenders to mount a counterattack against any besieging force.

Where the causeway leading to the castle reached the main gate, it entered a *barbican*, a small fortification that protected the approach to the gatehouse, and made a ninety-degree turn to slow down the impetus of any assault. Passage over the moat from the barbican to the gatehouse was by means of a drawbridge.[10]

CASTLE GATE. *As the primary point of entry in a defensive wall, the gatehouse controlled access to the castle.*

The massive structure of Dover's great gatehouse served more than military purposes. In peace as well as war, the gatehouse controlled access to the castle. A porter was always on duty, and prospective visitors were required to speak to him at the gate before gaining admission. Access to a castle was generally restricted to those having legitimate business within. To minimize intrusions into the castle grounds, many castles transacted business in the gatehouse itself. At Dover, the constable held a "Court of the Castle Gate" at which he handled business relating to his external responsibilities as a royal administrator. Like many officers in charge of castles, the constable of Dover used the gatehouse as his own residence, and it was furnished with extensive apartments to accommodate him and his household, as well as lodgings for the porter.

After dark, the Great Gate was closed entirely, and even the king was admitted only at the Fitzwilliam Gate on the far side of the outer wall, and that only with a few of his followers. The Fitzwilliam Gate was one of the castle's secondary gates, or *posterns*. There was another at the southwest edge of the castle, near the cliffs. These posterns were smaller than the great gate, and offered little access for an attacking force. Their principal purpose was to allow the defenders additional points of issue from which to harass a besieging force. For the same reason, there were even smaller sally ports in both the Great Gate and the Fitzwilliam Gate.

All of the gates dated to the reign of Henry III. They represented the very latest in military architecture and reflected a determination on the part of the constable that the gates should be adequately defended. He had reason to be concerned. In 1216, during the reign of John, the castle had been the object of a prolonged siege by King Louis of France. At the time, the only gate in the outer wall was at the north end of the castle, and it actually lay slightly below the level of the ground beyond it. Although the gate itself was complete, the barbican was not, and as the besiegers approached, the defenders fortified the barbican with a hastily constructed wooden palisade. The French identified this point as a promising weakness in the castle's defenses, and concentrated their efforts on it. The course of the siege was described in some detail by a Flemish monk who was present with the French forces:

> Louis . . . did not besiege the castle at once, but lodged himself in the middle of the town in a priory. Most of his troops lodged in the town and some in their pavillions. . . . Many times the men in the castle sallied forth from the gates. They had a barbican outside the gate, which Peter de Creon had under his command. This barbican was enclosed with very stout planks of oak, and he had it well ditched round about. . . . The men in the castle often came out in front of this barbican fully armed, so that the attackers saw them

clearly. Often Louis' crossbowmen went there to shoot. Once a very skilled crossbowman, named Per Ernaut, went there to shoot. He approached so close to them that they overran him, while he held his ground before them; thus he was captured, since he was given no support. Soon afterwards, Louis went up to join his forces, and laid siege the castle. One part of his men he had staying in the town, the better to fully encircle the defenders, and his ships returned to the sea, and in this way the men in the castle were surrounded on all sides. Then Louis had his trebuchets and mangonels set up to cast at the gate and the wall; he had made a very high tower of hurdles, with a gangway to lead to the wall. He had his miners go into the moat to mine the stone and earth under the palisade. Then he had the knights of his army attack; the barbican was soon taken. A squire named Huart Paon, who carried the banner of the Lord of Bethune, entered first. Peter de Creon, who led the defense of the barbican, had such an injury from it that he never recovered, and he died soon after. . . . Then Louis set his miners at the gate; they so mined it that one of the two towers fell. Then a large part of Louis's forces entered the castle; but the men within pushed them out again with great vigor, and then resealed the place where the wall had fallen with large timbers and with great logs laid across and with great planks of oak.[11]

The siege continued for the better part of a year, but no further direct assault was attempted, and eventually the siege was lifted and the invaders sailed back to France. Nonetheless, this vital castle had almost been taken by storm, and the constable was determined to leave nothing to chance. He had the old gate blocked up and an outwork constructed to protect the high ground north of the castle, with underground tunnels connecting it to the castle itself. He cut the new main gate through the western wall, on the steepest side of Castle Hill. Over the next half century, the outer walls were extended, and additional walls were added within the castle itself. Posterns and sally ports were also added to allow the defenders to attack the besiegers if they saw an opportunity, and to ensure that any future siege would have to stretch itself out around the castle in order to block the defenders inside.

The Outer Bailey

Once a visitor was cleared through the Great Gate, he came into the castle's outer bailey, which was in fact divided up into several enclosures separated by fortified walls. The main outer bailey extended around all sides of the inner bailey except the southeast side. This area was probably the principal space for the castle garrison. As with most castles, only the actual defenses at Dover are still standing, but building accounts, a few archeological remains, and comparison to other castles can offer a general idea of what has been lost. Traces of a large hall have been found along the northwestern wall adjacent to one of the wall towers, which itself shows signs of domestic use, including a privy. This may have been used by some of the soldiers of the garrison, and other structures may have stood along the walls next to the towers to serve as garrison accommodations. There were also stables, probably not far from the main gate, and perhaps others near the postern gate. Not only did every resident and visitor of any importance have a horse, but the garrison knights needed the facilities to accommodate their mounts. There was also a separate stable for carthorses, and at least one hayhouse.

The main outer bailey may also have been the site of the building used to store siege engines.[12] Castles were often furnished with siege weapons of their own, whether for use against a besieging force, or as a stockpile in case of war. Dover was furnished with a catapult, trebuchet, and ram in 1244, and there were several catapults in its stock in 1264.[13] The ram was a large tree trunk that could be used against the gate of a castle. The catapult and trebuchet were predecessors of the cannon and mortar, designed to lob massive projectiles at a large target. Such weapons were slow, and had a very limited range, typically around 150 yards, and they were only useful against large and stationary targets such as buildings or fortifications.

To the southeast of the inner bailey was another walled area enclosing the high ground that included the remains of the Roman lighthouse and the parish church of St. Mary. The presence of a parish church within a castle was unusual. Most castles had only chapels, although many castle lords tried to elevate their chapels to parochial status, since as a parish church it would be entitled to receive the tithes of its parishioners. The church probably ministered to the garrison and staff at large, and the enclosure in which it stood is likely to have served as a residential area for the castle's civilian population.

The most privileged civilian residents had their own houses. Given the relatively restricted space of the castle, these were probably multistory buildings comparable to medieval townhouses. Building accounts mention the thatching of the houses of Gerard the Crossbowman (probably the resident maker and repairer of crossbows) and Jocelyn de Oie, who supervised construction at the castle. In some cases these houses were owned by the occupants, who paid rent for the plot on which they stood.[14] The king provided Jocelyn with a subsidy to help with the cost of building his house, and payment was also made "to buy the house of Bartholomew the Porter, that had belonged to his wife, when they went to Jerusalem."[15]

Either in the enclosure around the church or in the main outer bailey there were workshops for resident craftsmen, and other utilitarian facilities similar to those found around a manor house. Dover had a smithy to provide the ironware necessary for the castle and its garrison.[16] There was a kitchen and a bakehouse, and a brewhouse for making ale, which suggests the presence of a kiln for malting grain. There was at least one garden, probably providing food and herbs; this had a wall to keep out livestock. The records mention a pond, probably used as a source of fresh fish for aristocratic residents and guests. Some castles even had

A ROMAN LIGHTHOUSE STANDS DIRECTLY NEXT TO THE PARISH CHURCH *on the Dover Castle grounds. In time, the lighthouse was converted into the church bell-tower.*

dovecotes. Dover's records indicate the presence of a barn and a granary. A castle of this size required substantial facilities for storage: some idea of the capacity at Dover may be found in an order by the king in 1255 to repay the constable for back wages with 227 quarters of wheat, 475 quarters of barley, 75 quarters of oats, 125 barrels of wine, and 500 lbs. of wax drawn from the castle stocks.[17] There were probably miscellaneous smaller storage buildings as well, like the locked toolshed mentioned in the building accounts. There was also a well in the outer bailey, and probably cisterns too.

At the southern end of the castle was a large undeveloped area that may have served primarily as pasture for the castle's livestock. There may also have been other facilities for husbandry, such as houses for the animals, and perhaps a dairy. This was also the site of a windmill, and perhaps of the "hermit's house" that was built at the king's expense in 1221. Between 1232 and 1265 there are references to a hermitess living in the castle on an allowance of 1½d. or 3d. a day from the king; in some entries she is named as "Emma the Recluse."[18] Such a resident in a castle was unusual, but not unique. Charity was an important part of the aristocratic way of life, serving not only as a means of helping the poor, but as a mark of the aristocrat's social status. In 1240, before Henry Ill's arrival on one of his visits to Dover, he ordered the royal hall to be filled with paupers, who were to have food for a day at his expense.[19] Eleanor de Montfort's accounts twice mention food provided for the poor, for thirty and forty-five people.

Most of the buildings on the castle grounds were timber-framed structures, whose walls were filled in with clay or wattle and daub, and covered with limewash. The floors may have been made of simple clay or of compacted earth mixed with sand and clay. Ordinary buildings were roofed with thatch or shingles, but some of the more important ones were roofed with lead sheets over wooden planks, which provided better protection against fire, a particularly important consideration during a siege. Lead roofing was used for the parish church, and at least some of the military and civilian structures were also covered in this way.

The Inner Bailey and Keep

In the middle of the outer bailey at Dover, a high mound had been built to create an elevated base for the inner bailey. The sides of the mound were steep, and the walls of the inner bailey towered over the outer bailey as the outer walls towered over the moat. This inner wall was closely studded with mural towers, and surmounted by crenellations to protect the defenders. Access to the inner bailey was through gatehouses at the north and south ends, each protected by its own barbican. The south barbican, like the Great Gate barbican, was approached at right angles to the actual entryway of the gate. The entry to the north barbican was instead offset from the gate, again to interrupt the impetus of an attack.

If the outer walls were taken by a besieging force, the garrison might retreat within the inner bailey, but during peacetime this area served principally as a residence for the castle's most privileged visitors, above all the king and his household when they came to visit. In the center of the bailey stood the keep, the great tower at the heart of the castle. The keep was always at the innermost point of the castle relative to the routes of access, requiring passage through each successive gate in order to reach it. At Dover, the keep was a freestanding square building, nearly 100 feet wide at the base and over 80 feet high, with walls around 20 feet thick, and corner

THE OUTER BAILEY, INNER BAILEY, AND KEEP OF DOVER CASTLE, *with the church of St. Mary and Roman lighthouse in the background.*

turrets rising 12 feet above the top. Inside the keep there were three main levels: a cellar for storage, and two residential floors above. These may originally have been built to serve the king and constable, with the royal apartments on the upper floor and the constable's below. By the mid-thirteenth century the king and constable had facilities elsewhere in the castle, and the keep may have been used mostly for guests.

The visitor to the keep entered by a series of external stone stairs. Halfway up the first flight of stairs was a landing with stairs leading down into the cellar. This direct entry to the cellar made it easier to bring in supplies, but although it was protected by a succession of three barred doors, it constituted a weak point in the keep's defenses, and suggests that even during its construction, the original idea of the keep as a crucial, defensible facility was being abandoned in favor of the simpler purpose of controlling access to the king. The cellar was divided into a number of large rooms that offered cool storage for foodstuffs and perhaps for military supplies as well. The keep also seems to have included prison facilities, which may have been in one of the cellar's corner rooms.

Past the turnoff to the cellar, the external stairs entered an enclosed forebuilding; the stairs were open to the sky, allowing them to be watched from guardposts above. At the corner of the building was a landing, with a chapel and a guardroom, probably used by a porter for the keep. Here the stairs turned to ascend the northeast side of the keep. Slightly beyond the landing was the door leading to the lower residential floor. Further up the stairs was a drawbridge and door, and at the top another guardroom. This forebuilding was particularly elaborate, but it was common for the entry to a keep to be above ground level, with access by means of external stairs. In many cases, the stairs were wooden, and could be destroyed in an emergency to impede access to the building.

At the top of the stairs in the forebuilding was a water room, with a lead cistern to collect rainwater from the roof. Water was a precious resource at this high point in the castle. On the opposite side of the stairs, at the entrance to the upper floor, was a well room, fitted with a pulley and bucket. Drawing water for the keep was a laborious task, as the water table lay 400 feet below. Next to the well was another cistern, from which water was distributed through lead pipes to the lower floors of the keep to provide running water on tap, a rare amenity in a castle.

Past the well room was the great hall. This was comparable to the hall of a manor house, serving as a public space where visitors to the household might wait, and where public meals and business might be transacted. The room was lit by window alcoves at each end. Beyond the southern alcove was a chapel, lying directly above the first-floor chapel but twice as large and even more ornate, with an attached sacristy for housing liturgical objects. At the north end of the great hall was a passageway leading to a privy. This privy was one of five in the keep, two back-to-back on each residential level, and one in the gallery above, all feeding into a single shaft above a cesspit chamber at the cellar level. A small hatchway in the outer wall at ground level allowed the cesspit to be cleaned periodically.

From the great hall, a door in the middle of the interior wall gave access to the great chamber, a room of similar design that would have served as a space for more private transactions. The great chamber was also lit by window alcoves, and it was heated by a fireplace on the southwest wall. Between the southern alcoves of the hall and chamber was a small room that may have been a service area. Built into the western wall of the great chamber were two rooms that appear to have been bedchambers. Both were lit by two windows and equipped with fireplaces. The one at the northeast comer also had its own privy and probably served as the king's bedchamber.

The floor below was built on almost exactly the same plan, but here, underneath the head of the external stairs, were two chambers that may have served as cooking facilities. One of them had a water tap fed from the floor above. However, much of the cooking for the keep may have been done in an external kitchen and bakehouse. Such an arrangement was common in castles, since it reduced the risk of fire. Access between floors in the keep was by a pair of spiral staircases that extended down to the cellar and up to the galleries. These galleries may have been used by the garrison. They had their own privy, and at the four comers were stairs leading to the roof of the keep. The roof was flat, and offered the garrison an unsurpassed view of the countryside and English Channel, allowing them ample advance warning of any approaching hostile forces.

Henry II built the apartments in the keep for his own use, but his grandson Henry III found them insufficiently appointed—or perhaps he disliked the long trek up the stairs of the forebuilding—for he had a new stone hall built into the wall of the inner bailey, comparable in design and use to the hall of a manor house. Construction of a new hall outside the keep was common in the thirteenth century, reflecting an increased demand for space and comfort among the upper aristocracy. In smaller castles, the inner bailey might be too small, and the hall was located in the outer bailey. At the lower end of the new hall at Dover were doors leading toward storerooms, a kitchen, and a bakehouse, and at the upper end was a chapel and chambers for the king. The king's chamber was particularly well appointed, with glass windows and wainscoted walls.[20]

GARRISON LIFE

The life of the castle can be divided into its military and administrative domains. The military function at a strategically important castle like Dover was especially prominent, and such a castle would have been maintained at a fairly high level of military preparedness at all times. A fourteenth-century assessment of Dover's defenses called for a garrison of 832 soldiers, based on a ratio of three men to every two battlements on the outer wall. Such an enormous number of soldiers was extremely expensive, and even in time of war, the garrison was probably never this large. During the siege of 1216, the castle was manned by 140 knights, plus an unknown number of ordinary soldiers, for a total probably not much over 500 men. In peace, a much smaller number was called for—the usual complement of knights seems to have been about two dozen, and the provision for the night watch calls for twenty soldiers, which may suggest a total of sixty watchmen, with perhaps as many crossbowmen. In a smaller and less-important castle, the garrison might include only a handful of men, and the military staff at many of the smallest castles in peacetime consisted only of a porter and a watchman or two, allowing for surveillance, but no sort of military action.

The Knight

The garrison included both aristocratic knights and common foot soldiers. Traditionally, the king assigned the knights from certain manors to garrison duty at Dover. In the twelfth century, the total number of knights was set at 174, of whom 118 were drawn from eight "honors" or baronies, each owing between five and twenty-four knights; the other fifty-six were from the Honor of the Constabulary, assigned to the constable of England for the defense of the realm, but eventually designated for Dover alone. Some of these knights were from manors as far away as Lincolnshire, a journey of over two hundred miles by land.[21] Similar arrangements were used in the castles of the nobility, who used their vassal knights to man their own castles.

The tour of duty at Dover varied enormously. The knights of the Honor of the Constabulary all served for a month each and were organized into twelve groups of four or five knights who did their service together. The services of the rest of the knights were less orderly. Many owed two or three one-month periods of service every year, others owed as little as five days. The knight for the manor of Hartanger served for two weeks just before Christmas and another two before the feast of St. John at midsummer, while his counterpart from Graveney served just after Christmas and St. John's; the knight from Down owed two weeks just before Easter. In all, almost 300 months of service were owed to the castle, suggesting that normally there were about twenty-four knights stationed at the castle at any given time.

During the reforms that followed the siege of 1216, it was decided that each manor that owed service should instead pay 10s. for each month of service owed, so that the castle could hire full-time garrison knights rather than having this continual turnover. This reform of knight service at Dover was part of a general shift away from traditional feudal arrangements. Feudal overlords were increasingly interested in hiring professional soldiers, while their vassals were happy to be released from the strictures of service in person. With the rise of a cash economy, it became easier to replace the older service arrangements with an annual monetary payment.

The Knight in Combat

Knights could form a formidable mounted force operating from the safety of the castle, responding with speed to dangers and opportunities in the vicinity. A military force on horseback could easily travel at twice the speed of foot soldiers, and man-for-man, the knights were vastly more powerful in combat. The combat advantage of the mounted warrior was lost in rough terrain, but even on foot the knight was a formidable figure, well armed and armored, and trained since childhood in the skills of battle.

Military technology was constantly evolving during the Middle Ages, but during the twelfth and thirteenth centuries the knight's equipment remained relatively constant. The principal material for a knight's body armor in this period was mail, consisting of a tightly packed surface of small steel rings, each interlocking with several of its neighbors in each direction, and riveted shut for added strength. Mail was particularly good at resisting the bite of a sword's edge, but it offered somewhat less protection against the crushing force of a blow, and it could be penetrated by the highly concentrated power of a crossbow bolt.

The knight's main body armor consisted of a long tunic of mail, called a *hauberk*, generally reaching to the knees, with a slit from hem to crotch in front and back, allowing him to sit in a saddle. Underneath the hauberk he wore a padded cloth tunic, called an *aketon*, that provided some of the impact absorption that the mail lacked. From the late twelfth century, the knight's hands were protected with mail mittens built into the hauberk, with slits at the wrists that allowed him to free his hands when needed. On his legs the knight wore long stockings of mail, protecting everything from his feet to his thighs. In the thirteenth century this armor was beginning to be supplemented with solid plates of steel at crucial points, particularly over the torso and knees. Additional protection was afforded by a shield strapped to the knight's left arm.

The head required the most protection, because of its importance and vulnerability. The innermost layer of head protection was a padded coif, secured in place by ties under the chin. Over this the knight wore another coif of mail, this one a full hood attached to the hauberk and covering the entire head, leaving only the face exposed. On top of this the knight wore a steel helmet. The helmet of the twelfth century was generally only a conical cap with a bar projecting downward in front of the nose, but in the thirteenth century it became common to wear a larger "barrel" helm that covered the entire head, with a horizontal slot in front of the eyes, and a grille of breathing holes in the area of the mouth and nostrils.

EXAMPLE OF
KNIGHT'S ARMOR
*from the twelfth
century.*

The barrel helmet weighed some six pounds, and the hauberk about twenty-five pounds. The combined bulk of the hauberk and aketon tended to impede mobility, as did the multiple layers of head protection, but they provided significant protection in close combat, and the knight's training gave him strength and skill to compensate for his encumbrance.

The knight's most powerful weapon was his lance. This was a wooden spear about nine to eleven feet long, with a steel point at the end. Medieval battle tactics typically began with a concentrated charge by the knights with their lances. A group of knights with lances tucked hard under their arms charging at their enemy en masse could deliver an enormously powerful initial shock, and it was axiomatic that no body of foot soldiers could withstand such an onslaught. Once combat was joined at close quarters, the lances were useless and were discarded.

The most common secondary weapon was the sword. The typical knightly sword of this period weighed about 2½ to 3½ pounds and had a blade a bit over thirty inches long. With a weighted pommel at the end of the grip to counterbalance the weight of the blade, it was a fairly handy weapon, and a well-trained swordsman could handle it with grace and skill. Some knights relied instead on a mace, a wooden or iron club with a heavy, weighted end. The mace's strength was its ability to deliver powerful crushing blows, taking advantage of the weakness of mail in protecting against impact, but the weapon was unwieldy in comparison to the sword, and its principal advantage was against armored opponents.

Knights in the Castle

The castle knights served not only as a mobile mounted force, but also as command staff for the garrison. Military leadership was considered the aristocrat's natural prerogative, and the knight's military training, combat experience, and social authority suited him to the task. In some cases, each knight had a certain part of the garrison soldiers under his command, and the group was based in one of the towers of the castle wall. Such a system may have been used at Dover, where the mural towers were named after the various baronies assigned to garrison the castle. The wall towers at Dover generally had built-in privies, and some may have had adjacent halls to provide lodging. Several of the fiefs that owed service at Dover are also known to have been responsible for the upkeep of houses or towers in the castle.[22]

The knights may have been lodged together, perhaps in the hall that once stood in the northwestern part of the outer bailey. If they were lodged with common soldiers under their command, they would have had special chambers set apart for their use, since it would have been inappropriate for aristocratic knights to mix with ordinary soldiers—this class distinction between officers and soldiers is still fundamental to the organization of modern armies, and fraternization is frowned upon to this day. Each knight would also be attended by one or more servants. One of these might be a squire, a younger aristocrat learning the military profession under the knight's tutelage, and providing the knight with service in exchange for his instruction. The squire was particularly responsible for assisting the knight with his armor—the name, derived from the medieval French *escuier*, means shield-bearer. For more menial sorts of service, the knight probably relied on an ordinary servant.

We know at least a bit about one of the knights who served at Dover, Peter de Burton, who was paid 12d. a day for his service. He appears to have been permanently stationed at the castle, for there is record of his presence from 1240 to 1261, and he and his wife seem to have been guests at Eleanor de Montfort's table in 1265.[23] Another knight named Robert de Useburn was receiving 2s. a day in 1262.[24] The duties of the knight were not restricted to standing guard at the castle. When the king sent his clerk with two servants to the nearby port of Whitesand to make payment to hired soldiers from Picardy, he sent one of the garrison knights of Dover to accompany them. The knights at Dover were professional soldiers, probably recruited from the younger sons of the aristocracy, and they shared many of the experiences of other professional wage earners, even downsizing and retirement packages: in 1255 the king decided to cut costs by having the "feeble and debilitated" surplus of the Dover garrison removed, although at least one of them, Robert de Torneboel, who had served from youth to old age, was granted an annual pension of £5.[25]

Foot Soldiers

The bulk of the garrison forces consisted of ordinary foot soldiers. These men were professional soldiers, paid a daily wage, and drawn from the landless peasantry and urban laboring classes. Their pay depended on what class of soldier they were. Crossbowmen were the best paid. At Dover, the standard rate appears to have been 3d. a day[26]; in other places wages were as high as 4d. to 6d. a day. These high wages—two to three times that paid to other soldiers—reflected the military power of the crossbow. The ordinary bow of the period was weak against an armored target—not until the English cultivated archery in the fourteenth century were they able to draw bows of sufficient strength to pose a threat to the armored knight. With an ordinary bow, the archer could only deliver as much power as he could bring to bear by drawing the string with his arms and shoulders, while trying to aim the arrow at the same time. The crossbow increased the archer's power by separating the processes of drawing and shooting. The crossbowman could draw the string using his entire body, holding the bow in place with his foot while pulling the string with his hands; some bows made use of a lever or even a winch to draw the string. Once the string was drawn, it was held in place by a catch, and released by pulling a trigger. The power of the crossbow was devastating. No matter how strong armor was made, a crossbow could always be made stronger to pierce it, and the weapon's range was some 300 yards. The crossbow was so deadly that the church tried to ban its use, but this attempt at arms control proved ineffective at restricting the use of a weapon that the aristocracy had cause to fear, yet could not bring themselves to forgo.

The crossbow was expensive, but its principal weakness in battle was its speed. Where a trained ordinary archer could easily shoot ten arrows a minute, the rate was closer to two or three for a crossbow, and the more powerful the bow, the slower its operation. This was a significant drawback in a field battle, where a few minutes might mean the difference between victory and defeat, but in a siege the pace was generally more leisurely, and here the crossbow excelled. For this reason, crossbows were deemed an indispensable part of a castle's defenses. Like other castles, Dover kept a stock of crossbows: a shipment from the Tower of London in 1237 included ten crossbows drawn with a single foot, fifteen double-foot crossbows, and ten that were drawn with a winch.[27] In 1242 the king ordered the authorities in London to furnish 120 crossbowmen for Dover,

EXAMPLE OF A MEDIEVAL CROSSBOW. *Crossbowmen were the best paid foot soldiers.*

along with 3,000 crossbow bolts.[28] There was even a resident crossbow maker to manufacture and repair them. The king issued periodic orders to have the crossbows tested to ensure that they were serviceable.

The other foot soldiers had less standing than the crossbowmen, and the ordinary soldier at Dover, called a watchman, received wages of 2d. a day. To provide additional firepower on the walls, some of these watchmen might be armed with bows. The ordinary bow had a maximum range of about 200 yards, and was significantly less powerful than a crossbow, but it was much cheaper, and offered an easy way to strengthen the castle defenses without breaking the castle budget. For hand-to-hand combat, the cheapest weapon for the ordinary soldier was a spear; other pole weapons such as axes were a bit more expensive, but were still cheaper than the sword, since they were simpler to make and required less steel.

The common soldiers were less well armored than the knights. Instead of a mail hauberk, they might wear a simple padded aketon. Instead of a full barrel helm, they might have only a conical helmet with a nasal bar, or a broad-brimmed kettle hat. In many cases, the helmet was not solid metal, but made of hardened leather reinforced by iron ribs.

A CRUSADER IS STRUCK BY AN ARROW *as his fellow soldiers attack a castle.*

The common soldiers were under the authority of the garrison sergeants, who, like their namesakes today, were given minor command responsibilities but were still classed with the ordinary soldiers rather than the officers. The ratio between soldiers and sergeants in the night watch was ten-to-one, and the same ratio may have applied to the garrison in general. Most of the soldiers probably inhabited quarters in the outer wall, either in the towers themselves or in adjacent buildings. Here they were out of the way of the daily business of the castle, but close to their posts in case of an emergency. The fourteenth-century plan for the castle garrison envisions three men for every two battlements on the outer wall, perhaps implying a system of three watches, with two on duty and one resting at any given time. The night-watch duty assigned to twenty soldiers each night must have been particularly difficult; the garrison rules stipulated that the two sergeants on duty were to tour the walls to ensure that the sentinels were awake. If any were found sleeping, the sergeant was to steal something from him or cut a piece off his clothing as proof. The offending soldier would lose a day's wages, but a sergeant who failed to report a sleeping watchman was to be imprisoned on bread and water, and then expelled from the castle garrison.

Garrison rations were fairly generous. English troops stationed in Scotland in 1300 were allotted a daily allowance of two pounds of wheat flour (probably in the form of bread), almost a gallon of ale, a pound of meat or a pound and a half of fish, and ten ounces of pottage made with peas, beans, and oatmeal, in addition to cheese, butter, onions, garlic, and spices.[29] A plan for provisioning the Dover garrison envisioned a similar diet; it specified that meat and fish dishes would be served as messes, each mess being shared by two soldiers. The plan also allowed for tallow candles.[30]

Boredom was probably a common feature of the garrison soldier's life, particularly in an age before the invention of military drill to keep the soldier occupied. There were various activities to while away the idle hours. Excavations at the twelfth-century castle of Hen Domen, on the frontier between England and Wales, revealed a board for tables (a class of games resembling backgammon). This board was highly decorated and probably belonged to one of the more privileged members of the garrison, but the bone dice found at the same site could have been used by an ordinary soldier, and a number of Nine-Men's Morris boards scratched into stone, and another for Tables, all recovered at Hen Domen, are probably the work of the castle's ordinary inhabitants.

Service Staff

In addition to military personnel, the garrison included a significant support staff of civilians. The kitchens required a crew to provide food for the garrison; the bakehouse and brewhouse had their own personnel; and there were stablehands, gardeners, herdsmen, and others to man the various facilities of the outer bailey. The highest-paid support staff were the skilled craftsmen. They included not only those responsible for making and repairing military equipment, but also those who oversaw the maintenance and improvement of the castle itself. In the case of Dover, there was an ongoing process of development for a century, so that the regular garrison and staff were augmented by a host of temporary laborers and craftsmen hired for specific projects. In 1266, Dover had a chief carpenter, John of Herting, who was paid 4d. a day and received two overgarments a year, and a smith, also named John, who was paid 3d. a day and received two overgarments as well.[31] Adam the Smith, who made crossbow bolts for the garrison, was paid 4d. a day in 1261.[32] The castle also had six priests serving the three chapels and parish church, all appointed by the king. The parish priest received £4 a year, and the chaplains £3.[33] The staff probably lived in buildings close to the facilities where they worked. The uppermost levels of the civilian staff had houses of their own, and even lived with their families. Others may have had private chambers, while the rest slept communally, probably in the same buildings where they worked.

THE HOUSEHOLD

At the apex of the castle community was the aristocratic household that governed it. At Dover, the castle lord was the king himself, who came to the castle periodically, sometimes staying for weeks or even months at a time. During his visits, the king stayed in the bailey, at first in the upper floor of the keep itself, and later in more convenient buildings built against the wall of the inner bailey. Such visits were major occasions, since the king might bring a retinue of hundreds of followers and use the castle as the base of royal administration during his stay. The provisions laid in at Dover for the king's stay over the Christmas season in 1254 give some idea of how elaborate a major royal visit could be. The king sent orders to the sheriffs of Kent, London, Essex, Hertfordshire, and Norfolk to procure supplies that included 20 deer, 23 boars, 40 pigs, 170 hares, 350 rabbits, 2 cranes, 10 herons, 12 geese, 16 peacocks, 31 swans, 36 pheasants, 50 ducks, 144 partridges, 5,500 chickens, and 12,000 eggs.[34]

During the king's absence, the ranking official was the constable, who maintained a substantial household of his own and used the castle as a base for his own significant administrative responsibilities. The constable probably also was lodged at first in the keep, but later was moved to the Great Gate. The constable's wages in the mid-thirteenth century were about £425. This sum was collected from the customs duties at the port of Dover and the payments from manors that had once owed knight service, and any difference was reckoned up at half-year intervals at Easter and Michaelmas.[35] It was an enormous amount of money, but the constable was personally responsible for paying his own expenses and the wages of the castle chaplains, servants, watchmen, and an engineer.[36]

In addition to regular inhabitants, the castle hosted visitors of importance, both aristocrats and high-ranking churchmen. Some of them brought substantial households and stayed for several months. One of these visitors was Eleanor de Montfort, countess of Leicester, whose record of household expenses during her stay in 1265 offers a particularly vivid glimpse of the life of the aristocratic household in a castle.

Eleanor was the sister of Henry III, and wife of Simon de Montfort, earl of Leicester. Simon was one of the most powerful noblemen in England, and in 1265 he was in rebellion against King Henry. Eleanor's loyalties lay with her husband, and during the troubles she took refuge at Dover, where the constable at the time was Henry de Montfort, her eldest son. As constable, Henry de Montfort was a royal appointee, but his loyalties were also with his father, and Eleanor could count on his assistance. She arrived at Dover in June with a

THREE MEN AND A BOY IN THE COURT OF A CASTLE, TO THE RIGHT THREE MEN ON A STAIRCASE. Leonhard Beck (German), ca. 1516. Woodcut. The head of the castle comes out to greet his visitors upon their arrival.

substantial following and gear—the household required about 140 horses as transport, and additional possessions were sent later.

Eleanor's household was sizable, although some of the people mentioned in her accounts were followers and allies not actually belonging to the household itself. A dozen men of aristocratic rank are mentioned, principally knights, and the accounts also imply that there were squires in Eleanor's retinue. During the latter part of Eleanor's stay, the accounts specify that there were six knights in her following. These men may also have had additional soldiers under their command: Sir John de la Warre is mentioned as having twenty-nine archers.

Most of the aristocrats were probably political supporters rather than paid staff, but the household also had a significant number of employees. Two dozen household officials are mentioned. The staff of a substantial aristocratic household commonly included a chamberlain, who administered matters relating to the private areas of the household, a steward, who oversaw matters relating to the hall and the household's public functions, and an usher, who controlled access to the lord himself. The logistical complexities of feeding a substantial establishment were supervised by a butler and a panter, who were responsible for the drinks and food respectively. Other common household administrators included a marshal to look after the horses, an almoner who supervised charitable donations (including the distribution of the household's surplus food), and a chaplain. In the countess's household, many of these would be prestigious positions, occupied by lesser aristocrats or privileged clergymen. Most of Eleanor's officials at Dover served generalized functions, and even Colin the Marshal, a smith in charge of looking after the horses, was sometimes sent on errands to buy food for the household. The records also name three clergymen, who may have served as household chaplains, but who were also sent on errands for the countess. The rest of the household consisted of servants of various sorts, including cooks, bakers, carters, personal valets, and chambermaids. Of the servants who are named, as many as nine appear to be messengers, with such picturesque names as Slingaway, Go-by-the-sty, and Truebody.

There were also women present. Several of the aristocrats and a few officials were accompanied by their wives, at least for part of the time, and Eleanor had her own women in her retinue, including her young daughter Eleanor. In fact, a number of children are mentioned in the accounts, apparently sons of the aristocrats, some of them young enough to require a nurse or boy to look after them.

For most of Eleanor's stay, she was supporting about twenty-five to thirty horses, giving an approximate idea of how many people in her household were aristocrats or important staff. The total size of the household was certainly over fifty, and may have approached one hundred. It was large enough that some had to be quartered in the town below, while the countess herself was lodged in the castle. We do not know where in the castle she stayed, but in the following description we shall suppose that she was lodged in the old royal bedchamber on the upper floor of the keep.

The Bedchamber

To a modern observer, Eleanor's life at Dover, like the life of medieval aristocrats generally, would seem a curious mixture of luxury and hardship. She rose each morning in surroundings at once sumptuous and spartan. The royal chamber measured a mere 10 feet by 22 feet, hardly palatial by modern standards, although it was built for a king who ruled most of the British Isles and half of France. The small size was dictated in part by the cramped quarters of the keep, and the room itself was built into the keep's thick outer wall. On the other hand, its size also made it warmer and less subject to drafts. The concern about drafts was also reflected in the room's limited window area—it was lit by only two small windows. The stone walls of the chamber were probably originally covered with a thick layer of white limewash, and perhaps painted with decorative designs, but in the thirteenth century the room was at least partially wainscoted.[37] The king's chamber at the Tower of London in the thirteenth century was decorated with the royal arms, and his chamber at Winchester had Old and New Testament scenes, while the Queen's chamber was wainscoted and painted with roses.[38]

The bed was not particularly soft by modern standards. At the base would be a wooden bedstead, probably with a latticework of cords woven across to provide a somewhat yielding surface for the mattresses.[39] There were several layers of mattresses, arranged in ascending order of comfort. At the base might be a mattress stuffed with straw, above it one or more filled with wool, and at the top, the softest mattresses stuffed with duck or goose down. Even with all these layers, the bed was not as soft as people are used to today—it was more akin to a futon than to a mattress with springs. The mattress ticking was made of heavy linen or canvas, its fabric woven in striped patterns, a feature of bed decoration of which vestiges remain today. Linen sheets, woolen blankets, and quilted or furred coverlets were laid on top, with a long bolster at the head surmounted by a feather pillow in a linen pillowcase. The countess's account books specifically mention the purchase of "blanchett" cloth: this was a coarse, undyed wool (whence its name, from the French *blanc,* white), that gave its name to the modern blanket. The bed would be curtained, partly for privacy, but mostly for warmth.

The furnishings were probably provided by Eleanor herself. Aristocratic households traveled frequently, visiting their various estates, conducting political business, and engaging in warfare. Most of the furniture traveled with the household—even the bedstead, a fairly large item, was bundled onto a cart or pack animal. This itinerant lifestyle dictated that furniture had to be kept to a minimum, and easily transportable. The total quantity of furniture and possessions in the home of an ordinary knight was probably comparable to that of a lower-middle-class wage earner today, and even the residence of a substantial aristocrat like Eleanor would seem spare in comparison to the wealthy and powerful today. Yet even this limited movable property was an indication of wealth, and what Eleanor's possessions lacked in quantity, they made up for in quality. She could afford to have well-made items, and displayed her wealth

PRESENT-DAY RECREATION OF THE KING'S CHAMBER ROOM *in the Dover Castle keep.*

in the richness of their decoration, with painted or carved woodwork, engraved, enameled or gilt metalwork, and intricately woven or embroidered fabrics.

The countess's bedchamber furnishings, aside from the bed itself, probably consisted principally of a number of wooden chests for storing clothing and personal possessions—these were not as convenient as the modern chest of drawers, but significantly easier to transport. The chests might be bound with iron and sealed with a lock if they contained valuables. There were no built-in closets, and instead of an armoire she hung her clothing over wooden rods suspended in the chamber—her accounts mention the purchase of a few of these during her stay at Dover.

The royal bedchamber was among the best in the keep, and had its own fireplace. Once a fire was lit, the chamber would be quite warm, but the fire would not be allowed to burn at night because of the risk of accident. For this reason, Eleanor may have been wakened each morning by the sound of a maidservant stoking up a fire on the hearth. The omnipresent servant reflected both the luxury and limitations of aristocratic life. No aristocratic household was without its staff of servants. Labor was cheap, and service involved minimal skills, so it was particularly inexpensive. The use of servants compensated in many ways for the lack of technological conveniences, or, to be more accurate, many of the conveniences invented in the past two centuries provide the work that aristocrats once assigned to their servants, allowing an "aristocratic" standard of living for a large number of people. An aristocrat did no manual work: cooking the food,

PRESENT-DAY RECREATION OF THE KING'S BED CHAMBER *in the Dover Castle keep.*

washing the dishes, laundering the clothes, cleaning the house, making the bed, were chores assigned to servants. Eleanor's servant who tended the bedchamber fireplace in the morning may also have helped her to dress, warming her night-chilled clothing at the fire before assisting her in putting them on. Eleanor would rarely be without a servant close at hand—even at night there would be servants sleeping close by, ready to rise should their mistress call for anything. Eleanor's maidservant may even have slept in the bedchamber with her.

Eleanor's bedchamber was particularly well appointed in that it had its own attached privy. Everyone else on this floor had to use the public privy attached to the great hall. Eleanor's accounts also mention the purchase of chamber pots. These were used principally for urine, and relieved traffic to the privies—there was, after all, only a single public facility on the entire floor, probably serving dozens of people. It also saved the user a long trip through the cold and dark keep in the middle of the night. After use, the chamber pot would have been left to a servant to empty, probably into the privy hole.

The Great Chamber

Once Eleanor had dressed, attended to her physical needs, and said her morning prayers, she would leave the seclusion of the bedchamber for the larger but still fairly private space of the great chamber. There was one other bedchamber adjoining the great chamber, similar in size to the principal bedchamber, and also furnished with a fireplace, but lacking a privy. This room may have been used by the other aristocratic women of Eleanor's household who stayed with her at Dover. A number of servants may have slept in the great chamber. The inhabitants of the keep were doubtless carefully segregated by sex, as this was always a priority in the aristocratic household. Male servants may have been lodged in the great chamber, the women in the bedchambers; or, perhaps more likely, the men may have slept in the great hall while the chambers were reserved for the women. Had the earl of Leicester been present, he and Eleanor would probably also have occupied separate chambers. As a married couple, there was no impropriety in their sleeping together, but it was customary at the upper levels of the aristocracy for husbands and wives to have separate rooms.

By the time Eleanor emerged from her bedchamber in the morning, the servants' bedding would have been cleared away from the great chamber. Like the rest of the castle, this room would be sparsely furnished. There would be a few tables, probably only boards mounted on trestles that could be cleared out of the way to make space when needed, and readily packed up when the household relocated. There would also be wooden stools and benches, but not many chairs. Chairs were harder to transport, and they were something of a status symbol, allowed only to the most privileged household members and visitors. There were probably a number of storage chests, and perhaps a few sideboards or cupboards for storing tableware.

The great chamber may have been richly decorated. Like other rooms in the castle, the walls would have been whitewashed and plastered, but on top of this there may have been paint. Bright colors like green, red, yellow, and blue were considered suitable for decorating castle interiors, and Eleanor's accounts also mention the use of gold stars for young Eleanor's chapel. Alternatively, the chamber may have been covered with painted cloths, which served to decorate and insulate the room.

Eleanor may have begun her morning with a religious service. A schedule laid out for a lady of the royal family in the fifteenth century envisioned her rising at 7 a.m. to hear Matins followed by a Mass, and prescribed a second Mass toward midday.[40] Regular devotions were also routine in the High Middle Ages, and there were two chapels in the keep at Dover, one of which (probably the lower) appears to have been assigned specifically to the countess's daughter.

The Working Day

After services, a table in the great chamber might be set up with a small amount of food and drink to sustain Eleanor for the morning. Substantial breakfasts were not customary in the Middle Ages, and she is more likely to have broken her fast with a few sops of bread dipped in wine. Even as she sat down for a quick morsel, she might begin the work of the day, for the great chamber was as much an office as a dining hall. The medieval environment made little distinction between public and private spaces, and it was a mark of Eleanor's status that she had even the tiny bedchamber as a place of retreat. In fact, she could probably have done a full day's work without ever leaving the great chamber.

Eleanor's work at Dover was considerable. There was a continual flow of messengers to and from the countess, who was busy supporting her husband's revolt against the king. She dispatched assistance to him, including a certain William the Engineer who was evidently a specialist in siege weaponry. She procured military equipment for her husband's use, maintained relations with a substantial body of military followers, and conducted negotiations with various third parties. Among the visitors who dined with Eleanor at Dover were leading citizens from the port towns of Sandwich and Winchelsea, whose support or assistance she was presumably trying to enlist, and she fostered relations with visiting ambassadors and merchants from overseas. In more settled times, a larger number of the countess's guests would be casual visitors. There were not many commercial inns, and certainly none that could accommodate a substantial aristocratic household on the move. Instead, the traveling aristocrat or important clergyman with a large entourage relied on the hospitality of other aristocrats. All of this was in addition to the ongoing work of maintaining and supporting the household itself: supplies had to be procured, sometimes purchased in the town or from the castle stores, at other times procured from one of the de Montforts' nearby manors.

Dinner

Toward noon the household took its dinner, the main meal of the day. This was served either in the great chamber or in the hall. It was traditional for the aristocracy to eat in the more public space of the hall, but during the course of the Middle Ages they increasingly retreated to more private rooms for their meals, and certainly the great chamber was of ample size for this purpose. During the latter part of Eleanor's stay, after the death of her husband at the battle of Evesham, the accounts note that she dined in the hall in the company of the garrison knights, which suggests that she had previously been using the great chamber.

As the mealtime approached, the servants would set up the necessary tables, covering them with tablecloths. All the places were laid on one side of the table, facilitating access for the servants from the other side. Food was eaten with knives and spoons only; the only forks in use were larger ones for cooking and

SERVANTS ATTEND TO THE LADY OF A CASTLE *and others at the dinner table.*
1873 illustration after a French illumination from a medieval manuscript.

serving. Knives may have been provided, but even in this aristocratic household it is likely that the diners had their own: the account books mention a scabbard purchased for the countess's knife. The civilian knife was quite distinct from the warlike dagger: the dagger was large and double-edged, with a crossbar to guard the hand, in contrast with the smaller, single-edged knife. The place setting also included a trencher, a round slice of bread from the bottom or the top of an old loaf, having a hard crust and serving as a plate. After the meal, the sauce-soaked trenchers were probably distributed to servants or the poor. Food was served on platters, commonly one platter to two diners, from which they transferred it to their trenchers. Each pair of diners shared a cup, and saltcellars were on the table, from which diners could take salt with their knives. Much of the etiquette of the medieval table related to the use of shared tableware, as is evident in the following thirteenth-century versified maxims on table manners:

> No-one should take food before the blessing has been made,
> Nor should he take a place other than that assigned to him by the one in
> charge of the meal.

Refrain from eating until the dishes have been placed before you,

And let your fingers be clean, and your fingernails well-groomed.

Once a morsel has been touched, let it not be returned to the plate.

Do not touch your ears or nose with your bare hands.

Do not clean your teeth with a sharp iron while eating.

The salt is not to be touched with the food where it sits in the salt dish.

If you can, I ask again, refrain from belching at the table.

Know that it is forbidden to put your elbow on the table.

It is ordered by regulation that you should not put a dish to your mouth.

He who wishes to drink must first finish what is in his mouth,

And let his lips be wiped first.

Nor can I avoid mentioning that he should not gnaw a bone with his teeth. . . .

Once the table is cleared, wash your hands, and have a drink.[41]

When the diners came to the table, a servant passed among them with a jug of water, a bowl, and a towel. The servant poured water from the jug over their hands into the bowl so that the diners could rinse them before eating. This was especially important since, in the absence of forks, much of the meal was eaten with the hands. A grace was recited at the beginning of the meal, and another at the end, at which point water was brought around again to rinse off the remains of the food.

The dishes served at an aristocratic table were far more varied than those available to the peasantry. Every meal involved bread, which appears on the countess's account books each day; the accounts also mention cakes. Meats served in Eleanor's household during her stay at Dover included beef, veal, mutton, and pork, as well as game, probably venison. Chicken and goose were also purchased for her table. She was conscientious about observing fast days: no meat was served on Wednesdays, Fridays, or Saturdays, or on the days before a major holy day. The alternatives on these days were diverse: in addition to eggs, cheese, and cheese tarts, the accounts mention an astounding variety of seafood, including plaice, sole, bream, cod, herring, bass, eel, shrimp, crayfish, and whelks. There were also mackerel and sturgeon, both of which seem to have come dried or salted from the castle cellars. Fish-day foods also included simpler fare such as gruel and pottages made with peas and beans. Fruits were served according to the season: Eleanor's household purchased strawberries in June, cherries in early July, and pears in late July and early August. Flavorings purchased by the countess included salt, pepper, ginger, cloves, saffron, parsley, fennel, anise, licorice, verjuice (a sour fermented juice squeezed from unripe grapes), and mustard. Sugar appears in the accounts as well, along with the spices. It was about as expensive as pepper, and was used sparingly as a spice, rather than liberally as a staple. Other cooking ingredients listed in the accounts included almonds, milk, butter, cream, and "colorings."

The other principal staple was wine, which appears in Eleanor's accounts on a daily basis. Both red and white wines were consumed by Eleanor's household at Dover, and in prodigious quantities. The accounts regularly distinguish between the best Gascony wine, served by the countess to her knights, and the mixed "bastard" wine served in slightly less generous amounts to the rest of the household. Ale was also purchased, chiefly for the benefit of the servants, although they were sometimes served wine instead.

The countess ate in the company of her fellow aristocrats and invited guests. Visitors from the area could dine with the countess at midday and still have plenty of time to return home before night. Dinner might therefore have been something of a working meal, an opportunity for Eleanor to confer with her allies and associates. In the late summer of 1265, after the defeat and death of her husband at the battle of Evesham, she regularly dined in the hall with all of her knights. The presence of all of her followers at these meals doubtless reflected the need for more consultation as the situation worsened, and these meals must have been the occasion of many anxious conversations.

Afternoon and Evening

After the midday meal, the countess could return to the work of running her affairs. Perhaps some time was allotted in the afternoon for rest and recreation, as a respite from a demanding cycle of work. The fifteenth-century schedule for a royal lady envisioned a fifteen-minute nap in the afternoon, as well as regular

THE STAG HUNT OF THE ELECTOR FREDERICK THE WISE. Lucas Cranach the Elder (German), 1529. Oil on linden wood.

time for entertainments. Hunting, one of the passions of the medieval aristocracy, may have occupied some of Eleanor's leisure hours. She had a servant named Jack who was in charge of keeping greyhounds, used for hunting hares. She might also have indulged in falconry, a form of hunting popular with ladies as well as men. Her accounts mention venison sent to various friends, although she may not have hunted these herself, since it was less common for women to participate directly in the hunting of large game. Jousting was another aristocratic pastime that was principally for men, although women often took part as spectators. More sedentary activities included dice games and board games such as chess and tables. Eleanor might also have engaged in needlework, which was one of the characteristic pastimes of aristocratic ladies.

At the close of the day came supper, the second principal meal, which tended to be smaller than dinner, with lighter but more expensive food. This might be taken somewhat less formally in the great chamber, but if there were important guests, the meal might be served in the hall. Hired musicians might play during the meal, and afterward the countess might call for entertainments to relax her after the demands of her day's work. Aristocratic account books are full of payments made to musicians, acrobats, animal trainers, and similar entertainers. Dancing was popular with the aristocracy, including circle and chain dances similar to those of common folk, as well as couple dances, which seem to have been an innovation of the High Middle Ages. Storytelling was another beloved pastime, and the aristocracy especially favored long tales in verse about chivalric adventures. Stories of King Arthur and his knights were particularly popular and enjoyed by aristocrats across Europe.

At the close of the evening, the countess retired to her bedchamber, where a maidservant helped her undress; she may have worn her shift as a nightshirt. Eleanor would say a prayer before retiring, while her maidservant hung her clothes on their rod and covered up the fire for the night, perhaps leaving a candle on the hearth to provide light. Once the household was squared away, the servants retired; the only creatures still stirring would be the ones on four feet. Like other castles, Dover had a problem with mice, and one of Eleanor's earliest purchases after her arrival was a household cat.

PREDICAT: EADWINVS FAMA PER SECCULA VIGO · INGENIVM CVIVS LIBRI DECVS IND SIM COGA LITTERA CLACO ALITTER TE TVA SRIPTVRA QVEM SIGNAT PICTA FIGVRA

6

MONASTIC LIFE

The Monastic Tradition

The institutions of the village and castle discussed in the previous two chapters had their roots in native European traditions, either of classical Rome, or the barbarian tribes of the north. Medieval Europe was also profoundly affected by a third cultural tradition, that of the ancient Near East, imported to Europe during the centuries of Roman ascendancy. The medium for this influence was Christianity, which began its life as a sect within Judaism but soon attracted converts outside the Jewish community; in time it came to be adopted as the state religion of the Roman Empire and subsequently as the official religion of the nascent kingdoms of medieval Europe.

Judaism had traditionally been a religion concerned primarily with the present life and with governing conduct in the material world. By the time of Roman ascendancy in the Near East, certain sects among the Jews had begun to gravitate toward a more otherworldly form of spirituality, rejecting the things of the physical world as evil; most famous among these sects is the Essenes, the secluded community of religious Jews who wrote the Dead Sea Scrolls. Christianity drew on such trends toward otherworldly Judaism, as reflected in Christ's admonition to the just man who wishes to seek a perfect life: "If you would be perfect, go, sell what you possess, and give to the poor, and you will have treasure in heaven; and come, follow me" (Matthew 19:21). The otherworldy aspirations of Christians found ample scope in the first few centuries of Christianity, as sustained official persecution made the profession of their faith an invitation to hardship, ruin, and

THE MONK EADWINE. Unknown miniaturist (English), ca. 1150. Illumination on parchment.

even death. The official toleration of Christianity in 313 and its establishment as the state religion in 380 meant that a new path had to be found for those who wished to seek salvation through hardship.

The new path lay through the deserts of Egypt. Already before the edict of toleration, it appears that some Christians in Egypt were retiring from the world to the solitude of the desert. The Greek word for desert, *eremia,* gave these recluses the name "hermits." Their course of life attracted even more followers in the fourth century, and before long there were communities of hermits living semisolitary lives in loose association, gathering only for communal religious services. Some of these communities began to adopt a more formalized structure, living under the authority of an older, experienced hermit, called *abba,* the Syriac and Aramaic word for father (hence the word "abbot"). Such a community was known in Greek as a *koinobion,* "communal way of life," and its members were termed coenobites, but their origin as solitary hermits was reflected in an alternative term, *monachos,* from the Greek *monos,* "one," the origin of the English word monk.

During the fourth and fifth centuries, these institutions were exported to other parts of the Roman Empire, including Western Europe. Eventually, Western monasticism acquired a definitive shape, articulated by Saint Benedict of Nursia in the sixth century. Benedict, an Italian abbot, laid out a plan for monastic life and organization that ultimately became the standard in Western Europe. Benedictine monasticism was ascetic, requiring monks to live with minimal possessions, simple food, and austere accommodations, yet it avoided the excesses of heroic self-denial, stressing instead the role of communal cooperation as a means of achieving personal spiritual improvement. Benedict's rule for monastic life was concise and pragmatic, offering both a viable organizational structure and a healthy degree of flexibility. The Benedictine monk sought communion with God through a combination of physical labor and a daily cycle of communal worship that came to be known as the Divine Office. Over time, the Divine Office took precedence over other monastic activities, although some forms of work, particularly reading and writing, continued to play an important part in the monastic routine and ethos.

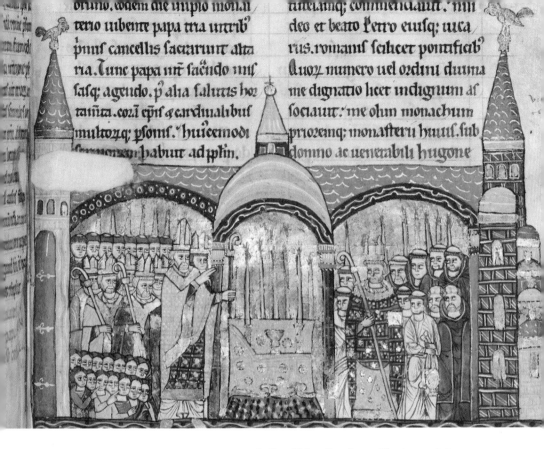

THE CONSECRATION OF CLUNY ABBEY *by Pope Urban II, a former Cluniac monk, in 1095. Illumination from a Book of Offices, twelfth century.*

Among the Benedictine monasteries of high medieval Europe, Cluny, lying in the Burgundy region of France, was of outstanding importance and influence. Very little of the medieval monastery survives, as most of the complex was dismantled during the French Revolution, but the site has been excavated in the twentieth century, revealing a great deal of detail about its physical layout, and the life of its inhabitants is richly documented in surviving texts from the Middle Ages. Although Cluny's extraordinary wealth and importance set it apart from most other monasteries of the period, they also made it a particularly complete example of the monastic ideal. As an unusually rich establishment, Cluny was able to afford multiple renovations and improvements that continually changed its appearance during the centuries of the High Middle Ages. This chapter will focus on the monastery as it was in the early twelfth century.[1]

Monastic Orders

The earliest monasteries were communities of laymen. By the High Middle Ages, it was common for monks to be priests as well, but monasticism and priesthood were oriented toward different goals. The priest served principally as an intermediary between God and man, while the monk sought to achieve spiritual purity. The monks were termed "regular" clergy, meaning that they lived a communal life according to an established set of regulations, called a monastic rule (in Latin, *regula*). Those monasteries that followed the rule of St. Benedict were considered part of the Benedictine order, although there was no unifying organizational structure among them beyond the rule itself. There was some leeway in how the rule was interpreted, and in many cases the monastery codified its interpretation and elaboration of the rule as a "custumal," essentially a set of by-laws that applied to that monastery alone. Our knowledge of life at Cluny around the year 1100 owes much to a custumal compiled by the monk Ulrich in the late eleventh century.

For most of the early Middle Ages, the Benedictines were the only monastic order in Western Europe. Over the centuries, monasteries of the order became lax in applying the rule and less vigorous in their sense of religious vocation, and in the tenth century a major reform movement was initiated with the founding of Cluny. Cluny's first abbot was energetic and enthusiastic, and brought a renewed sense of zeal and discipline to the monastic world. Over the next two centuries, many new monasteries were established under Cluny's guidance, while older ones were placed under the authority of Cluny to help them reform. Cluniac monasteries still used the Benedictine rule and belonged to the Benedictine order, but where previously every Benedictine monastery had been a self-contained unit, Cluny sought to maintain its reformed version of Benedictinism by retaining authority over the monasteries it founded or reformed.

The Cluniac movement emphasized stricter adherence to the Benedictine rule, but there were many who saw the enormous wealth, power, and feudal involvement of Benedictine monasteries as grave obstacles to a virtuous life. Partly in response to Cluny, a new reform movement arose toward the end of the eleventh century at the nearby abbey of Cîteaux. The Cistercians established a new rule of their own, rejecting the opulence of the traditional Benedictine monastery and its reliance on income from feudal manors. The new Cistercian monasteries were much plainer in decoration, and the monks made their living by farming their own lands through hired labor and lay brothers, members of the monastic community who lived semimonastic lives, but were not actually monks.

Other reform movements led to the founding of additional monastic orders, and there were also other organizations that emulated the monastic ideal. It became increasingly common for cathedral canons to adopt a communal style of life under a formal rule, and eventually these "canons regular" established houses of their own, institutions that in some cases were hardly distinguishable from monasteries. In the twelfth century, the crusading zeal of the European aristocracy was conjoined with monastic asceticism and organization to create the military orders of the Templars and Hospitallers, knights who lived in communities under a quasi-monastic rule, but whose primary purpose was warfare in defense of the Christian states established by the Crusaders in the Holy Lands. In the thirteenth century, the revitalization of urban life fostered new versions of communal living in the form of the mendicant orders, or friars, discussed in Chapter 7.

ORGANIZATION

Monasteries varied greatly in size. Cluny's population rose from 200 monks in the mid-eleventh century to 460 in the mid-twelfth, and even after the population declined again to 200 a century later, Cluny remained an outstandingly large establishment. Something under a hundred monks was more typical for a moderately large monastery. At the lower end of the scale, there were countless small monasteries consisting of a dozen monks under the authority of an abbot, and even smaller communities not qualifying as actual monasteries, composed of as few as three or four monks living together. Overall, monks constituted a very small portion of the medieval population— probably well under 1 percent.

The potential size of a monastery was limited by its income. The physical facilities at Cluny were comparable to those of a major castle, and at its height, the population was that of a small medieval town. Such an institution required a substantial and reliable source of income, and as in other church institutions, this money was provided by endowments of property from the monastery's lay patrons. The properties were often in the form of rural manors, which the monastery held as manor lord, receiving income in cash and in kind in much the same way as did the landed aristocracy. Cluny's landholdings ranked it as a major feudal lord, and constituted hundreds of manors widely dispersed through southern and eastern France. Nearby landholdings were used principally as sources of agricultural produce to supply the monastic population. Cluny had about thirty of these holdings, called *granges*, most of which were within twenty-five miles of the monastery, although a few were up to seventy miles away. More distant holdings were administered as feudal manors, with the monastery receiving cash profits to support its operating costs.

Other patrons donated urban properties, yielding cash rents to the monastery as landlord. In some cases a patron might donate a parish church that lay in his possession, providing income in the form of tithes. All of these sources of support tended to entangle the monastery in the secular world that the monks were theoretically supposed to have left behind. As a property holder, the monastery had to manage its estates, and often defend its rights by law. Since manorial properties generally entailed feudal obligations, many monasteries were obliged to engage knights to serve the lords from whom the manors were held. As holders of parish churches, monasteries had to collect tithes and hire a parish priest. Their involvement in parishes often brought them in conflict with the hierarchy of the secular church, since monasteries themselves were independent of the authority of the regional bishop, but as parish rectors they were subject to episcopal oversight.

The Abbot

The administration of the monastery, both as a religious institution and as a political and economic entity, involved a hierarchy of specialized officers. The rule of St. Benedict achieved flexibility by relying heavily on the discretion of the abbot. The abbot was the absolute authority within the monastery. He was required by the rule to consult the older and wiser monks, but he was not obliged to follow their advice. The abbot was normally chosen by the senior monks, but once in place only his superiors in the church had the right to countermand his will or remove him from office. If the order to which the monastery belonged did not have an organizational hierarchy, this would require direct intervention by the pope. Usually an abbot was expected to hold his post until prevented by death or debility. The abbot was chosen from within the monastery's order, but not always from within the monastery itself. Nor was he necessarily an old man. At Cluny it was common to choose a monk in his late twenties, who could provide years of stability and continuity during his long years of life.

The abbot had principal responsibility for the monastery's interaction with other monasteries and with the world at large, including attending meetings of the order, dealing with lay patrons, and overseeing the monastery's legal rights and obligations. The abbot of a major monastery like Cluny was an extremely important political figure, comparable in power and status to a substantial feudal lord—the abbot of Cluny even had the right to mint coinage. Within Cluny, the monks were expected to do great reverence to the abbot. They were obliged to bow deeply when they encountered him, kiss his hands when giving or receiving anything from him, and when his name was mentioned in a letter as it was read aloud, all were to bow toward him.

The Priors

Since the abbot had so many responsibilities outside of the monastery, the day-to-day running of internal matters within the monastery often fell to his second-in-command, the prior. Some monasteries, particularly the smaller ones, had no abbot at all, and were instead under the authority of a prior—these were called priories as opposed to abbeys. Cluny was so large that it required two priors.

The grand prior was responsible for overseeing the abbey's affairs as a feudal landholder. He was aided by a number of deacons who oversaw the manorial granges that supplied Cluny with its food. The claustral prior was charged with the administration of Cluny's monks. He had a number of inspectors who helped him make the rounds of the monastery each day. He also oversaw the work of the masters of the oblates and of the novices.

Other Officers

A large monastery like Cluny had a substantial roster of monks in administrative offices, termed "obedientiaries," sometimes with additional subobedientiaries to assist them. Cluny's obedientiary staff was typical of a large monastery. Two officers were assigned to the needs of the monastic church. The precentor oversaw the celebration of divine services, and since this was drawn from liturgical books, he was also in charge of the library and scriptorium. The material needs of the church, as well as the offerings made by visitors, were the concern of the sacristan.

Other officers looked after the monastic population. The chamberlain was in charge of collecting and distributing monastic income and property, and especially attended to the monks' personal clothing and gear; he was assisted by one or more deputies. The cellarer was responsible for the monastery's supply of food, drink, and fuel for its fires. He was assisted by a deputy cellarer, a keeper of the granary, a keeper of the wine, and a gardener. The refectorian was in charge of the dining hall where the monks took their meals. The infirmary was in the hands of an infirmarian, assisted by three lay brothers.

Other officers were responsible for charity and hospitality. The keeper of the guest house saw to the needs of privileged guests, while the almoner looked after ordinary travelers and oversaw the monastery's charitable activities. Horses and other riding beasts were in the hands of a stable master. One of the older monks would serve as porter, lodging in the monastery gatehouse so that he could supervise the arrival of visitors.

The obedientiaries' responsibilities were very time-consuming, and they could be excused from the Divine Office to allow them to fulfill their official duties. A few offices rotated on a weekly basis, including the priest in charge of celebrating communal masses, a reader responsible for reading during meals in the refectory, and four cooks who prepared food in the monastic kitchen.

The Chapter

Although the monastery was not a democratic institution, it was fairly participatory by medieval standards. Every morning after mass all the monks assembled in the chapter house where they handled current business. If there were novices to consider for admission to the monastery, it was discussed at this time. This was also an occasion for administering discipline. Monks were expected to report on one another's misdeeds, and a monk who had transgressed was required to prostrate himself before the abbot. At the abbot's discretion, he might be beaten, and for more serious offenses he might be placed under a regime of punishment involving exclusion from communal activities and even imprisonment. The daily meeting of the community was termed the chapter, and the abbot was expected to consult with the chapter on important matters, allowing the monks to voice their opinions, although the function of the chapter was principally advisory, and the final word always rested with the abbot himself.

THE MONKS

Monks were sworn to a life of personal poverty, but this does not mean that they were recruited from among the poor. In fact, they were predominantly drawn from the aristocracy. Recruits were expected to bring a significant donation to their monastery, and it was the upper classes who had land and money to offer. While monks were individually poor since they were not permitted to own personal property, the monastery collectively was a rich institution, and monks enjoyed a standard of living far above that of ordinary medieval people. They had regular and sufficient meals regardless of the state of the harvest; they had wine to drink and occasional fine foods, at least at Cluny and other establishments that took a moderate approach to asceticism; they lived in well-constructed stone facilities with good sanitation; and there was ample provision for them in illness and old age. The monastic way of life was austere, but it offered enough advantages that there was always a demand among the aristocracy for monastic positions.

LADY PRESENTING MONKS FROM WEINGARTEN
ABBEY *with a sacred relic. Illumination from a 1489
German manuscript.*

Aristocratic parents with multiple sons needed to find an appropriate career for the younger ones, and sending them to monasteries was a good option, offering an acceptable standard of living, a stable future, and even prospects of prestige and power. Of course, this practice of treating monasticism as a career rather than a vocation meant that many monks were not deeply committed to the monastic ideal, to the detriment of monastic discipline.

Most monasteries recruited their population principally from the surrounding region. This was less true in the case of a major establishment like Cluny, the highly esteemed head of an extensive international order. Cluny attracted a more diverse population than most monasteries, drawn from across Western Europe. Some of its monks came from other Cluniac monasteries, sent by their abbots to live at the mother house. Some came from other monastic orders. A monk was generally expected to remain in his monastery for life, but he was permitted to leave a less strict house for a stricter one, and Cluny had a high reputation for its adherence to the Benedictine rule. Some recruits came to the monastery from a life as secular clergymen, others as laymen. Although the bulk of Cluny's population were presumably native French speakers, the daily language of the monastery, as of the church in general, was Latin. The monks used Latin among themselves, and any new monk who was ignorant of the language had to learn it. Monks might need the local vernacular to communicate with lay brothers and visitors, but since communication with nonmonks was strictly limited, a monk could spend his lifetime at Cluny without knowing French.

Oblates

The process of admission to a monastery depended on the situation of the candidate. Some monasteries, including Cluny, accepted children, generally from the ages of five to seven or later. These children, called *oblates* ("offered ones"), were principally a feature of Benedictine monasteries. They were not numerous at Cluny, having been reduced to six in the eleventh century. By the thirteenth century, the church had decided that a boy could not be bound permanently to the monastic life by his parents, so that when he came of age he could choose whether to become a monk or not. The later reformed orders generally refused to accept oblates at all, since the presence of children could easily disrupt monastic discipline, and the practice disappeared in the course of the thirteenth century.

The oblates at Cluny had minimal contact with the monks. They were under the watch of two or more masters and were never allowed to be alone: they were always required to operate in pairs at least, with a master walking between them. If one woke up in the middle of the night needing to use the latrine, he woke the closest master, who lit a lantern, roused another boy, and walked between them to the latrine. The oblates were integrated into the liturgical life of the monastery, with particular roles assigned to them in the execution of the Divine Office and other communal devotions. They lived according to a moderated version of monastic discipline. They were allowed more food, and very small boys might even have extra rations brought to them in the cloister between meals. At mealtimes each boy was sent to eat at one of the tables of the monks, where he took his food standing across from a reliable monk who would report him for discipline if necessary. The Cluny custumal also made provision for a small table to be provided for any boy for whom the effort of standing was too difficult, and the twelfth-century statutes of Cluny abolished the custom of requiring the oblates to stand, on the grounds that it was too hard for young children. The oblates had their own chapter, in which they were expected to reveal one another's misdeeds as did the monks. Instead of the monk's tunic, they wore a linen shirt, with a hooded gown over it; when the abbot judged them ready, the hood was removed, and they were given a cowl. They were taught the skills necessary for a monk: reading, writing, arithmetic, and Latin, as well as singing and reading music so that they could take part in the Divine Office.

Novices

Anyone who joined the monastery at the age of fifteen years or more became a novice. The novitiate began with a ceremony of initiation followed by a mass, during which the novice was shaved and given the tonsure, the distinctive hairstyle of the clergyman, which involved shaving the crown of the head to leave a circle of hair just above the level of the ears. The novice wore the same clothes as the oblate, with a monk's tunic substituted for the linen shirt. The novitiate lasted one year, during which the novice participated to a limited degree in monastic activities and learned the requirements of monastic life. The novices were separated from the monks at most times, with their own dormitory, refectory, and latrine, and, like the oblates, they were never permitted to be alone. At the end of the year, the novice was allowed to take his vows, pledging himself to the monastic life and becoming a full member of the monastic community. During the ceremony of initiation, the novice's hooded gown was removed, and replaced by the monastic cowl. For the next three days, the new monk was required to keep the hood of the cowl over his head, sleep in his full habit, and keep continual silence. On the third day, the priest of the week kissed him and pushed back his hood, at which point he be-

SAINT BENEDICT FREES A NOVICE MONK FROM A DEMON. *Spinello Aretino (Italian), 1387. Fresco.*

gan the customary life of the monk. In the twelfth century, Cluny tightened its rules on the admission of monks, requiring them to be at least twenty years of age. Most novices were youths, but they also included older men who chose to retire to monastic life.

Monks

The monk's vows were considered permanently binding, and the new monk was in principle bound to the monastery for the rest of his life—he was not even permitted to pass the cloister gate without permission, or to talk with any lay person, even the lay brothers who worked within the monastery. Everything the monk needed for the rest of his days was provided within the precincts of the monastery. In this way, the monk could leave behind the outside world. In practice, however, many monks did have contact with the world beyond the cloister. Monastic officers were required by their work to interact with laymen and spend time in the outer areas of the monastery, or even beyond the monastery walls, serving as ambassadors from the monastery or administering its business affairs. In some cases a monk was permitted to transfer to a new monastery, either for his own spiritual benefit, or to provide experience or expertise for an institution in need. During the thirteenth century, with rising educational standards in the secular world, many monasteries began to send monks to university, and some monasteries established houses at universities to serve as residences for members of their order—Cluny had such an establishment in Paris.

Lay Brothers and Laborers

Not all of the inhabitants of the monastery were monks. Like other monasteries, Cluny had a supplementary population of lay brothers, recruited from the lower classes, who provided manual labor for the monastery: the monastery's bakers, launderers, and wood gatherers were drawn from the lay brothers. The lay brothers lived under a quasi-monastic rule and wore the tonsure, but they had limited participation in the monastic life: they observed but did not take part in the Divine Office, and they were probably illiterate in almost every case. The lay brothers at Cluny resided in a building in the outer courtyard of the monastery, with its own dormitory, refectory, and latrine. Monasteries that lacked lay brothers relied on hired labor instead, and even Cluny made some use of hired workers.

THE MONASTERY

The Cloister

Although monasteries varied greatly in size, wealth, and ethos, the idea of a typical medieval monastery has much more meaning than it does for villages, castles, or towns. Monasticism evolved with a degree of planning, coordination, and even deliberate standardization that was not possible for secular institutions. The standardization of monastic life is especially evident in the physical layout of the monastery. The typical monastic ground plan shows the influence of the Roman villa. Its distinctive feature and the central point of its physical space was the cloister, a sheltered arcade surrounding a square open area, recalling the characteristic square courtyard of Roman times. The entry to the cloister lay at its northwestern corner, toward the main gate of the monastery. Monks were not permitted to pass from the cloister to the outer area of the monastery unless their official duties required it, and visitors were only allowed within the cloister by express permission. Lay visitors were only admitted to the cloister when the monks were in church, and women were forbidden at all times. The contrast between the pure space of the cloister and the sinful world outside is evoked in a story told about Cluny by Peter the Venerable, one of the monastery's twelfth-century abbots:

> There was an Italian brother named John, who disliked the severity of monastic discipline, and went so far as to contemplate fleeing the monastery. Then the devil himself came to him in the likeness of an abbot. For two demons, under the appearance of monks, followed this brother to a secluded spot in the monastery, where he sat deep in thought. Then the devil, believing that he had found an opportune moment for deception, appeared to him, and sat by his side, and said, "I came this way now, brother, for the purpose of visiting with my hosts, but having chanced to see you, I perceived that you

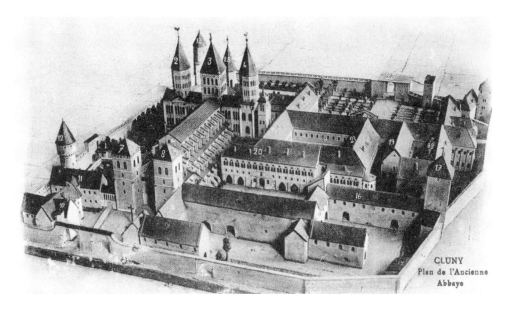

LAYOUT OF CLUNY ABBEY, *a Benedictine monastery in Saône-et-Loire, France, built in the Romanesque style between the tenth–twelfth centuries. From a postcard, ca. 1900.*

LEGEND

1. Grand Church
2. Belfry of Bisans
3. Bell Choir
4. Clocher de l'Eau Bénite ("Holy Water Belfry")
5. Clocher de l'Horloge ("Clock Belfry")
6. Narthex, or entry vestibule
7. Tower of Archives and Treasure
8. Tower of Justice
9. Main entryway
10. Palais Jean de Bourbon
11. Palais Jacques d'Amboise
12. Fabry Tower
13. Round tower

14. Entrance to the stable yard
15. Stables
16. Storehouse
17. Tour des Fromages ("Cheese Tower")
18. Refectory
19. Chapel of the Virgin
20. Palace of Pope Gelasius II
21. Monastic buildings
22. Garden facade
23. Garden doors
24. Passage for the Palace of the Church Abbot
25. Clocher des Lampes ("Lamp Belfry")

are afflicted with great distress. . . . Therefore, tell me, your interested friend, who you are and why you are unhappy." This brother feared to open the secrets of his heart to an apparent stranger, and responded only that he was Italian by birth, to which this devil in monk's clothing responded, "I am also an abbot of the same region, and I can help you well in all things. For I know, although you remain silent, that the abbot and the others of this monastery treat you poorly, nor do they respect you as you deserve, and what's more, they constantly vex you with outrage and insults. Therefore I advise that you take heed, leave this utterly horrible place, and come away with me. For I am prepared to take you away from these evils, and lead you to my abbey, which is called Ironvault, and exalt you with every honor." To these things the brother responded, "I can hardly leave this place, because the gate of the monastery prevents it, and I am surrounded by a multitude of other monks." Then the devil said, "Nor can I help you, as long as you remain here. But find some means to get past the enclosure of the monastery. Once you have done that, I will be there at once, and will take you to my place as I said." But merciful God . . . did not let the enemy proceed any further. . . . For while this was taking place, the community of brothers was sitting in the refectory for their customary dinner hour. When it was finished, the prior struck once a little bell as is the custom. When this sound was heard, at once the demon . . . was made by divine power to rush away from the brother to whom he was speaking. It ran at full tilt toward the latrines that were nearby, where in full sight of this brother it cast itself into the bottom of them. Thus God's mercy rescued the brother from the temptation of the most evil enemy, and cast the filthy spirit out of his house through a place suitable to his filthiness.[2]

The arcade of the cloister served as a general utility area for the monks. The oblates had their school here, and the monks read, talked, and worked in this area. A whetstone was suspended in the cloister for the monks to use in sharpening their knives, and there was a large trough for laundering clothes. At Cluny's cloister gate was the almonry, where eighteen indigent laymen resided, living semimonastic lives supported by the monastery. The building on the west side of the cloister, called the cellar, was used to store supplies brought in from outside; it also served as lodging for the cellarer and his wine keeper. At the southwest corner of the cloister were the food preparation facilities, including a bakehouse and two separate kitchens. The monastic kitchen, which faced the cloister, was staffed by monks, and at Cluny it provided only vegetable stews and beans—not even other legumes were cooked in this kitchen. The lay kitchen, facing the outer courtyard, provided food for the lay brothers and guests of the monastery, as well as fish, spiced dishes, and other foods permitted to the monks but not allowed in the monastic kitchen. The kitchens had running water, and access to the stream running as a drain underneath.

On the south side of the cloister was the monks' refectory, where they took their meals. This was a particularly fine hall, well lit with thirty-six large glazed windows, and decorated with wall paintings that included scenes from the Old and New Testaments, a large figure of Christ surrounded by the principal founders and benefactors of the monastery, and a depiction of the Last Judgment. The monks ate at six long tables running lengthwise along the room, while across the head of the room were three tables for the chief officers of the monastery: the abbot's table on a dais in the center, with the grand prior's table to his right and the claustral prior's table to his left. Clerical guests of the monastery also sat at these tables. There was a small bell in the refectory, used to signal mealtimes for the monks. Just outside the refectory was the *lavabo*, a large basin at which the monks washed their hands before every meal. There were three towels at the lavabo: one for the monks, a second for the oblates, and a third for the lay brothers. These were changed twice a week, and the water replaced once a week.

Next to the refectory was the calefactory, a heated room where the monks went to warm themselves. It also functioned as a service area where work was done that might otherwise disturb the tranquility of the cloister—for example, monks who missed the communal shaving might be shaved in this room. At the southeast corner of the cloister was the chamber, a workshop used by the chamberlain and his staff. On the east side of the cloister was the parlor, a room where monks could hold conversations, and the chapter house, a large room that served for the daily communal meeting of the monks. Above the rooms on the east side of the cloister was the dormitory, the long hall in which the monks slept. The dormitory at Cluny was a particularly fine room, with ninety-seven glazed windows, each over seven feet tall and two-and-a-half feet wide. These windows provided ample light during the day, and at night three oil lamps burned constantly to dispel the darkness—the twelfth-century statutes of Cluny emphasized that monks should not sleep in the dark. At the north end of the dormitory was the night-stair leading into the church, which allowed the monks to attend nighttime devotions without venturing into the cold outdoors. A day-stair led down into the cloister.

At the south end of the dormitory a short walkway led to the latrine, built close to the dormitory but as a separate structure. This was divided into forty-five cubicles, each illuminated by a window two feet tall and half-a-foot wide; two oil lamps were kept lit in the room all night. A pile of straw lay on the floor, so that the monks could grab a handful to wipe themselves after defecating. The latrine was built over a drainage channel of running water.

The north arcade was the warmest and brightest part of the cloister, since it faced southward. Like other monasteries, Cluny used this area as a scriptorium where the monks might read and write, and it was equipped with large high desks called carrels. At the eastern end of the scriptorium was the large cupboard in which the precentor stored the monastery's books.

Adjoining this arcade was the monastery church. This was principally for the use of the monastic community, although at some monasteries it served as a parish church as well. At Cluny, the church was accessible to the public, although visitors were allowed only in the nave, at the western end of the church, where they had no contact with the monks in the choir at the eastern end. In monastic churches the choir was elongated, and had stalls equipped with seats to allow the monks to rest during the Divine Office. The church was lit in the day by a hundred and sixty windows, and at night by four large chandeliers with wax candles. Additional candlelight was provided at ground level close to the monks, to allow them to read their chants. An enormous new church was begun at Cluny in about 1085; its high altar was consecrated in 1095, but the building itself was not finished until the twelfth century.

The buildings of the cloister were the heart of the monastery, and were more or less common to every substantial establishment. Not all monasteries followed precisely the same plan: in a few cases, the cloister was on the north side of the church, with the entire complex laid out in a mirror image. This reversal was sometimes dictated by local topography, and it was the normal arrangement in nunneries. On the whole, monastic ground plans were more noteworthy for their consistency than their variety, and even nonmonastic orders, such as the mendicant friars, followed much the same pattern.

Ancillary Buildings

The rest of the monastery supplemented the buildings of the cloister. Cluny's wealth was reflected in its unusually complete collection of additional buildings. In a smaller monastery only some of these facilities might be found, as multiple functions were combined in a single structure. Where additional buildings existed, their layout generally resembled that of Cluny. To the east of the cloister was the infirmary, housing ill or aged monks. At Cluny this included a dormitory with its own kitchen, refectory, and latrine. The infirmary had five chambers, one of which was reserved for the dying. The capacity of the chambers may be judged by the older infirmary, replaced in the late eleventh century, whose four chambers for sick monks each held eight beds. Also in this area Cluny had a secondary church and the monastic cemetery with a chapel. All of these buildings were connected by a series of covered walkways: unless he passed the cloister gate, the monk at Cluny was never obliged to walk on open ground.

To the south of the main cloister at Cluny were additional monastic buildings. These included the lesser cloister, reserved for meditation and quiet work; a cloister and dormitory for novices; and facilities for craftsmen employed in precious work for the church such as glazing and goldsmithing. Also nearby was a "privy washing room," with water on tap, where the monks could launder their braies, and a bathhouse equipped with twelve barrels in which the monks could bathe at appointed times. Like other monasteries, Cluny had a garden to supply the community with herbs and vegetables, as well as ponds to stock fish for the table; this appears to have been at the eastern end of the complex, near the infirmary.

To the west of the cloister were the exterior areas where the monastery interacted with the outside world. The whole monastic complex was encircled by a wall, with access through a gatehouse. The wall served in part to separate the monastery symbolically from the sinful world outside, but it also helped to minimize and control contact between the monks and the exterior world. At times it might even serve a military purpose. In 1125, Pons de Melgueil, a former abbot of Cluny who had been forced to resign his office, assembled a following of mercenaries and fugitive monks and marched on the monastery. The grand prior, himself a former knight of some distinction, shut the gates and prepared to defend the enclosure, but Pons's forces broke down the gates while his supporters within the monastery overthrew the prior and welcomed the invaders. Military action against a monastery was uncommon but not unknown; in the latter part of the twelfth century, new fortifications were built around Cluny in response to depredations in the area by the count of Chalon.

Adjoining the gatehouse was a large building that held the stables and a hostel for travelers, with adjacent latrines. Between the main gate and the cloister were the lodgings for Cluny's lay brothers, again with their own latrines, and a refectory that they shared with visitors lodged in the hostel. To the north of this was the guest house for privileged visitors. This building had a dormitory at each end: the one for male guests had forty beds, the women's dormitory had thirty, with as many cubicles in the latrines adjoining each dormitory. Between the dormitories was a joint refectory, equipped with fine curtains and bench covers for use on special occasions. On the south side of this building was the palace, a special facility for the monastery's most important guests. Adjoining the guest house were workshops for the monastery's tailors and shoemakers, and a cemetery for lay members of the monastic community.

Monastic Architecture

A well-endowed monastery might be the site of a great deal of ongoing development even after the basic complex was complete, with new structures added or old ones replaced; the tranquility of the monastic environment could be disrupted for years at a time. At Cluny, the new basilica begun in the late eleventh century required twenty years to finish. Monastic construction materials and techniques represented the highest standards of the time. During construction, temporary facilities of wood were erected, but the finished

THE THIRD CHURCH OF CLUNY ABBEY, *viewed from the northeast.*

buildings were of stone. Ideally, this consisted of solid stone blocks; less expensive was stone rubble held together with mortar. In either case, the surface was covered with limewash and plaster, and rubble walls were adorned with horizontal and vertical lines to make them resemble solid blocks. A Benedictine monastery like Cluny might also be elaborately decorated. The wall paintings of the refectory have already been mentioned; there were also marble columns in the cloister arcade, and innumerable carved decorations in the monastery's stonework. Such opulence was criticized by the Cistercians, whose buildings were more simply adorned, although equally well constructed. As in other medieval buildings, the floors at Cluny were strewn with rushes, which the custumal says were changed six times a year.

One of the most striking features of the monastery was its sanitation system. In an age when running water was unusual even for an aristocratic household, it was a more or less standard feature of monastic planning. Cluny was typical in having diverted a stream into a channel that ran through its south side. This channel served all the working areas of the monastery, passing under the kitchens, where a hole in the floor allowed direct access to the water, and then past the bathhouse and underneath the monks' latrine. Other channels served the other latrines in the complex. In addition, Cluny, like other monasteries, had a raised cistern. From this cistern a system of conduits provided water to various points in the monastery, with water pressure provided by gravity. Some monastic cisterns were fed by wooden, ceramic, or lead pipelines from an elevated source such as a spring, and some even had a system of settling tanks to ensure the water quality.

The setting of the monastery varied. Usually it was founded on land granted by a lay patron; the complex was then constructed somewhere on the donated land. The monastery was often sited on the floor of a river valley, which provided flat ground on which to construct the monastic buildings, as well as ready access to water for the needs of the monastic community. Some monasteries were founded in rural settings, others were adjacent to towns. In time, the monastery itself proved a base for urban development. The demand for goods and services at a substantial monastery was a significant spur to economic activity, and during the early Middle Ages the monastery was in many cases the most stable political force in its district. By the High Middle Ages, many towns had grown up around monasteries, and in others a monastery on the outskirts of a town gave rise to a significant suburb. When the monastery of Cluny was founded, the place was little more than a manor house and village, but by 1100, the village had become a substantial town.

MODE OF LIFE

Living conditions within the monastery varied. The rule of the order and the customs of the monastery might be rigorous or lenient; some abbots were stricter than others; and at various times and places the trend in monastic practice leaned toward easing the rules or toward reforming laxity. At a time when most people worked extremely hard to maintain a fairly low standard of living, and when even the privileged classes lived in somewhat spartan conditions in peacetime and under genuine hardship in time of war, the rigors of monastic life were probably less significant than its stability.

Food

The approved monastic diet was simple but adequate. In fact, monks had the highest dietary standard of the Middle Ages as judged by modern nutritional science. Meat was forbidden except for the sick, although fish was permitted. The bulk of the diet was derived from grains, legumes, vegetables, and fruits. The basic monastic meal at Cluny consisted of bread, wine, boiled beans flavored with a bit of fat, and boiled vegetables according to the season; the ordinary seasoning was salt. In addition to their basic diet, every two monks shared a plate of supplementary food on Mondays, Wednesdays, and Fridays, and each had a plate of his own on Tuesdays, Thursdays, Saturdays, and Sundays. Each monk also had an additional plate on certain holidays and special occasions of celebration, as when the abbot returned from a journey. A variety of supplementary foods were permitted. Eggs, cheese, and fruit were regularly included in the diet, and on certain holidays there might be dumplings, pancakes, cakes, and other special breadstuffs. On Thursdays, Sundays, and certain festive occasions, the additional plate consisted of seafood. A range of seafoods are mentioned as monastic fare in the Cluny custumals, including eel, lamprey, salmon, pike, and trout. Flavorings included honey, pepper, and mustard. The staple drink at Cluny was wine; ale was not common in this part of France, but it was consumed at other monasteries. On special occasions the monks were issued *piment*, a flavored wine mixed with honey and spices. The monks ate two meals a day during the summer, but only one during the winter and on fasting days. The daily ration was a pound of bread, but on days when two meals were served, the monk could have an extra half ration if he finished his portion during the first meal.

The diet at Cluny was fairly generous. Some monasteries, notably those of the Cistercian order, were more austere, while others were extremely lax. Abbot Peter the Venerable of Cluny commented acerbically on the diet in use at many monasteries:

> Beans, cheese, eggs, and even fish have become loathsome. . . . Roast or boiled pork, a plump heifer, rabbit, and hare, a goose selected from the flock, chicken, in fact every kind of meat and fowl cover the table of these holy monks. But now even these things lose their appeal. It has come to . . . royal and imported luxuries. Now a monk cannot be satisfied but on wild goats, stags, boars, or bears. The forests must be searched, we have need of huntsmen! Pheasants, partridges, and pigeons must be caught by the fowler's cunning, lest the servant of God should die of hunger![3]

Clothing

Monks wore uniform attire derived from lay clothing of the late classical and early medieval period. The basic garment of Cluny's monks was a plain woolen tunic girded with a leather belt. Over this the monk wore the cowl, a loose sleeveless garment reaching to the ankles in front and back, with a deep hood attached. The hood helped keep the monk's head warm in the cold environment of the monastery, while submerging the identity of the individual into his monastic character. It also served as protection against the evils of the outside world: when the monks of Cluny traveled through a large town, they were required to lower their hoods over their faces.

On top of the cowl the monk wore a loose gown with broad and very long sleeves that helped keep him warm in winter and minimized visible flesh—the sleeves usually covered his hands. During the winter he wore a sheepskin mantle on top of the gown or instead of it. The color of his outfit depended on the order. Cluniac monks wore the Benedictine black habit, while the Cistercians wore undyed white wool. The rule and custumal both required that clothes were to be made of plain, inexpensive fabric.

The monks at Cluny also wore hose and shoes. For underwear they wore a pair of linen drawers like the braies of the layman. The Cistercians differed from other monks in permitting no underwear, a peculiarity that their detractors were quick to mock. Each monk at Cluny was allotted two gowns, two cowls, two tunics, two pairs of braies, three fur-lined mantles, a furred hood, five pairs of socks, two pairs of day shoes, a pair of wooly night shoes for winter, and a lighter pair for summer use. He received a new gown and cowl every Christmas, new socks at Martinmas,

MOURNING MONK. *French, ca. 1450. Notice that the monk wears a cowl and long, loose gown.*

new shoes on Maundy Thursday, and a new mantle every other Michaelmas—the new clothes were placed by the chamberlain on each monk's bed. The tunic, braies, and other items were replaced as necessary: the monk washed the old garments and handed them in to the chamberlain, who then provided new ones. The discarded garments were distributed to the poor. At his discretion, the chamberlain might also provide additional warm clothing for an infirm monk, such as sheepskin shoes or puttees for the shins. The monk's garments were marked with his name in ink, but on the braies, which were washed periodically in hot water, his name was stitched in thread.

The monastery had elaborate provisions for laundry. The monk who needed to wash his braies removed them from under his outer clothes, folded them at once, wrapped them in a tunic, and tied up the bundle with the tunic's sleeves. He then proceeded to the monastic kitchen to fetch the brass laundry cauldron in which washing water was heated and mixed with lye. There was a laundry trough in the cloister, carved into separate compartments so that the braies could be washed separately from the other garments. The water was poured into the trough and the laundry left there to soak during the chapter meeting. In the afternoon the monk washed his clothes, then hung them to dry in the cloister. Clothes hanging in the cloister had to be taken down before the next meal. Alternatively, the monk deposited his clothes into the common laundry chest, located below the dormitory. These clothes were collected every Tuesday, and returned on Saturday afternoon. When a monk's shoes needed oiling, he could wash them and leave them for the assistant chamberlain to collect, or go to the kitchen where he received cooking fat to oil them himself. If a monk's clothes needed mending, he put them in a chest especially for this purpose in the chapter house, where the assistant chamberlain picked them up and delivered them to the monastery's resident tailors.

Gear

In addition to clothing, the Benedictine rule provided that each monk be issued a knife, a pen, writing tables, a needle, and a handkerchief. The rules at Cluny also mention a linen belt for the monk's braies, a leather belt to gird the tunic, a wooden comb with case, a sheath for the knife, and a needlecase and thread. The rule also allowed each monk a mattress, bedsheet, blanket, and pillow; the mattress was to be stuffed with straw, although feather mattresses were among the most common violations of monastic discipline. Monasteries like Cluny, in colder climates than Saint Benedict's Italy, allowed additional bedclothes. The Cluny custumals mention sheepskin, catskin, or rabbitskin coverlets, a felted woolen blanket, and a bed cover. Each monk at Cluny also had a cup and a dish, and a measured flagon to receive his daily ration of wine.

Bodily Care

Monastic hygiene was reasonably good in comparison to the rest of society. Running water was common in monasteries, and monks were required to wash their faces every morning and their hands several times each day. The kitchen had a special conduit that provided detergent (perhaps a mild lye) so that the staff could wash their hands frequently. On certain days, the monks who had served as cooks the previous week ritually washed the feet of the rest of the monks, and provision was also made for washing the monks' feet after any barefoot procession. Full bathing was much rarer, since bathing was regarded in ascetic circles as a dangerous physical indulgence. Cluny permitted baths only twice a year, just before Christmas and Easter. Other monasteries also allowed a bath at Pentecost. Additional bathing required permission. This was probably below the usual standard of the upper classes, but above that of the peasantry. In spite of monastic mistrust of bathing, Cluny had a rather well-appointed bathhouse, with twelve tubs.

The monk's tonsure required periodic shaving. Shaving gear was kept by the chamberlain in a locked box at the entrance to the dormitory. At permitted times, at the discretion of the chamberlain, the monks gathered in the cloister, seated in two rows, one against the wall of the cloister, the other against the pillars of the arcade, ready to be shaved. Razors were distributed down one line, shaving basins down the other, and the monks on one side shaved the others while singing psalms. Beards were also shaved at this time, although the interval between shavings meant that the monks usually had some facial hair.

Perhaps the most prominent source of bodily discomfort, at least at night and during the winter, was the chill. Few rooms in the monastery had fires—principally just the kitchen and calefactory—and the cold was pervasive. The twelfth-century monastic chronicler Orderic Vitalis was sometimes unable to write because his fingers were too cold to grip the pen.[4] The custumal of Cluny allowed monks to enter the kitchen to thaw frozen ink, and mentioned visits to the kitchen by the abbot to warm himself.

Care of the Sick

One of the most remarkable aspects of monastic life was its provision for the sick and the elderly. A monk who felt unwell could ask to be excused from his monastic duties. If after a few days he had not recovered, he was sent to the infirmary. He stayed there under the care of the infirmarian and his assistants, and if his condition was beyond the capacity of the infirmarian, a practitioner might be brought in from the outside to examine the monk. While in the infirmary, the monk was allowed more food, even meat, to help him regain his strength. Once recovered, he was obliged to prostrate himself in the chapter meeting, and ask for forgiveness for his lapse from monastic discipline. A termi-

nally ill or enfeebled monk received care for the rest of his days, and even had a lay brother assigned as his full-time attendant during his final decline. When death approached, the community was summoned to the infirmary—one of the rare times monks were permitted to run—to observe the traditional ceremony for a monk's passing, in which the dying monk was placed on a goat-skin strewn with ashes, while the community chanted psalms to aid his passage to heaven.

DEATH AND ASCENSION OF ST. FRANCIS. Giotto (Italian), ca. 1325. Monks pray over St. Francis on his deathbed.

Monastic Etiquette

Life at Cluny was governed by an elaborate code of decorum that in part may have reflected the monks' aristocratic background. Other than the imminent death of a member of the community, the only circumstance in which running was permitted was a fire in the monastery. While riding, the monk was also required to keep his mount at a walk. The custumal of Cluny even instructed the monks in how to walk, sit, and stand. Walking, the monk was expected to keep his head bowed; standing, he was to have both feet even; and seated, he was to be at least an ell's distance from his neighbor, with his habit drawn up into his lap so that his feet were visible and the skirts of his garments did not touch the floor. Between psalms of the Divine Office, a monk was allowed to rest on the seat of his stall, but only if the monks next to him were standing. Although the rules of monastic behavior were demanding, they were also pragmatic. When the bells rang to summon the monks to services, they continued long enough to allow for a visit to the privy before entering the choir. The custumal also made provision for monks who needed to leave the choir during the Divine Office in instances of urgent need, such as a sudden nosebleed.

The monks of Cluny had a distinctive bow that the custumal of Ulrich describes with great precision. It was called "before and behind," because the monk bowed so deeply that he began looking forward but ended looking backward, inclining his body from the waist, with his back straight, not arched. The monk bowed repeatedly in this manner during the course of the day: to greet a superior; on entering the church, chapter house, or refectory; before sitting down to a meal. When he spoke, the monk was required to say "our" instead of "my," except when speaking of his mother or father. When speaking of another monk, he added the title *Domnus* (from the Latin *dominus*, lord) to his name; for oblates and himself, the title was "Brother."

Much of the etiquette of the monastery was oriented to ensure that a minimum of skin was visible. In the morning, the monk dressed himself under the covers, and if he needed to remove his cowl during the day to have it cleaned, he was required to have his mantle or gown on over it. Yet although monastic discipline and attire sought to minimize attention to the body, it was also customary for monks to kiss one another as the usual form of welcome, a practice that was also common in medieval society in general.

When traveling, the monk was expected to adhere to a daily routine of hymns and prayers. He was to have a fellow monk with him at all times, and was not permitted to sit at table with a woman or accept anything from her hands. He was enjoined not to beat the lay brother who accompanied him, nor to make conversation with him while eating. While riding, he was obliged to wear his gown over his cowl, and if he removed his cowl at night, he had to keep it within arm's reach.

Monastic Silence

One aspect of monastic life that would be striking to the modern observer is the rarity of ordinary speech. Conversation was forbidden at all times in the church, monastic kitchen, dormitory, and refectory. It was allowed in the cloister in the morning after the chapter meeting, and in the afternoon after the midday meal. Even when conversation was permitted, it was governed by strict rules. Monks who wished to converse were expected to take a book and sit, and their conversation was to be quiet and only about spiritual matters, "or of those things which are indispensable to this temporal life."[5] Monks were not allowed to talk with nonmonks—even lay brothers—without permission, unless they held office in the monastery.

To facilitate essential communication when speech was forbidden, monks developed the use of sign language. The custumal of Cluny describes the hand signs for several dozen words that were taught to novices. Most are nouns related to food, but the custumal indicates that the full vocabulary was much more extensive. Excessive signing could itself be a problem, as one observer noted after visiting the priory of Canterbury: "They gesticulated with fingers, hands, and arms, and whistled to each other instead of speaking. . . . It would be more consonant with good order and decency to speak modestly in human speech than to indulge ridiculously in this mute chatter."[6]

The restrictions on conversation did not mean constant silence. Even in parts of the monastery where ordinary speech was forbidden, the sound of human voices chanting hymns and psalms and reading religious texts was heard frequently. Monks spent much of their day in church performing the Divine Office, and even outside the church devotional singing and recitation was a constant feature of daily life. During meals, while the monks ate silently, one of them was assigned to read aloud from a suitable text, and the custumals specify which hymns and psalms are to be sung even during such mundane activities as shaving and washing the dishes.

SINGING MONKS. Simone Martini (Italian), ca. 1322–1326. Detail from a fresco.

Communal Life

The silence of the monastery and other customs that restricted interaction among the monks may have compensated somewhat for the constant lack of privacy in monastic life. Within the monastery, monks slept, ate, and worked communally, and when they were outside of the monastery, whether traveling on a mission or residing at a small monastic establishment or grange, they were always supposed to be in pairs at least. This aspect of monasticism would be hard on many modern people, but it was not all that remarkable in a society where even the upper classes had relatively little private space, taking their meals in the great hall and sleeping in close proximity to servants and other members of the household. Yet even the monks seem to have found their communal life difficult at times. The twelfth-century statutes of Cluny made provision for two monks to be appointed as overseers of the dormitory, "for frequently because of the lack of overseers, and the great number coming together there, large quarrels break out, which often cause their clothes and other monastic trappings to be lost, nor can they be easily found again."[7]

The Sign Language of Cluny

For the sign for bread, make a circle with both thumbs and index fingers, since bread is usually round. . . .

For the sign for beans, place the tip of the index finger on top of the first joint of the thumb, and in this way make the thumb stick out. . . .

For the sign for pottage made with vegetables, draw one finger over the other like someone who is slicing vegetables to be cooked.

For a general sign for fish, imitate the motion of the fish's tail in the water with your hand.

For the sign for cuttlefish, divide all your fingers from each other, and move them around in this way, because cuttlefish similarly appear to have multiple parts.

For the sign for a salmon . . . make the sign for a fish, and at the same time place your fist with the thumb standing upwards underneath your chin, which is the sign for pride, because the proud and rich are the ones who most usually have such fish. . .

For the sign for honey, stick our your tongue just a bit, and apply your fingers to it as if you were going to lick them.

For the sign for raw leeks, stick out your thumb and index finger together.

For the sign for garlic or horseradish, open your mouth slightly and extend your finger toward it, on account of the sort of odor that comes from it.

For the sign for water, place all your fingers together, and move them sideways. . . .

For the sign for wine, act as if you were dipping your finger, and place it against your lips.

continued on page 190

For the sign for piment, shut your hand, and act as if you were
grinding. . . .

For the sign for mustard, place your thumb on the joint of your little
finger.

For the sign for vinegar, stroke your throat with your finger, because
bitterness is tasted in the throat.

For the sign for a dish, hold out your hand flat. . . .

For the sign for the tunic, hold its sleeve with three fingers, the little
finger and the two next to it.

For the sign for braies, do the same thing, and at the same time pull
your hand up along your thigh like someone who is putting on his
braies.

For the sign for the gown, take its sleeve in the same way one does with
the tunic.

For the sign for the cowl, do the same, and at the same time pull back
on the hood with two fingers.

Sign used by someone asking permission to leave early from a meal: He
rises from the table, comes toward the dais, and with his hand
stretched out, draws it away from his chest.

Sign used by someone wishing to see a priest for confession: Taking his hand
out of his sleeve, he places it on his chest, which is the sign for
confession.[8]

The Monastic Day

The monastic routine was built around the daily cycle of the Divine Office.
The cycle began before the night was over, with the bell ringing at about 2 or
3 A.M. to summon the monks to sing Nocturns (also called Matins) and Lauds.
The monks, who slept in their tunics, put on their cowls under the covers

before rising from bed. Then they rose, pulled up the bedclothes, donned their night shoes, and drew their hoods over their heads. At this point they might visit the privy before proceeding down the night stairs into the church. Once in the church they took their places in the choir and began the chant. Drowsiness was a predictable problem at this hour, and provisions were made for a lantern bearer to pass among them at certain points in the service to find any who were asleep, and silently wake them by waving the lantern three times before their faces. If a monk did not wake after the third time, the watcher roused him and left the lantern with him; the monk was then required to take over the job.

If it was winter, the monks returned to bed after Lauds until first light; during the summer the interval between Lauds and first light was too short to warrant this. At first light the church bells were rung to summon the monks to Prime. During the winter, this occurred late enough in the morning that the monks might rise beforehand to celebrate private masses or begin their tasks for the day. At Prime, the monk put on his day shoes and knife, and proceeded down the day stairs to the wash stand near the refectory to wash his face and hands and comb his hair before entering the church. After Prime there was time for reading and work. At about 9 A.M. came Terce, a fairly short office, followed by the morning mass. After mass the community assembled in the chapter house. The meeting began with the reading of a passage from the Bible and a chapter from the order's rule (hence the meeting was called the chapter). This was followed by a sermon or discussion by the abbot or the prior. Then the community dealt with organizational business and handled disciplinary matters.

The chapter was over by about 10 A.M. Afterward, the monks had time for various activities. Conversation was permitted during this interval, or a monk might attend to mundane matters, such as trimming his nails, washing his tableware, sharpening his knife, washing his clothes, or visiting sick monks in the infirmary. At midday the monks returned to the choir for the brief office of Sext, followed by the High Mass of the day.

The Shape of the Monastic Day

2 or 3 A.M.

Nocturns (Matins) and Lauds
Winter: sleep, tasks, private masses

Daylight: 4:30 A.M. in summer;
7:30 A.M. in winter.

Washing face and hands
Prime
Silent working period

9 A.M.

Terce
Morning mass
Chapter meeting
Nonsilent working period

Midday

Sext
High Mass
Summer: dinner
Summer: silent working period
Winter: nonsilent working period

Afternoon: 2:30 P.M. in summer,
1:30 P.M. in winter.

None
Summer: drink
Summer: nonsilent working
  and rest period
Winter: dinner
Winter: silent working period

Evening: 6 P.M. in summer,
4:15 P.M. in winter.

Vespers
Summer: supper
Summer: silent contemplative
  period
Winter: light meal

Night: 8 P.M. in summer,
6:15 P.M. in winter.

Compline
Bed

Meals

In summer the High Mass was followed by the principal meal of the day. At mealtimes, the community all washed their hands and proceeded into the refectory. Prior to their arrival, the tables were set by the refectorian's three assistants. Each place had a spoon and bread, and if the bread was burnt, the scorched part was shaved off with a knife. Just before the monks entered, the wine was served. As they came in, they took the places assigned to them on the basis of seniority, bowed, and stood waiting for the arrival of the abbot or prior, who pronounced a blessing and rang a bell to signal the beginning of the meal. At this point the reader for the week began to read from an approved text, and the monks began to eat. No conversation was permitted in the refectory, although the monks used their sign language to communicate. The monks were not allowed to fetch anything other than water or salt; the food was brought by the cooks of the week. Each monk was expected to ensure that not even the smallest crumb fell to the ground. After the meal, he gathered the crumbs on the table with his knife, so they could be brushed into a plate; these crumbs were used to provide food for the poor. The monks were expected to remain at their tables until the meal was over, but a monk who needed to leave could ask the abbot for permission to go, and a monk who arrived late similarly needed permission to join the meal.

THE MONK'S REFECTORY. *Illumination from a fourteenth-century Italian manuscript.*

Food was eaten only in the refectory. A monk who was unwell or felt greatly in need of food might come to the chamberlain at midday or after Compline to ask to be let into the refectory. The monk might drink between mealtimes, but this was to be done seated, with both hands on the bowl. During the summer, water was provided for the monks every afternoon in the refectory.

Afternoon and Evening

After midday the monk had time to read or sing hymns and psalms. He was also allowed to bring a book to the dormitory and read in bed, although he was not permitted to converse with other monks here, even in sign language, or even to glance at them in their beds. At about 3 p.m. came the office of None, again fairly short. In summer, the monks gathered after None for a drink. In winter and on fasting days the sole meal of the day was taken at this time. During the longer summer days the monks might be allowed a brief rest period in the afternoon. The latter part of the afternoon was given to another period for work, study, or private masses.

In the evening came the office of Vespers, which was fairly long. In summer, this was followed by the second meal of the day; in winter, a small bite of food was allowed before Compline. After the evening meal, the monks went to the dormitory to remove their knives and change their day shoes for their night shoes. In summer, they then returned to sit in the cloister, where they might read or write. At this time absolute silence was enjoined: the monks were commanded to ensure even that their pens made no noise on the parchment, and any monk who entered the cloister late had to walk slowly and make no sound. Compline, another brief office, took place at dusk. At the end of Compline the monks were sprinkled with holy water and covered their heads with their hoods. Then they retired to bed, leaving their hoods up until they were under the covers. Once under the covers, the monks removed their cowls, folding and placing them at the head of their beds for the next morning. The rules at Cluny allowed a monk to uncover only his feet and arms at night if he was hot. While the monks were retiring, the claustral prior toured the cloister to see that all was in order, ensuring that the doors were closed and locked, inspecting the dormitory, and even checking the latrines.

In addition to the major cycle of monastic offices, there were other devotions. The monks might recite prayers for the dead and supplications to the saints, especially on behalf of a patron, and in the morning before daybreak, ordained monks might celebrate private masses in smaller chapels in the church. There were also special masses and observations on the occasion of major church feasts, as in ordinary parish churches. Particularly important in the life of Cluny were the processions made by the community every Sunday after the morning mass, passing from the church to the infirmary, then around the cloister past each of the monastic buildings.

NUNS

Although male monasteries had the highest profile in medieval society, monasteries for women were also an important feature of the medieval world. In most respects the life of nuns was very similar to those of their male counterparts. The typical nunnery was laid out along much the same lines, albeit in mirror image, with the cloister on the north side of the church. The nuns themselves were recruited from the upper levels of society; in fact, nunneries tended, if anything, to be more socially exclusive than monasteries. This was perhaps because of a higher demand for places in nunneries. The son of a nobleman might make his living in a number of ways: he could inherit his father's position, rise through military service, or enter the secular clergy, in addition to the monastic option. For daughters there were only two principal choices: marrying a man who could support her, or entering a nunnery.

Like monks, nuns passed through a novitiate, and some were admitted as oblates. The reforms that curtailed the offering of boys to monasteries never went as far in the case of girls, in part because a female oblate who reached the age for taking vows was unlikely to have alternative options. Some aristocratic women also entered nunneries in their later years. Nunneries might also include lay sisters, but they relied more heavily on the hired labor of both female and male workers.

The nun's habit was a long tunic, with a veil that covered her head. Instead of the tonsure, her hair was cropped short. The veil was traditionally worn by married women as a sign of modesty, and this practice was adopted by nuns, not only for modesty, but as a symbol of their status as the brides of Christ. Most nuns were Benedictines. Monks were expected to refrain from excessive contact with women, and the various reformed orders from the tenth century onward were ambivalent about the idea of accepting affiliated orders of nuns, although a few new orders of nuns did arise in the High Middle Ages. Even Cluny had its misgivings: the monastery's statutes in the twelfth century forbade the founding of a nunnery within four miles of a Cluniac house.

The organization of the nunnery was similar to that of a monastery, with authority vested in the hands of an abbess, assisted by a prioress and obedientiaries. One major difference was that nuns could not be priests, since the priesthood was forbidden to women. As a result, every nunnery needed the services of a priest who could celebrate mass for the nuns. The activities in a nunnery were similar to those in a monastery: the daily cycle was built around the Divine Office, and the nuns' work often featured reading and writing. In addition, nuns were often called on to use their aristocratic skills in needlework to furnish richly embroidered cloths for liturgical use.

FUNCTIONS OF THE MONASTERY

The Divine Office lay at the heart of the monastery's purpose, but the institution also fulfilled a variety of additional functions. We have already seen the political and economic activities of monasteries, which tended to distract from the monastery's spiritual functions, although they did allow some monks to contribute to society by bringing their own spiritual perspective to bear on the world outside the cloister. Other monastic activities were more directly related to the monastery's spiritual purpose. Almsgiving was considered an essential part of a virtuous Christian life and was integrated into the monastic routine. Surplus food and clothing were saved for distribution to the needy, and the almoner made a weekly tour through the town of Cluny, bringing bread and wine to any paupers who were sick. Cluny also supported eighteen paupers within its walls on a permanent basis, lodging them in the almonry at the gate of the cloister. Some monasteries had facilities for the long-term housing of the elderly, typically people of substance who had given money or property to the monastery, or promised it as a legacy, in exchange for support during the donor's old age. Other monasteries simply furnished food and support to nonresident pensioners on similar terms.

The monastery also provided hospitality for travelers in an age when inns were not always easy to find. Many of the monastery's visitors were aristocrats, particularly lay patrons and other important figures, but others were ordinary folk, in many cases pilgrims making a journey to a shrine. Some of these were visitors to the monastery itself. Cluny attracted a constant stream of pilgrims who visited the abbey's collection of holy relics, most notably the ashes of Saints Peter and Paul. In the twelfth century Cluny also acquired a fragment of the Cross, a finger of St. Stephen, and a tooth of John the Baptist. Guests were allowed to stay overnight, receiving a pound of bread and a measure of wine on the day of their arrival, and half a pound of bread with wine on the second day. Pilgrims to Cluny were given a penny on their departure, provided they had not previously visited during the same year.

Also important was the monastery's role in learning and literacy. Christianity was a religion based on written texts, and literacy was essential to allow the monk to fulfill his spiritual obligations. During the early Middle Ages, literacy in the secular world was largely limited to priests, who were too few and too isolated to have much impact on the general level of learning in their society. Monasteries by contrast were concentrated literate communities that served as focal points for study and education. Monastic schools were especially influential during the early Middle Ages, at a time when other educational institutions were practically nonexistent; even some secular students acquired their learning in schools run by monasteries outside the cloister. During the High Middle Ages, other types of schools became more common, and literacy spread among the upper levels of lay society, so the predominance of monasteries as intellectual centers declined, although they still remained important participants in the intellectual life of medieval society. Cluny in particular had a high reputation for learning in the twelfth century.

A part of the intellectual importance of monasteries was their contribution to the study, preservation, and composition of written texts. The Benedictine rule made provision for work as an integral part of monastic life. Saint Benedict envisaged manual labor as an important part of monastic work, but by the High Middle Ages, the aristocratic population of the monasteries had largely abandoned physical work in favor of the more genteel occupations of reading and writing. In some monasteries each monk was assigned a suitable text to read each year, which he was required to finish by the end of twelve months. The copying of books was also regarded as appropriate work for a monk. In principle, the monk was expected to read and copy only texts that advanced the spiritual goals of the monastery. In practice, this definition was extended to include a wide variety of secular writings: histories, because they showed the unfolding of God's plan for humanity; medical treatises, because they helped the monk attend to the sick; literature, because it taught styles of writing that the monk could employ in his own writings. Monastic copying contributed enormously to the availability of books in their own time, and to the survival of texts into the present day. Indeed, access to classical Roman literature today is largely due to the efforts of monastic copyists. Monastic production of books was especially important as all books had to be copied by hand, and for much of the Middle Ages the secular audience for books was too small for significant secular resources to be devoted to this labor-intensive work. Continual copying by monastic scribes meant that some monasteries assembled substantial libraries, in an age when such facilities were extremely rare. The library at Cluny held 570 volumes in the twelfth century, at a time when even a hundred books constituted a respectable institutional library, and two hundred and fifty was outstandingly large.[9] The monks were also the authors of important works of their own, and as with the books they copied, these were not exclusively spiritual in nature: much of our knowledge of medieval history derives from the works of monastic chroniclers.

Copying books is just one of the ways in which monasteries helped maintain Europe's link to its classical Roman heritage. The monastery, as an institution deliberately isolated from the outside world, was less directly affected by the decay of Roman institutions than was the secular church that served society at large. Of course, as institutions without military resources for self-defense, they were especially vulnerable to the violence of the times, yet they also had internal resources that made for institutional strength, many of them reflecting their Roman origins. Their emphasis on constitutional structures and on the authority of written rules provided direction and stability, an aspect of the monastery that was emphatically Roman in spirit. Ironically, these spiritual institutions might be said to represent the heirs in the West to the warlike legions of Rome. They fostered a sense of purpose and discipline through a highly regimented lifestyle. This aspect of monastic life may in part reflect the background of Saint Pachomius, one of the principal authors of the monastic system, who was himself an ex-soldier of the Roman army. A powerful strain of military imagery runs through monastic language and thought, characterizing the life of the monk as a kind of spiritual warfare waged by the monastic army, evoked in the Benedictine rule itself:

A SCRIPTORIUM MONK *copies a text from a book on his writing-table.*

> My words are now directed to you, who, renouncing your desires, are taking
> up the very mighty and splendid arms of obedience to fight for the lord king
> Christ.[10]

Such language doubtless had a special appeal for the medieval monk, now cloistered, but remembering a childhood in the martial atmosphere of the aristocratic household.

7

TOWN LIFE

THE COLLAPSE OF THE ROMAN EMPIRE AFFECTED URBAN LIFE even more profoundly than other aspects of society. Roman civilization had been distinguished by a high level of urban development, and the Germanic invasions of the late Roman period, by disrupting commerce and overthrowing the governmental structures that had once provided coinage, undermined two of the most crucial supports that made urban life possible. Cities were depopulated, sometimes to the extent of complete abandonment. Yet they never fully ceased to exist. Some major cities like Paris, Marseilles, Naples, and Rome itself remained in continuous occupation as urban centers, albeit in a decayed state, as did a number of lesser cities of the empire. Even at the time of the invasions, commerce never entirely dried up, and the barbarians themselves had learned the use of coin from their Roman neighbors. Urban life slowly reestablished itself over the course of the early Middle Ages. By 1200, cities and towns were numerous and prospering, and although the number of city dwellers was small in relation to the population at large—probably no more than 10 percent at any time in the Middle Ages—the towns wielded social and cultural influence well beyond their size.

No town in northern Europe better reflects the range of medieval urban activity than Paris. Already a substantial city in the Roman period, by the thirteenth century Paris had become a leading political, religious, cultural, and economic center, and arguably the most important city in Europe north of the Alps. Very little of medieval Paris survives after centuries of warfare, political turmoil, and economic development, but a rich body of documentary evidence allows a fairly detailed glimpse of Parisian life.

SCENE OF MEDIEVAL TOWN LIFE. *Detail from the mural* The Blessings of Good Government. *Palazzo Pubblico (Italian), fourteenth-century.*

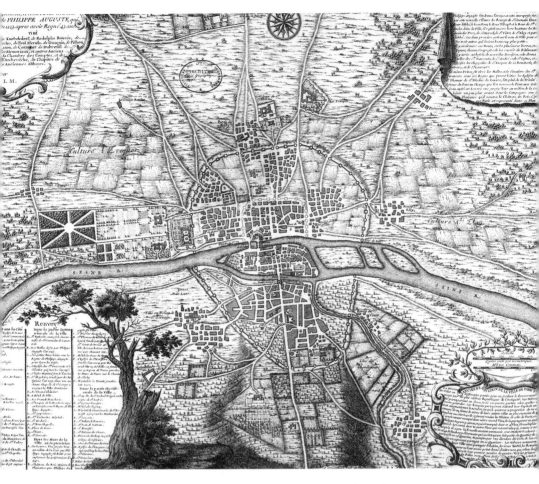

MAP OF PARIS IN 1223. *Created by Jean-Baptiste Bourguignon d'Anville in 1705.*

The city is by far the most complex human environment of the Middle Ages, so to bring medieval Paris into focus, we will see it as it might have looked through the eyes of one of its households, that of Pierre le Normant, in the late thirteenth century. The household is mentioned in the Paris tax assessments of 1292, 1296, and 1297, among the residents of the street called the Juiverie in the parish of

Ste.-Madeleine on the Île de la Cité. The later assessments mention only Pierre himself, but the one of 1292 lists a few members of his household:

> Pierre le Normant, baker, 70 *sous*.
> Thomassin of Chaumont, his *valet* [journeyman or servant], 3 *sous*.
> The sister of Pierre's wife, 34 *sous*.[1]

Behind the brief and businesslike language of the tax assessor lies a lifetime of personal experiences of real flesh and blood people. By integrating the information of the tax assessment with other data on thirteenth-century Paris and on medieval towns in general, we can reconstruct an informative portrait of Pierre le Normant's world.

URBAN SOCIETY

Immigration

Pierre le Normant's name (the Norman) suggests that he, or more likely his father or grandfather, was an immigrant to Paris from Normandy. Surnames were in use among bourgeois families of the time, but they were sufficiently new and unstable that Pierre's name was unlikely to have been handed down for more than a generation or two. Surnames were even less well established toward the lower levels of society, and Pierre's servant Thomassin of Chaumont was almost certainly an immigrant, as were most inhabitants of medieval towns. The majority of urban immigrants were generally laborers from rural areas, usually within a radius of twenty to thirty-five miles of the town. A major city like Paris also attracted a more diverse spectrum of immigrants from a wider area. Surnames from Parisian tax assessments of the period suggest that while most immigrants came from nearby towns, there was also a significant number from Normandy, Brittany, England, the Low Countries, Germany, and even Italy. There are several places in France named Chaumont: Thomassin probably came from the closest, Chaumont-en-Vexin, a small town about thirty-five miles northwest of Paris.

Immigration was stimulated by various economic forces. The eleventh and twelfth centuries were a period of rapid growth in the rural population. As the rural population grew, opportunities shrank, prompting many to seek their fortunes in the towns. The consequent growth in town populations in turn spurred immigration from smaller towns to major cities like Paris. Urban centers, for their part, were a rich market for the surplus population of the country. Poor urban living conditions kept the death rate above the birth rate, so that the medieval town was perennially unable to maintain its numbers without constant immigration.

Immigration to a town offered particular advantages for serfs. According to a custom widely observed from the twelfth century onward, anyone who lived in a town for a year and a day became free. Even if a serf's lord caught up with him within that time, the lord still had to prove the serf's status before he could be returned. It was also possible for a serf to live in a town with his lord's permission, and although this arrangement did not lead directly to freedom, it might in time loosen the manorial bond.

Population

Immigration to the town not only maintained urban population levels but led to rapid urban growth, particularly in the larger cities. Medieval towns varied enormously in size, from the metropolis of international standing to the local market town that was scarcely more than a village. Paris in the early twelfth century probably numbered under 25,000, hardly impressive by modern standards, but still larger than any other town in northern Europe. By the early fourteenth century its population had boomed: historians have offered estimates ranging from 80,000 to 200,000 people. The latter figure is almost certainly too high, but the population may well have approached or exceeded 100,000. Urban populations were rising significantly in the twelfth and thirteenth centuries, reflecting the new dynamism of town life. In 1100, the largest Western cities, generally numbering around 25,000, were mostly in the south. These included Florence, Genoa, Milan, Venice, Padua, Bologna, Naples, and Palermo in Italy, and Barcelona, Cordova, Seville, and Granada in Spain. London at the time had

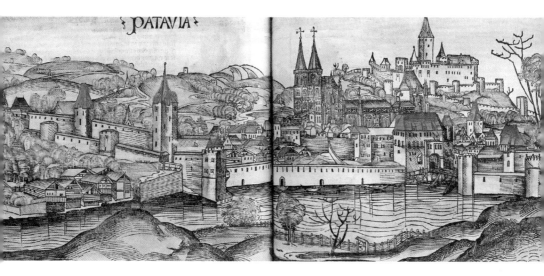

PADUA (PATAVA). *From the Nuremberg Chronicle, an illustrated book published in Germany in 1493.*

only about 10,000 inhabitants. By the early fourteenth century the population in all of these towns was upward of 50,000, and Milan had reached 100,000.[2]

At the low end of urban development was the ordinary market town, consisting of a cluster of houses grouped in a few dirt streets. The smallest of these towns might have fewer than 500 inhabitants, making them less populous than the largest villages. Such a town was distinguished from a village not by its size but by its facilities. The town would have a large open area that served as a market place, as well as a range of tradesmen's shops not represented in a village, and in many cases there were also establishments catering to travelers.

Social Classes

Pierre le Normant was one of the wealthiest men in the Juiverie and must have enjoyed a prestigious social position in his community. Although town dwellers were usually free commoners by definition, their society was highly stratified. At the top were the wealthy and powerful who dominated city politics. Some of these were great merchants, men whose fortunes were made by major commercial enterprises. Others were important administrative officials who derived their power from the feudal or ecclesiastical hierarchy. The elite in a town might also include resident aristocrats, particularly in Italy and Spain, where many of the aristocracy had their primary homes in the town.

The middle layer of the urban hierarchy consisted of independent heads of smaller commercial establishments. Some were artisans, producing manufactured goods for sale to local buyers—whether from within the town or from the hinterland—or for export to other urban centers. Others were tradesmen such as lesser merchants, food sellers, and tavern keepers. People at this level were considered citizens of the town, with commercial privileges and usually some degree of participation in municipal government. They enjoyed a reasonable measure of comfort and security, and possessed the means to support themselves, but they were still far below the opulence of the upper stratum and lacked the substantial capital and political influence that made the fortunes of the urban upper classes. The Parisian tax assessment of 1292 generally assessed people of this middle layer at some 5 to 30 *sous*, so Pierre le Normant's assessed tax of 70 *sous* suggests that he was an outstandingly prosperous baker who was making his way into the urban elite. His sister-in-law's assessment at a hefty 34 *sous*, equivalent to the tax bill of a well-to-do tradesman, is a further indicator of Pierre's social success.

The middle and upper echelons of urban society required the labor of a lower stratum of hired staff. Some of these might be fairly prosperous themselves, if they were well-placed functionaries in the pay of the upper classes. Among those who worked for the middle layer of urban society, the most fortunate were the journeymen and apprentices. Apprentices were usually teenagers, placed in service to a master for a certain term of years in order to learn a trade. On completion of their apprenticeship, they became journeymen, entitled to sell their services to any master, typically for a daily wage (in French *journée,* day). The journeyman might in principle achieve economic independence, since as a fully qualified practitioner of his trade he could eventually set up his own shop. In practice, opportunities were limited by the journeyman's access to capital and working facilities, and unless he was heir to an established tradesman, he might well spend his working life in the employ of others. Thomassin of Chaumont's assessed tax of 3 *sous* is comparable to that of the lowest stratum of independent tradesmen. He is designated *valet* by the assessor, which could mean either a servant or a journeyman. His relative wealth as a wage earner suggests that he was no mere household drudge, but a well-paid assistant to his master, probably a journeyman who played an important role in running Pierre le Normant's bakery. Pierre probably also had apprentices living with him, as well as nonresident journeymen who came to the house to work.

Not every employee had even these prospects of social and economic advancement. In addition to the skilled labor represented by journeymen and apprentices, a town drew on a pool of unskilled workers employed as day laborers and servants. This class constituted a majority of the population in a medieval town, and in an age when labor was cheap and plentiful, such people led a hand-to-mouth existence, with minimal employment security and little surplus income to make provision against unemployment, disability, or old age. Pierre le Normant probably employed a number of laborers. Some would be household servants and chambermaids assigned such tasks as waiting on the family, cooking the food, and maintaining the home. Others would be hired hands in Pierre's bakery. In addition to the journeymen and apprentices, the regulations of the Parisian bakers mention the services of sifters, bolters, and kneaders, whose low-skill work would command only minimal wages.

At the lower end, the laborers shaded into the class of the chronically poor— the unemployed, the underemployed, and the unemployable. Many of the poor were dependent on charity. The most fortunate might a find a place in one of the town's charitable foundations, of which Paris had several, generally administered as religious institutions on behalf of lay founders. One of the largest, the Hotel-Dieu ("Hostel of God"), stood just down the street from Pierre le Normant's house. Most other charitable houses were on the populous right bank. The Trinity supported pilgrims and sick paupers. The Hospital of Ste.-Avoie was founded by a priest and a pious lay woman to support forty widows. Saint Louis, the former king of France whose grandson Phillip the Fair occupied the throne

SAINT ANTHONY DISTRIBUTING HIS WEALTH TO THE POOR. Master of the Osservanza (Italian), ca. 1430–1435. Tempera on panel.

in the 1290s, established the Hospital of the Fifteen-Score, a residence that served three hundred blind men. The Filles-Dieu (Daughters of God) was established north of town to take in reformed prostitutes.

Yet even the numerous charitable houses of Paris were insufficient to address the needs of the poor in so large a city. Many who did not find places in charitable establishments lived by begging. Those who were not obviously disabled were unlikely to receive charity at all, since alms were generally reserved for those who lacked the capacity to support themselves, such as orphans, widows, the elderly, the handicapped, and the infirm. In an age when rural populations far exceeded the opportunities for rural labor, the surplus gravitated toward the more fluid economy of the town, but many of them found insufficient work even there and ultimately contributed instead to urban crime.[3]

Women

Pierre le Normant was the head of his household, but to some degree his authority was shared with his wife. She is not named in the tax assessment of 1292, but the language of the assessors suggests that she was still living. Women in the city, like their counterparts in the countryside, were active participants in the economic life of their community. Like the peasant woman, the urban wife was responsible for household affairs such as cooking, cleaning, and raising children, but she might have also earned money through a trade. The Parisian tax records yield many examples of householding tradeswomen, always a minority, but still significant in number. Pierre le Normant lived just a few houses away from a butcher named Beatrice.

Like many tradeswomen, she may have acquired her trade from her husband. The wife of a journeyman stud maker in Paris was allowed to practice the craft if her husband had been a journeyman for a year and a day. A lace maker's wife could also practice the craft and even help her husband to train apprentices. The labor of women was less valued than that of men, and even crafts that permitted wives to practice often placed restrictions on them. In some cases a wife was not allowed to train apprentices, or engage in the trade after the death of her husband or if she remarried someone who did not belong to the trade.

Some trades could be practiced by a woman in her own right. The regulations of the poulterers of Paris allowed women to purchase the right to practice the trade "as freely as a man in all things." The daughter of a currier could be apprenticed to the trade, and a currier's widow was permitted to take apprentices of her own. The regulations of the linen drapers made provisions for female journeymen, trained in a six-year apprenticeship. In some cases, a husband might even learn his trade from his wife. Some trades were practiced principally by women, including the spinners of silk thread, the makers of silk ribbon, and veil makers. Such trades might be governed jointly by male and female overseers, as in the case of the silk ribbon-makers, or by women alone, as were the veil makers. At the lower end of the social scale, many women earned their living as laborers. Heavy physical labor was generally reserved for men, but there was always domestic work for women as chambermaids and laundresses, and as hired workers performing the unskilled labor required in tradesmen's shops.

WOMAN WORKING AT A TRADESMAN SHOP *within a covered market.*

We can only guess at the situation of Pierre le Normant's wife. Like many other urban women, she may have taken an active part in her husband's business, or her energy may have gone into running the household. Since her husband was quite well-to-do, she would have done very little physical work herself, leaving the manual work of cooking and cleaning to the servants and laborers.

THE URBAN HOME

The Household

A wealthy tradesman like Pierre le Normant probably had a fairly large household. Not only were there servants and apprentices, but he might well have had a substantial family, including not only more children than poorer families, but perhaps even other relatives. Pierre hosted his sister-in-law in 1292, although her substantial tax of 34 *sous* makes it clear that she was not living on Pierre's charity. A woman of such means would have been considered highly marriageable, and it is not surprising that when the tax assessors came around again in 1296, she was no longer present. In all, there easily could have been a dozen people or more living in Pierre le Normant's home. People at the lower end of the social scale had correspondingly smaller households, while those at the top had larger ones.

The House

The building in which Pierre le Normant's household lived and worked probably represented the latest in urban architecture. Townhouses underwent a great deal of change during the twelfth and thirteenth centuries. In the early Middle Ages, the typical urban home was not very different from a rural one, essentially no more than a small cottage on a single floor. As urban populations and wealth grew, the value of urban land rose and the sophistication of urban architecture increased. New styles of construction were developed to make more efficient use of available space, particularly by building taller houses. By the latter part of the thirteenth century, the townhouse had developed a characteristic design as a narrow timber-framed structure with multiple floors heated by one or more fireplaces with chimneys. Typical of such buildings was the house bought by a Parisian carpenter in 1293, consisting of three stories in all, with a chimney and privy on ground level, a chamber above, and a garret at the top. Such a multistory building required a fireplace and chimney, but central hearths with smoke escaping through the roof were still found in the older style of single-story townhouses.

Street frontage was at a premium, requiring deep properties with a short end facing the street. Medieval urban properties commonly ranged from forty to sixty feet in width, and extended sixty to one hundred feet back from the street. In most cases the property's frontage was divided among two or more residences. Most of the houses of the Juiverie were probably around ten to fifteen feet wide, which was typical of houses in the urban core of a medieval town—fifteen feet was about the maximum length for an architectural timber without a supporting pillar in the middle. One of the houses on the Juiverie appears to have been only about seven feet wide. The rear of the property was used in many cases as an herb and vegetable garden for the household, and perhaps also to raise poultry. There was often a privy at the far end. Ordinary urban houses did not necessarily have cellars, and in some cases lacked even foundations: the timbers were set directly into the ground or rested on padstones at key points. The walls of the house were usually a variant of the wattle-and-daub technique used in peasant cottages, with plastered interiors. Roofing materials were similar to those used in the country. Many towns banned thatched roofs because of the fire hazard, although these rules were not always obeyed. Preferred roofing materials included tiles, shingles, or boards, the latter covered with a layer of lead to seal them and reduce the risk of fire. In some cases, thatching reeds were coated with plaster to reduce the fire hazard.

The townhouse of a nobleman or well-to-do merchant was larger and finer, perhaps built of stone rather than wood, with a foundation, a cellar, and a tiled or leaded roof. Some of these buildings used the same basic ground plan as the tradesman's townhouse. Pierre le Normant's house was very likely of this sort, and it might well have resembled a rare surviving Parisian townhouse of the period. The building consists of two ground level stone shop fronts with four timber-framed stories above plus a garret. The most opulent urban residences were often built as compact equivalents of the rural manor compound, consisting of a cluster

PRESENT-DAY PHOTOGRAPH OF THE OLDEST HOUSE IN PARIS, *built in 1407. Note the timber-framed architecture.*

of buildings grouped around a courtyard, with street access by means of a passageway through the street-side building. Such complexes had many of the same facilities as the manor house, including a hall with adjacent solar, stables, separate kitchens, storage buildings, and a cellar.

Property values in Paris were high, and in general urban land was quite expensive. In twelfth-century Milan, property in the city cost about thirty-six times the going rate in the surrounding rural areas.[4] In principle, each urban tenement was held from the town's feudal lord, but unlike most rural landholders, the urban landholder had a perpetual right to his holding and could buy and sell it freely. Because of the cost of urban land, few people could afford to become landholders. Most householders rented or leased their property. The building and the land were not necessarily owned by the same person, and in many cases there were multiple layers of tenancy between the occupant of a building and the feudal lord's tenant. Those at the lower end of the social scale might rent a floor or room in a private house or in a house divided for multiple tenants. Such arrangements were common in Paris: a floor in a house in the center of town rented for about 12 to 15 *sous* a year, while out near the city walls the rent was about 10 *sous*.

The house of an urban tradesman like Pierre le Normant provided both living and working spaces. Pierre's shop would lie at the front of the house, adjacent to the street to facilitate customer access. It would have a large shuttered window next to the front door, and when the shop was open, a vending stall would be set out at the window to display the baked goods, with a wooden awning above it as protection against rain. Inside would be the bakery, with ovens toward the back of the building. The ground floor may also have had a kitchen to supply food for the household. Since Pierre was so wealthy, he may also have had a cellar for extra storage space.

The living spaces for Pierre's household would be on the upper floors. The hall, an all-purpose room like its equivalent in the manor house, was often on the floor directly above ground level, along with a chamber for the master and mistress of the house. There may have been additional chambers on higher floors, including the one allotted to Pierre's sister-in-law. Thomassin would probably have slept toward the top of the building. Directly under the roof was a garret that could serve as additional storage space, or accommodations for children, servants, or lodgers. Stairs provided access to the upper floors, although toward the highest levels of a house they were so narrow and steep that they were scarcely more than ladders.

A substantial townhouse like Pierre's certainly had its own privy. In many cases it was at ground level at the back of the yard, although a man as wealthy as Pierre probably had some arrangement to spare him a trip to the backyard: he may have had an attached privy with a chute to a backyard cesspit. In lesser dwellings, a single privy was shared by multiple tenements, or the privies in several tenements had chutes leading to a joint cesspit. The cesspit was lined with timber or stone, and had to be cleaned out from time to time, an unpleasant task that was generally performed by a professional cesspit cleaner. Kitchen as well as human waste was dumped into the cesspit. Other sorts of detritus were often dumped into a pit on the property, although in the later Middle Ages it became more common for the community to arrange for the public disposal of waste.

The Île de la Cité: The Urban Environment

Pierre le Normant's house stood on the Île de la Cité, an island in the middle of the Seine that had been the heart of Paris since Roman times. The street on which Pierre lived was part of the main north-south street that had once formed one of the axes of the Roman city, and sections of the old Roman ramparts were probably still visible around the edges of the island. The location of the Cite served an obvious military purpose, since the water constituted a natural barrier to an attacking force. In fact, the Cite had survived a year-long siege by the Vikings in 885. The Viking raids were ancient history by Pierre's time, and now the Cite constituted only a

PARIS AS THE CROW FLIES. Jean-Jacques Champin (French), 1852. Engraving.

small part of the urban area of Paris. The bulk of the Parisian population now lived on the right bank of the Seine, to the north of the Cite, with a less-populous, but equally large, urban area on the left bank.

The siting of Paris also owed something to economic considerations. Most major medieval towns were located next to rivers. Not only did the river provide an ample supply of water for domestic and industrial use, it was the best available means of commercial transport. Since the medieval town relied on external supplies, transportation was one of its primary needs, and water transport was generally much cheaper and more efficient than roads. Paris depended heavily on water transport. The Seine was one of France's principal rivers, wide enough to carry a great deal of traffic. Upriver was a network of waterways connecting Paris to the rich agricultural lands that provided much of the city's grain and wine; downriver were Normandy and the English Channel. River traffic was served by three substantial wharves in the Cite, and there were others on the right and left banks.

Bridges

As an island, the Cite had ready access to water, but the island itself also facilitated land transportation. The site of riverside towns like Paris was often determined by the availability of a crossing. Sometimes the crossing was in the form of a ford, reflected by the many towns in Europe with names like Oxford or Frankfurt. In other places, including Paris, it was based on the suitability of the site for construction of a bridge. The Île de la Cité made the Seine easier to bridge by reducing its breadth and dividing it into two branches, making Paris an important crossroad in France's inland transportation system. Two of the three bridges that connected the Cite to the mainland were located just down the street from Pierre le Normant's home. To the north was the smallest, a wooden footbridge called the Planches de Mibray (Mibray Planks). To the south was the Petit-Pont (Small Bridge), which led to the left bank. The third, to the northwest, was the Grand-Pont (Great Bridge), the main route to the right bank.

These bridges were not merely thoroughfares, but important commercial properties. The Grand-Pont and the Planches de Mibray supported a large number of watermills that harnessed the power of the Seine to grind flour for the Parisians' bread. The Grand-Pont and Petit-Pont were lined with commercial buildings along each side of the bridge itself. Bridges were an important feature of many towns, either joining its various quarters, as in Paris or Florence, or connecting the city to the world beyond, as in London, where London Bridge led to the road toward Dover and the Continent. As in Paris, these bridges were often substantial stone structures built wide to accommodate housing, and real estate on these key points of transportation was some of the most expensive in town. A bridge was an expensive installation, and many charged some sort of passage: the Petit-Pont, for example, levied a toll on merchandise brought across the bridge.

Trade

Ready access to transportation was crucial, not only to furnish necessary foodstuffs, but also to connect the town to its customers, since its principal economic function was as a commercial hub. Smaller towns offered commercial services for the hinterland, providing goods for rural buyers, particularly manufactured items such as clothing and household wares, and receiving from them the agricultural produce needed to sustain the urban population. Larger towns engaged in the same sort of trade, but they were also involved in interurban commerce, exchanging commodities over longer distances with other urban centers.

City Streets

Pierre le Normant's neighborhood lay in the very center of Paris. The population here was particularly dense, and lived in a network of small streets lined with tightly packed houses. The layout of the streets in this part of Paris was fairly regular, in part reflecting the street patterns of the Roman city. Outside of the Cite, the streets were more haphazard, the product of centuries of evolution rather than distinct stages of urban planning. Although some medieval cities had an area where the older Roman street system survived, few were dominated by the gridwork layout typical of the planned cities of the Roman or modern world. Growth in the medieval city tended to be by accretion, with neighborhoods clustering around important centers such as major streets, water supplies, and markets.

The list of households assessed for taxes in the Juiverie section of the parish of Ste.-Madeleine offers a glimpse of the neighborhood in which Pierre le Normant lived:

The Street of the Juiverie [west side]:

Euvroin Aalart	100 sous
Macy Aalart	4 livres 12 sous
Jehannot of Pontoise	18 sous
Robin Aalart, their valet	12 deniers
Guillaume the Shearman	4 sous
Michiel of Verdi, draper	4 sous
Jehannot of Beauvais, draper	15 sous
Geubert of Beauvais; Jeannot the Small, his brother; Denise, their sister	15 sous
Guillaume the Strong, baker	10 sous
Adenot the Tailor	2 sous
Rogier of London	10 sous
Alison, his stepdaughter	3 sous
Henri of Germany	30 sous
Richardin, his valet	2 sous
Dame Agace the Marshal	40 sous

On the other side of the street [east side]:

Thomas l'Ami [the Friend], baker	12 deniers
Guillaume the Small, baker	9 sous
Richard de l'Espoise, baker	18 sous
Guillaume Graffart, baker	30 sous
Guillaume l'Ami, baker	12 sous
Robert of London, baker	100 sous
Jehan Paquier	22 sous
Jehanne, the wife of the late Michiel the Master	7 livres 15 sous
Dame Agnes aux Fèves	50 sous
Geffroi, the servant of Dame Jehanne the Mistress	5 sous
Jehannequin the English, baker	58 sous
Guillaume of Douai, baker	30 sous
Guillaume de la Roche, baker	12 sous
Thomas the Oilpresser	14 sous
Richardin, his valet	5 sous
Pierre le Normant, baker	70 sous
Thomassin of Chaumont, his valet	5 sous
The sister of Pierre's wife	34 sous
Nicholas the Shaven, wheat-merchant	12 sous
Tierri of Lambale, shoemaker	8 sous
Gautier the Shearman	5 sous
Phelippe Aalart, draper	36 sous
Beatriz, the Butcher-Woman	5 sous
Jehannot of Montfort, baker	12 sous[5]

Next spread: PLAN OF PARIS *by Truschet et Hoyau, 1550.*

Icy est le vray pourtraict naturel de la ville, cité, vniuerſité & Fauxbourgs de Paris, ou ſont juſtement figurées toutes les Rues & Ruelles correſpondãtes l'vne à l'autre, ainſi qui ſont de preſent ſituées, qui ſont en nõbre deux cens quatre vingts & ſept. Pareillement ſont figurées toutes les Egliſes, & Monaſteres, qui ſont en nombre cent quatre. Auſſi ſont figurez tous les Collèges, qui ſont en nõbre quarante neuf. Et pour ⟶ gnoiſtre auecſes Rues, Ruelles, Egliſes, Monaſteres & Collèges, vous trouuerez ⟶ſom eſcripts à chãſur ſon propre endroict. Cõme plus amplement vous pouez voir cy deſſus.

A Paris, par Oliuier Truſchet, & Germain Hoyau, demourans en la Rue de Montorgueil, au Chef ſainct Denys.

There may have been other residents not mentioned by the tax assessors. In the assessment of 1297 five additional tradesmen in the Juiverie are named in a separate list of "lesser people" assessed at 2 to 5 *sous* each. There may also have been lodgers and other lesser residents of the street whose means were insufficient to be taxed. Even among the households judged taxable, we can see a vast discrepancy in wealth between the widow Jehanne, assessed at the equivalent of 155 *sous* and Thomas l'Ami, who owed only 1 *sou*. This diversity of wealth in a single street was typical of the medieval town. Where modern towns tend to be divided into neighborhoods according to the wealth of the inhabitants, rich and poor town dwellers in the Middle Ages lived cheek by jowl.

While the residents of the Juiverie were diverse in wealth, they were strikingly consistent in profession. Almost half of the households belonged to bakers; another seventh belonged to drapers. This clustering of trades was also characteristic of the medieval neighborhood. In some cases it was influenced by local conditions or opportunities. Tradesmen who served travelers were often found near the gates on important roads, like the horse sellers and tavern keepers who clustered near the northern gates of Paris by the main road toward St.-Denis, or the innkeepers who lined the rue St.-Jacques on the left bank. There was another cluster of taverns near the market at the Grève, the principal landing-place for wine coming into the city. The greatest number of book-related trades were found near Notre-Dame and on the left bank, close to the cathedral schools and university. In the case of the Juiverie, the large number of bakers may be explained in part by the proximity to the watermills on the north arm of the Seine and by the presence of a weekly wheat market in one of the buildings on the street.

There were many other clusters of trades for which no external influence can be identified, but in all cases clustered trades helped facilitate administration and quality control. Many of the core trades that supported city life, such as the sellers of foodstuffs and clothing, and politically or economically important trades, such as armorers, sword makers, and goldsmiths, were found in large numbers in the Cité and on the right bank near the Châtelet, close to the centers of regulation. The presence of both the bakers and drapers in the Juiverie reflected the need for official oversight of these core services.

The Juiverie was one of the better-appointed streets in Paris. Many city streets, like those of smaller towns and villages, were simply dirt, and tended to become muddy in wet weather. The better streets were cobbled with stones or bricks, usually slanting toward a gutter in the middle. The Cité still had Roman foundations under its streets, but centuries of dirt and refuse had covered them over by the late twelfth century. A chronicler of the reign of Phillip Augustus offers an account of the king's decision to improve the streets of Paris:

> King Phillip Augustus was staying at Paris, and was pacing around in the royal hall meditating on the affairs of the kingdom. He came to the windows of the palace, where he liked sometimes to watch the river Seine to revive his spirit, but the horse-drawn carts that travelled through the city, churning up the mud, raised an intolerable stench. The king, pacing about in his hall, was unable to bear this, and he conceived of a very arduous but necessary plan, which none of his forebears had dared to approach because of the great difficulty and expense of the work. He called together the burgesses and provost of the city, and ordered by the royal authority that all the streets and roads of the whole city of Paris should be laid with hard and strong stones.[6]

The project was not an unqualified success. One chronicler remarks that the burgesses "would have done it with much more joy had it not been at their own expense."[7] In fact, the paving of Paris was a gradual process, beginning with the principal streets of the Cite, like the Juiverie, and major thoroughfares, such as those leading to the city gates. At any given time, only a portion of the city streets were paved, and new urban development always brought with it new unimproved streets.

Important streets were fairly wide, sometimes wide enough to accommodate a market. Others were narrower, and many were no more than alleys: Unicorn Alley (ruelle de la Licorne) and Four-Basset Alley (ruelle du Four-Basset) off the Juiverie were each about four feet wide. There were no street signs. Street names were never official and could change over time. The cross street just north of where Pierre le Normant lived sometimes appears in the records as the rue de la

Madeleine, sometimes as the rue des Marmousets (street of the jesters—named after a house that bore jesters for a sign). The street behind his house was known as the rue de la Licorne (street of the Unicorn—also named after a house) or the rue des Oublaiers (street of the Waferers). Some streets had no accepted names at all. The Juiverie itself was quite short. Beyond the rue de la Madeleine, the street was usually known as the rue de la Lanterne (the street of the lantern), and in the other direction it was known as the Marché-Palu (Marsh Market). The streets of Paris listed in the tax returns of the late thirteenth century include some that were named after important residents, like the rue Sire Guillaume Bourdon. Others are named after topographical features, like the rue aux deux portes (the street of the two gates), or named after their destinations, like the rue St.-Germain and the rue St.-Martin, that led from the center of town toward the peripheral areas of St.-Germain-l'Auxerrois and St.-Martin-des-Champs. Others have more curious designations, like the rue ou l'en cuit les æufs (the street where they cook eggs). Many street names reflected a clustering of crafts: the Heaumerie (Helmery) was heavily populated by armorers, the Peleterie (Furriery) was home to many furriers, the Selerie (Saddlery) had numerous saddlemakers and other makers of riding gear, the rue aux Ecrivains (street of Writers) had a concentration of parchment makers. Individual houses were not numbered as is the modern custom, but some had names, reflecting the building's appearance, use, or current or former owner. Many were known by the name of a decorative emblem on the façade. Houses in Pierre le Normant's neighborhood named in thirteenth- and fourteenth-century sources included the Rose, the Scales, the Lantern, and the Unicorn.

Sanitation

The state of Parisian streets that prompted Phillip Augustus's interest in paving was just one part of the problem of medieval urban sanitation. Even contemporaries sometimes complained of the bad air of the city: one wrote around 1200 that "He who lives amidst stench no longer perceives it; he must depart and return for the stench to affect him. . . . This can be proven by the inhabitants of Paris who forget its evil odor and only notice it when they return from a journey."[8] Households made use of cesspits and rubbish pits on their property for disposal of waste, and the excess was sometimes carted outside of the city for disposal elsewhere, but much of the city's refuse ended up in the streets. Inadequate drainage meant that towns were often subject to flooding, so that waste in the streets could easily contaminate drinking water.

The sanitation conditions in the cities were not improved by the omnipresence of animals. Horses, oxen, and donkeys were common in the streets, since they were essential to transportation. Many houses kept pigs, dogs, or poultry. Pigs and dogs were a serious hazard for young children, since they were often left to roam the streets and entered open houses, sometimes attacking unattended infants. The animal population was no respecter of persons: in 1131, Prince Phillip, heir to the throne of France, was riding through Paris when his horse was startled by a pig; rider and horse fell to the ground, and the prince died of his injuries.

The concentrated population supported other animals even less subject to human control. Rats and mice were common, as were flies, fleas, and lice, all agents for the propagation of disease. The fleas and rats eventually brought devastation by transmitting the plague that came to Europe in 1347. The plague killed some 25 to 50 million people in its first three or four years, representing about a quarter to a third of the total population. Local mortality was sometimes much higher: in the city of Lübeck in northern Germany, the plague killed 90 percent of the inhabitants. Overall population loss in the fourteenth century was about 50 percent, and recurring epidemics continued to depress the population levels, which did not resume growing until the late fifteenth century. The plague was the greatest demographic catastrophe to strike medieval Europe, but even before its arrival, disease was a chronic feature of urban life.

Churches and Religious Houses

The most imposing building in the Juiverie was the parish church of the Madeleine, which stood near the corner, a few houses away from Pierre le Normant's home. The Madeleine was one of the most important churches in

Paris, but the parish, like most in this ancient district of the city, was tiny, consisting of the northern part of the Juiverie and parts of three other small streets. Residents of these streets were assigned to the church of Ste.-Madeleine, a total of perhaps some 600 to 700 people. As in the village, the parish church served not only religious but social functions, since it was usually the only public building in its neighborhood.

The parish church might also provide burial grounds, although many of the churches in Paris, including Ste.-Madeleine, were relatively new establishments with insufficient land to provide graveyards. The surplus of corpses generally ended up in one of the older and larger graveyards, of which the most important was Saints-Innocents, on the right bank near the Halles market. The Innocents, lying so close to a major marketplace, constituted something of a health risk. The ground in this area was marshy and muddy, which was part of the reason why it had never been developed. This made effective burial difficult, and the city's pigs were notoriously given to rooting among the corpses, although this problem was reduced in the late twelfth century, when the cemetery was enclosed by a wall, with gates that were shut at night. Since the cemetery was one of the few public green spaces in the city, it attracted both commerce and recreation. The Innocents was used as an informal marketplace for vendors and was often frequented by merrymakers. Prior to the construction of the wall, it also served as a nighttime business area for prostitutes.

Medieval towns often had monastic houses as well as secular religious establishments. Just up the street from the Juiverie was the canonry of St.-Denis, and a bit to the west was the priory of St.-Eloi. On the right and left banks there were several sizable monastic houses, most of them founded at a time when they were still at a distance from the urbanized area of Paris. These included the abbeys of St.-Germain-des-Prés and St.-Magloire, the Cluniac priory of St.-Martin-des-Champs, and the canonries of St.-Honoré, St.-Germain-l'Auxerrois, Ste.-Geneviève, St.-Marcel, and St.-Opportune. Perhaps most impressive of all was the Temple, the complex to the north of the city walls that served as the European headquarters of the Knights-Templar. The buildings of the Temple included not only the usual monastic facilities, but an enormous fortified

SAINTS-INNOCENTS CEMETERY, CA. 1550. Theodor Josef Hubert Hoffbauer (French), late nineteenth century. Engraving.

keep. Many of these religious establishments enjoyed seigneurial authority over their neighborhoods, and contributed to the complex patchwork that made up the urban political structure. Pierre le Normant's home probably stood in a part of the Juiverie whose feudal lord was nominally the priory of St.-Eloi.

Paris and Its Feudal Lords

By far the most imposing structures in the Cite were the complexes at either end belonging to the city's chief feudal lords, the king of France and the bishop of Paris. Feudalism pervaded medieval society, even here in the city, but there was a fundamental disjuncture between urban life and feudal organization. Feudalism was oriented toward land as the principal source of wealth, and presupposed a fairly stationary population to maintain the personal relationships by which feudalism was structured. Such arrangements were incompatible with the needs of an urban community founded on commerce, which required a mobile population and flexible labor market. Nonetheless, feudal lords recognized the advantages of having urban centers in their territories as sources of taxation revenue and as centers for trade and manufacture, so they found ways to mediate between the feudal and urban worlds.

The pattern that emerged was one in which the town became a semi-independent entity granted certain freedoms from the usual constraints of the manorial system. Urban property owners held their land in "burgage tenure," essentially a form of freehold that allowed them perpetual rights to the holding, along with freedom to sell or bequeath it as they pleased. The urban community was also allowed some measure of self-government and authority to handle minor legal matters. The precise terms of the town's rights were in many cases laid out in a written charter issued by the feudal overlord. This model of the town as a free zone within the feudal domain predominated in the feudal heartland of northern Europe. In the south, particularly Italy and Spain, the town retained something of its Roman character as a regional capital. In northern Italy, the towns were dominant political entities: cities like Rome, Florence, Venice, and Genoa exercised authority over large surrounding territories, and were distinguished by a highly urbanized aristocracy.

The Royal Palace

In Paris, the principal overlord was the king himself. Paris had been a royal residence for centuries, and by the High Middle Ages it had emerged as the principal seat of royal government. The west end of the Cite was the site of the royal palace, which covered a third of the island and included gardens, a great hall with adjoining chambers, the royal chapel, and other buildings serving both residential and administrative purposes. The entire complex was fortified with a keep and an encircling wall; the main gate was just down the street from the north end of the Juiverie. The palace served as the center for royal administration of the city. Because of the importance of Paris, the king kept the city's liberties on a short leash, allowing it rather less independence than was granted to many other cities in France. Paris had no charter, and for most of the High Middle Ages it possessed only minimal institutions for self-government, although the city began to acquire more independence during the course of the thirteenth century.

When the king was in Paris, the palace also functioned as the seat of national government. Government in this period followed the person of the ruler, and the king was rarely

LA CONCIERGERIE, *a former royal palace in Paris, located on the west end of the Île de la Cité.*

stationary, so although Paris was the most important governmental seat in France, the government was not always present. King Phillip Augustus, who reigned in the late twelfth and early thirteenth centuries, made some sixty-five visits to Paris during his forty-three-year rule, each lasting no more than a month or two at most.

The Episcopal Complex

At the far end of the island from the palace was the complex belonging to the bishop of Paris, consisting of the bishop's palace, the buildings used by the cathedral chapter of canons, a charitable residence called the Hôtel-Dieu, and the episcopal cathedral, Notre-Dame de Paris. The bishopric of Paris had been founded in the late Roman period and had acquired feudal power in the vacuum of authority left by the empire's collapse. Although the bishop's authority predated that of the king, the city's political importance was such that the kings of France did not allow the bishop more than a junior partnership in the city's government. In towns where authority was shared between the bishop and a lesser lord, the distribution of power was less uneven, while some towns were entirely subject to the local bishop as feudal lord. In Paris, the bishop received some of the city's feudal taxes and enjoyed particular rights over certain quarters of the city, such as the neighborhood of St.-Germain-l'Auxerrois, where he had legal authority in all cases except murder and rape. Pierre le Normant, as a baker of Paris, was required to purvey three halfpennies' worth of bread each week for the city's feudal lords—a halfpenny loaf on Wednesday and a penny loaf on Saturday. The bread went to the king two out of three weeks, and to the bishop in the third.

The Cathedral

The symbolic center of the bishop's authority was the cathedral, the bishop's church that housed the ceremonial chair that represented his episcopal status (in Latin, *cathedra*, "chair"). New architectural techniques in the twelfth century

PRESENT-DAY PHOTOGRAPH OF NOTRE-DAME DE PARIS CATHEDRAL, *located on the east end of the Île de la Cité.*

allowed cathedrals to become the skyscrapers of their day, and the cathedral of Notre-Dame towered over the Cité, dwarfing every other building in Paris; it was visible for miles around the city. The interior vaults of Notre-Dame rose to a height of 110 feet (equivalent to about ten stories today), the towers to 210 feet, and the spire over the body of the church to a dizzying 325 feet above the ground—this in an age when even an unusually tall secular building, like the keep at Dover, measured less than ninety feet. The building covered an area roughly the size of Pierre le Normant's entire parish. Yet the achievement of the new architecture, known as the Gothic style, went beyond sheer scale. The skill of twelfth-century architects allowed the cathedral to support its weight without the bulky walls and pillars of the earlier Romanesque style. As a result, churches like Notre-Dame had a grace and delicacy unlike any other buildings of their day, with large open interiors and enormous windows, in contrast with other contemporary structures whose rooms were usually small and dimly lit. Only a large castle could begin to compare with Notre-Dame in scale, and none matched it in beauty. Perhaps most important, the cathedral was a public space, accessible to people who might never see the inside of a castle. Notre-Dame can easily accommodate 9,000 people, and has been known to accommodate significantly more. For medieval people, this outstanding feat of architecture and decoration must have been an overwhelming sight.[9] The royal palace at one end of the Cité reminded Pierre le Normant of the greatness of the king, but the cathedral at the other end reminded him of the even greater majesty of God.

The Cathedral Chapter

To facilitate the bishop's work, the day-to-day affairs of the cathedral were in the hands of a body of canons, collectively termed the cathedral chapter. At Notre-Dame, there were about three or four dozen canons, in addition to the chapter officers, who included a dean, a cantor, a sub-cantor, three archdeacons, and a chancellor. The chapter lived a communal life in facilities similar to those of a monastery, although unlike the monks they were not tied to their cloister. In fact, the cloister had accommodations for only three dozen canons; the rest were lodged in external houses belonging to the chapter in the Cité. The canons dwelling in these houses lacked the constant supervision of those who inhabited the cloister, although there were rules governing their conduct. They were not allowed to receive women in their houses except for close relatives and important ladies, and no women at all were to be admitted at night. The canons were forbidden to sell wine except by the barrel (a rule intended to prevent them from using their residences as taverns), and they were specifically forbidden to keep bears, stags, monkeys, or crows in their houses.

Like monks, the canons maintained a daily cycle of worship services in the cathedral, but they were also charged with assisting the bishop in the administration of the diocese. The chapter also possessed secular rights and responsibilities within Paris, and substantial feudal and ecclesiastical authority outside the city as well. Chapter responsibilities also included running the cathedral school, and as a result they acquired responsibility for overseeing the University of Paris as it emerged in the twelfth and thirteenth centuries: the chancellor of the modern university ultimately owes his title to that of the chancellor of the medieval cathedral chapter.

The Right Bank: Economic Life

The Cité had been the old commercial heart of Paris, but by the High Middle Ages the economic center had shifted across the Grand-Pont to the right bank. This area had become the new administrative center of Parisian commerce, and Pierre le Normant's work must have taken him frequently to the right bank, both to buy and sell goods, and to play a political role as one of the town's wealthier tradesmen. Just at the end of the Grand-Pont itself was the Grand-Châtelet, a fortified keep that initially was built to guard the entrance to the bridge, but now served principally as the center for royal administration of the Parisian economy; it also housed one of the city's principal royal prisons. The Châtelet was the headquarters of the provost of Paris, an official appointed by the crown to oversee the conduct of the various trades practiced in the city. Nearby was the Parloir au Bourgeois, a building that served as a meeting place for the leaders of the trades of Paris. The church of St.-Leufroy, also in this area, served as the repository for the city's official weights and measures.

The Guilds

Each trade in the city had its own structure, with rules governing its practice, customs as to the tradesmen's rights and responsibilities, and a greater or lesser degree of communal self-government. These trade associations had their roots among urban social fellowships called guilds that appeared in the eleventh century. Early guilds provided town dwellers with some of the social functions that were furnished by village and kinship communities in the country, such as arranging social feasts and religious festivals, and providing charitable services for their members, especially funerals and support for widows. In the twelfth century, guilds began to appear that were restricted to the practitioners of a certain craft, and by the thirteenth century the institution of the trade guild was well established.

Trade guilds tended to be grouped by their raw materials as much as by their products. In Paris, a distinction was made between the makers of iron buckles and those who made them of copper or brass. There were separate regulations for the various makers of prayer beads, depending on whether they worked in bone and horn, coral and shell, amber and jet, or in copper and its alloys. The structure of Parisian trade guilds varied, but usually each craft was overseen by one to three guildmasters, in some cases assisted by a couple of journeymen. The guildmasters were supervised by the royal provost of Paris. Michiel the Master, whose widow lived a few doors down from Pierre le Normant in 1292, may have been the guildmaster of the bakers: in 1297, Guillaume, the master of the Bakers, was living in about the same place. The guildmasters were generally assisted by a body of jurors who helped adjudicate matters of controversy. The bakers had some twelve jurors, chosen by the guildmaster. Pierre le Normant may well have served in this capacity, since the regulations of the bakers stipulate that the jurors should be chosen from among "the most judicious men of substance . . . who are good at assessing bread." The jurors of the bakers were required to swear upon holy relics "that they will look after the trade well and faithfully, and that in judging bread they will not spare either kinsman or friend, nor will they condemn anyone wrongfully for hatred or ill-will."[10]

Some trades in Paris enjoyed a fairly high level of autonomy and corporate identity; the bakers were one of these. Their guildmaster had authority in matters of petty justice involving members of the craft, including civil suits except those pertaining to property, and cases of battery that did not involve bloodshed; he was also authorized to collect fines on behalf of the guild. Most trades were less independent, and many do not seem to have constituted an identifiable organization that might be considered a guild. The rather limited autonomy of the Parisian trades reflected royal unwillingness to relinquish too much authority in France's principal city. Elsewhere, trade guilds evolved more quickly. Although there was some opposition from established authorities, some of whom saw the guilds as potentially dangerous conspiracies of disenfranchised tradesmen, the guilds eventually became an accepted part of urban life, and in many towns the trade guilds enjoyed considerably more autonomy and had a more fully developed identity and organizational structure than was the case in Paris. In such places, the guilds often had their own administration buildings, that were used in some cases for business transactions.

Functions of the Guilds

The trade guilds continued to fulfill some of the social and charitable roles of the earlier guilds. The regulations of the cooks of Paris made provision for a third of the fines levied by the craft on its members to be used "to support the old folk of the said craft who have declined through outcome of commerce or through old age."[11] Most guild regulations related directly to the work of its members. Each guild had its own rules regarding the process of admission to the trade. To become a baker in Paris, Pierre le Normant had to pay the king for the right to ply the trade. Once admitted as a baker, he had to pay 10 *deniers* to the king each Christmas, 22 *deniers* at Easter, 5 ½ *deniers* at the feast of St. John, and 6 *sous* at Martinmas. His first four years were a kind of probation period during which he paid a higher tax at Christmas. In each of these years, at Epiphany, he met with the tax collector who collected his payments and made a notch in a tally stick that served as a record of the probationary period. Pierre le Normant may have held his own tally stick next to that of the tax collector to mark the notches in both sticks, a common medieval method of making verifiable duplicates of a tally. The end of the four-year period was marked by a lively ceremony:

> The new baker . . . shall take a new clay pot and fill it with nuts and wafers; and he shall come to the house of the master of the bakers, and he shall have with him the tax-collector, and all the bakers, and the master-journeymen. . . . And this new baker shall hand his pot and nuts to the master of the bakers, and say, "Master, I have finished and completed my four years." And the master shall ask the tax-collector whether this is true. And if he says that it is true, the master shall hand the new baker his pot and nuts, and command that he throw them against the wall, and then the new baker shall throw his pot and nuts and wafers against the outside wall of the house, and then the master, the tax-collector, the new baker, and all the other bakers and journeymen shall enter the master's house, and the master shall provide them with wine and a fire, and each of the bakers, and the new one, and the master journeymen, all owe a penny to the master of the bakers for their wine and the fire.[12]

Product quality was one of the major concerns of guild regulations and was especially important for a core trade such as the bakers. The master of the bakers was expected from time to time to summon the jurors of the craft to accompany him on a tour of inspection of the city's bakers. The master took with him at least four jurors and a sergeant from the Châtelet:

> And at the windows where they find bread for sale, the master takes the bread and gives it to the jurors, and the jurors examine it to see if it is adequate or not, and if it is adequate, the jurors return it to the window, and if it is not adequate, the jurors put the bread in the hand of the master; and if the master determines that the bread is not adequate, he can confiscate all the rest of it, even that which is in the oven. And if there are several types of bread in a window, the master will have each one assessed. And those which are found to be too small, the master and jurors will have them donated to charity.[13]

The bakers were one of the most highly regulated trades in a medieval town since their product was the community's main staple food. Bread was to be sold in loaves at specific prices: halfpenny bread, penny bread, and twopenny bread. The actual weight of the bread varied with the price of grain according to an official schedule of weights and prices. To prevent the selling of underweight loaves, each

BAKING SCENE *from a Book of Hours, ca. 1500.*

baker was required to keep a set of approved standard weights. Inspectors also looked for adulterated bread: unscrupulous bakers were known to include sand in their loaves to increase weight at less cost.

Some guilds also regulated the terms of competition. The makers of purses and braie belts were not permitted to leave their shops to show their merchandise to a customer who was at a neighboring shop; the cooks were forbidden to call to a customer at a neighbor's stall or shop; and the saddlemakers were forbidden to shout or gesture. The cooks were also forbidden to make false criticisms of one another's food.

Many regulations concerned the training of apprentices. The linen weavers required the jurors of their craft to investigate masters who wished to hire apprentices, to ensure that they had the required money and skill. Most trades limited the number of apprentices a master might take on (usually only one or two), and stipulated the minimum number of years of apprenticeship. The regulations themselves emphasize the time and attention needed to train an apprentice, but such laws also served to limit access to the trade, lest a glut of tradesmen lower the value of their work. The dyers of Paris complained in 1297 that they were "so burdened with great numbers of journeymen that often there remain half in the place who cannot find work," and accordingly they decided to require a five-year apprenticeship.[14] Yet the guild might take a real interest in the treatment of apprentices. An apprentice linen weaver who left his master because of inappropriate treatment might complain to the guild, or send a friend to do so on his behalf. If the charges were justified, the guild might summon the offending master and order him to "treat the apprentice honorably like the son of a proper householder, providing him clothing and shoes, and drink and food, and all other things, within the next two weeks," and if the master failed to satisfy them, a new master would be found.[15]

Guilds also exercised authority over the tradesman's work schedule. The regulations of the bakers forbade Pierre le Normant to bake on Sundays or on major holy days, including the day after Easter and the two days after Christmas. On Saturdays and the eves of holy days he was also forbidden to bake unless the bread was already in the oven by the time candles were lit in the evening. The only exception was on Christmas Eve, when he could work late into the night, until Matins was sounded by the church bells of Notre-Dame, allowing him to build up an extra supply of bread for the three holidays ahead. On Mondays he was permitted to bake again as soon as Matins was rung. In other crafts, work on Saturday might end as early as None (about 3 P.M.), and work might be forbidden on all days after dark or before dawn. As a baker, Pierre's work would normally begin long before dawn so that the bread would be ready for morning buyers; his work was considered too important to be prohibited late at night except on holidays.

Regulations restricting the hours of work served in part to prevent masters from overworking their staff. Several by-laws specifically mention the journeyman's right to rest. The makers of metal thread even allowed their journeymen to take a month's leave from work in August—probably not an actual holiday, but an opportunity to make higher wages working at the harvest. Prohibitions against nighttime work also helped ensure product quality. Many of those who were forbidden to work at night were the practitioners of difficult crafts, such as cutlers and locksmiths, and the by-laws of the lace makers explicitly state that candlelight was too weak for the practice of their craft. The metalsmiths who forged buckles were required to work during the day with their doors open, since work done at night or in secret might contain hidden flaws. A few crafts were permitted to work at night, either because their work was too important to be restricted, like the armorers, or because it was fairly simple, like those who cast buckles and other small wares in copper and its alloys.

Guilds and Government

In time, the guilds came to be dominant forces in city government. Some cities, like London, developed a municipal government in which a number of guilds participated. Others were dominated by a single guild, most often the guild of merchants, who were among the most wealthy and powerful guildsmen in the town. This was the case in Paris, where the water merchants' control over Parisian trade on the Seine brought them to prominence in the twelfth and thirteenth centuries. In 1221 they were assigned authority over petty justice and the salt and grain measures in the city. In 1260 the king constituted the four jurors of the water merchants as the city's magistrates, and the guild of water merchants effectively became the municipal government of Paris. To this day, the symbol of Paris is a medieval ship derived from the seal of the water merchants.

Markets

Pierre le Normant's home doubled as a retail shop, but much of his business was done beyond his door. The presence of a public marketplace—whether an indoor hall, an open square, or just a wide city street—was one of the defining characteristics of the town. Small market towns held their markets one day each week. Large cities had multiple marketplaces and hosted markets several days a week, perhaps even daily. The thirteenth-century regulations of the trade guilds of Paris mention markets on every day of the week except Tuesday and Thursday. These markets catered both to wholesale and retail trade, providing Parisians and visitors with goods for personal use, as well as offering a setting in which traders could buy and sell merchandise for resale.

The two principle markets of Paris were on the right bank, reflecting the district's commercial importance. The Grève (Strand) was, as its name suggested, on the bank of the Seine. Here the barrels of wine shipped to Paris from upriver were unloaded and sold. Since wine was a staple, the wine trade was of immense

THE GRÉVE, *in front of the Hôtel de Ville de Paris, late sixteenth century.*

economic importance, and much of the commercial life of Paris gravitated toward the Grève; eventually the town hall was located here.

Toward the northwest end of the city was the Champeaux (Little Fields). This market was vigorously developed by Phillip Augustus in the late twelfth century. According to one chronicler, the king ordered the construction of

> two large halls where the merchants could remain when it rained, and sell their wares more properly. He had them enclosed and shut in, so that the merchandise that stayed there overnight could be kept safe. Outside he built lodges and stalls, and had them well covered above, so that when it rained they would not have to cease selling, and so that the merchants would not not suffer loss from the rain.[16]

The area later became the financial center of Paris, and the king's buildings are still recalled in the district's modern name, les Halles. The Halles were an important source of royal income, and many trades were required to bring their wares there for the principal weekly market on Saturday, paying an annual rent for their stalls ranging from 2 to 12 *sous,* plus a daily fee on market days of about 1½ to 1 *denier.* Pierre le Normant probably took part in the Saturday market, which was one of the principal bread markets of Paris. There were also markets at which he was permitted to dispose of imperfect bread:

> The bakers living within the region of Paris can sell their defective bread (that is their rejects, such as damaged bread that rats or mice have gnawed on, excessively hard bread, burnt or scorched bread, overrisen bread, doughy bread, ill-turned or undersized bread, which they are not allowed to sell in the stall) on Sunday in the Halles, at the place where iron is sold in front of the cemetery of Saints-Innocents; or, if they like, they can sell it on Sunday between the portico of Notre-Dame and St.-Christopher. The bakers . . . can carry their bread on Sunday in these places in their baskets or in their panniers, and carry their stall or boards or tables, provided the stalls are no more than 5 feet long.[17]

The right bank and Cité were home to several smaller markets, and there were even markets on the less-commercial left bank. Some specialized in certain products. Those on Sunday at the Halles, in front of Notre-Dame, and at Place-Maubert on the left bank were for bread; there were butcher markets near the Châtelet, at the Petit-Pont, and in the Cité at Massacre-Moyenne. The market hall in the Juiverie, across the street from Pierre le Normant, had once been the principal wheat market in Paris, but in Pierre's day most of that trade had shifted to the Champeaux, and the Juiverie market was mostly used for wheat brought in from the Beauce and Hurepoix regions, lying in the direction of Orléans.

Wares were also sold by itinerant vendors. The regulations of many of the trades of Paris made provision for tradesmen selling their goods in this manner, or for having them sold by hired vendors, which was probably more common. This was a prominent part of the Parisian economy, but the regulations treated it with some misgiving. Tradesmen who had stalls at the Halles were generally forbidden to have wares sold in this manner, at least on market days, lest the king's market suffer from the competition. Some by-laws required that itinerant vending on market days should take place within the market area, while others stipulated that the vendors were not to stop in front of the tradesmen's stalls. The tallow chandlers were permitted to hire only two itinerant vendors. The regulations of the hosiers forbade new stockings to be sold in this manner," on account of the frauds in such matters, since the vendor is unknown, so they sell hose made of waste and other bad materials; and when the buyers think they have purchased good wares, and they realize that they have been deceived, they do not know where to find the vendors, and so they lose their money—something that they would not do with vendors in stalls.[18] This sort of problem seems to lie behind the subjection of itinerant vendors of used clothing to the fripperers, shopkeepers who dealt in the same sorts of wares.

Fairs

As part of his program to develop the Champeaux, Phillip Augustus made it the new site of the annual fair of St.-Lazare, which had formerly taken place near the Hospital of St.-Lazare to the north of the city. The St.-Lazare fair ran for eighteen days beginning on November 2, and it was the only fair to take place within Paris itself. The Lendit, the largest fair in the area, ran for about three weeks every June at the monastery of St.-Denis a few miles north of Paris. Until 1278 there was a third local fair, that of St.-Germain-des-Prés, which ran for eighteen days each year beginning two weeks after Easter, but the fair was suppressed because of brawling among university students.

The twelfth and thirteenth centuries were the heyday of the fair. The right to hold a fair, like the right to hold a market, was bestowed by the feudal lord. It was not accorded to every town. Larger towns were more likely to have a fair, and some of them even had more than one. The fair took place each year at the same time, usually lasting three days to a week, or in some cases lasting several weeks. Some fairs attracted vendors from great distances. Those in the Champagne region in northeastern France served as one of the principal centers for European commerce in the thirteenth century, and even fairs of less importance were visited by merchants from all over Western Europe. They were also frequented by local country folk, who often preferred to buy their household goods at fairs, since they offered a better selection and more competition than the local weekly markets. Many people traveled up to twenty miles to attend the fair—a full day's journey on foot, involving at least two nights' lodging.[19]

Jews

The economic activity of the right bank attracted a significant Jewish community. Jews were primarily town dwellers in medieval Europe, and their status was unstable. They constituted a highly educated and dynamic segment of the population, and their services as moneylenders (in many places one of the few occupations open to them) were invaluable to many in the upper levels of society, especially after 1179 when the church forbade Christians to lend money to each other at interest. At the same time, the Jews were few in number, and they could never be truly integrated into a society that regarded church and community as indivisible. Their rights were invariably restricted, and the wave of religious enthusiasm kindled by the first Crusade in 1095 led to an outbreak of anti-Semitic violence that remained endemic in Europe for the centuries that followed.

The ambivalence of Christian attitudes toward the Jews can be seen in the conduct of the kings of France, who were chronically in debt to Jewish moneylenders. King Phillip Augustus expelled the Jews from France in 1182. The main Jewish quarter at the time, the Juiverie (Jewry), was the very street on which Pierre le Normant was living a century later. Phillip Augustus bestowed the houses of the Juiverie on the drapers—a few were still there in Pierre's day—and the local synagogue was replaced by the parish church of St. Mary Magdalene, while other Jewish houses near the Champeaux were destroyed to make room for the Halles. The Jews were recalled in 1196, and periodic expulsions and readmissions recurred during the following centuries—a technique typically used by the French kings as a means of extorting money from the Jews as a condition of their return. The darker implications of medieval piety were reflected in the order by Saint Louis that the Jews wear a yellow badge so that they could be easily recognized.[20]

The Left Bank: The Church in the Urban Age

Pierre le Normant's business may have been oriented toward the right bank, but his position in the Cite right near the Petit-Pont made him well placed to cater to the growing market of the left bank as well. The Parisian left bank had developed much more slowly than the right, and even in Pierre's day it still supported vineyards within the city walls. The left bank underwent substantial development during the course of the thirteenth century, but it took a very different shape from that of the right bank, deriving its impetus from religious rather than commercial institutions.

Education

In the early Middle Ages, the church had been dominated by its monasteries, but during the twelfth and thirteenth centuries the revitalization of urban life was reflected in a renewed vigor in religious institutions rooted in the towns. One of these institutions was the cathedral school. Cathedrals traditionally maintained schools to provide basic training for parish priests, but by the end of the early Middle Ages these schools had also become centers for the advanced studies that supplied the church with its intellectual leaders. Initially, teaching was in the hands of the cathedral canons, especially the chancellor, but as demand increased, the chancellor licensed other teachers to provide instruction. During the twelfth century, the teachers in Paris acquired an international reputation, and the scholastic population boomed. Parisian scholastic life was originally confined to the area of the Cité near the cathedral, but in time it expanded into the houses of the Petit-Pont, and eventually spilled over onto the left bank beyond.

The University

By the late twelfth century, the Parisian masters, or teachers of advanced studies, had coalesced into professional associations—comparable to those of the trade guilds—that represented the faculties in each discipline. The chancellor of the cathedral chapter at first resisted the rise of these associations, but eventually the pope ordered an arrangement by which the associations were placed under the general authority of the chancellor, while being accorded a high degree of

HENRICUS DE ALEMANNIA IN FRONT OF HIS PUPILS.
The eminence of early universities depended primarily on the fame of the teachers who came there to teach.

autonomy in teaching and assessing the qualifications of others to teach. By 1200 these associations were collectively termed the University of Paris; the Latin term *universitas* means entirety, and it originally referred to the entire body of teachers in the associations.

Comparable educational institutions appeared in other European cities, especially in the south. Montpellier in southern France and Salerno in southern Italy emerged as leading centers for the study of medicine. The cities of northern Italy excelled in the study of Roman law. In twelfth-century England, Oxford emerged as a university on the Parisian model, and Cambridge came into existence in the early thirteenth century when a conflict with town authorities prompted a number of masters to leave Oxford. There were a few other universities in France, but none in Germany or the Low Countries before 1300. In general, the university was found in only a few cities, although a certain measure of advanced learning was available at cathedral schools.

University Life

A student arriving in the city to begin his university studies was typically about fourteen years old, although some were younger and others older. Most students at Paris came from France, but the university's reputation always attracted a large number of foreigners, especially in countries that lacked universities of their own. At Paris, and in northern Europe generally, the student was classed as a cleric, and his education fell under the auspices of the church. Many went on to the priesthood, although for some the goal was an administrative position in the church or a life of scholarship. Prior to his arrival, the student needed to have at least a grammar school education, since courses were conducted in Latin, and this was the principal language of communication among scholars who did not necessarily share any other common language. The university area on the left bank of Paris is known to this day as the Latin Quarter.

On arriving in Paris, the student needed to arrange long-term accommodations. The university regulated the teaching activities of the masters, but the daily lives of the students were largely in their own hands. The student might rent a room, preferably in the Cité or on the left bank, with the rest of the university community. In many cases, a group of students rented a place together, and it became increasingly common for a significant number of students to rent an entire building for a long term, the dwelling remaining in student hands even as the population changed from year to year.

The new student also needed to choose a master. The master was also young, typically in his early twenties, and perhaps pursuing an advanced degree. The master was the student's main source of lectures during his years of study and had general responsibility for seeing that the student fulfilled his requirements for the degree. Since the master-student relationship was so important, the student was well advised to take some care in his choice. The masters, for their part, relied on their students' fees for their income, so they were keen to market their services. It was common to allow a student to sit in as a guest at a few initial lectures to sample the quality of the master's teaching, and many masters even hired older students to visit newly arrived scholars and advertise the master's services.

The first level of university studies for every student, equivalent to the modern undergraduate degree, consisted of the Seven Liberal Arts, inherited from the classical period: Grammar, Rhetoric, Logic, Music, Arithmetic, Geometry, and Astronomy. To receive a degree, the student was required to attend lectures on a prescribed curriculum of books in each of these subjects. Within this framework, the student acquired a wide knowledge of medieval scholarship. The lecturing master read the text to his class, expounding on the content as he went. This format allowed for considerable breadth: a lecture on rhetoric might be based on a Roman epic poem, and range from versification to geography and classical mythology.

Advanced education in the twelfth century was still fairly informal, relying principally on the master-student relationship. By the latter part of the thirteenth century a more systematic means of verifying the student's work had taken shape. After about two years, the student was required to certify that he had attended the necessary lectures, after which he underwent an oral examination and took part in a public debate on a set topic. If the masters judged his performance satisfactory, he was granted the status of Bachelor, which entitled him to engage in some limited teaching. After two more years, the Bachelor was examined by the chancellor, who issued the license to teach; a license from Paris and other accredited institutions was internationally recognized through the authority of the church. Within the following year, if the other masters were satisfied with him, he was admitted to the status of master. At Paris, the new master was required to teach for at least two years. It seems that few students failed to pass the oral exams and debates. Those who failed at school were more likely to drop out beforehand, and indeed a student had to be recommended by his master prior to examination.

A student who had completed the course in arts might undertake an advanced course of study in one of a few specialized fields. The particular strength at Paris was theology, and the theology faculty at Paris were often called upon to adjudicate important disputes regarding church doctrine. The other advanced fields were medicine, canon law, and civil (i.e., Roman) law. Civil law was not taught at Paris, and the student who wished to pursue this field had to choose a different university. The students in the advanced courses of study, having already been students in the faculty of arts, were generally in their twenties or even early thirties. A degree in medicine required about six years of additional study, theology about fifteen.

The medieval university had no buildings of its own. Lecture spaces were generally rented, and administrative meetings were held in local churches. Books were owned by the masters and students themselves, and could also be purchased or rented from booksellers—in this way, booksellers functioned as commercial libraries. To ensure that the university's needs were met, booksellers were placed under the regulatory authority of the university, receiving access to the lucrative academic trade in exchange. Students who had more time than money could also choose to make their own copies of the texts they wanted.

The economic status of the students varied enormously. Some were from privileged families, sent to Paris to acquire the education or political connections that would set them on the path to a powerful position in the church. Many were clergymen who already held office in the church and were supported by the income from their positions while they were away at the university acquiring an advanced education. There were also students from poorer backgrounds. Some supported themselves by teaching or tutoring on the side. Others were promising scholars sent to the university at the church's expense. In such cases, funds might be provided by the student's diocese of origin, where he was expected to return, bringing with him the skills and knowledge acquired during his advanced studies.

Providing the church with its intellectual leaders was considered a charitable act, and during the late twelfth century benefactors began to devote resources to the support of scholars. One of the first was a Londoner named Jocius, who purchased a room at the Hôtel-Dieu and established an endowment to support eighteen poor scholars. During the thirteenth century, donors began purchasing or constructing buildings to house endowed students. These institutions were called colleges, the most famous example of which was the college founded for sixteen theological students by Saint Louis's chaplain Robert de Sorbon in the mid-thirteenth century, which came to be known after its founder as the Sorbonne. The colleges closely regulated the conduct of the students, making possible a degree of control over student life that had not been feasible through the university system itself. Eventually colleges became the predominant model for university organization, and students were required to reside in them.

The daily routine of the medieval student was built around attendance at lectures. These were much smaller than is often the case today, since the lecture hall was usually an ordinary room in a private house and accommodated only a limited number of students. The statutes of the University of Paris in the early thirteenth century required the lecturing master to wear a black cape that reached to his heels. Student attire was less formal; university authorities fought an ongoing battle to prevent these clerics from wearing the more ostentatious styles of contemporary

PRESENT-DAY PHOTOGRAPH OF THE SORBONNE, *Paris's preeminent university, founded in 1257 by Robert de Sorbon. This particular building was renovated in 1626.*

secular dress. Both master and student were tonsured: by wearing the tonsure, they ensured their status as clerics, which conferred significant advantages, including immunity from secular legal authorities. The students literally sat at their master's feet: it was considered prideful for a student to sit on a bench, which put him at the same level as his master.

A student typically attended two principal lectures during the day. "Regular" lectures were delivered by the masters in the morning, probably at around 6 A.M., and were on the assigned texts of the curriculum. "Cursory" lectures took place in the afternoon. They might be delivered by a master or a bachelor, and they could be on other texts not actually required for the degree. In between lectures there was time for meals: dinner was taken at about 10 A.M., the evening meal at about 5 P.M. The school term generally started at the beginning of October and lasted until Easter, with a few days off at Christmas and Easter, and other holidays on major feasts.

Then, as now, students somehow found time for play amidst their studies, as one might expect in a community of teenagers suddenly freed from constant adult oversight. In Paris, the Pré-aux-Clercs (Field of the Clerks), near the priory of St.-Germain-des-Prés, was designated for the use of the university community as an area for recreation. The sports that took place here were probably tame compared to the drinking, gambling, and other pastimes pursued by students in Paris at night. Not the least of their preferred pastimes was violence. There was constant tension between the inhabitants of the city and the university community that sometimes escalated into deadly incidents. One major clash occurred in 1229:

The Monday and Tuesday before Ash Wednesday, on which days the scholars customarily relax with recreations, a number of scholars went from Paris out to St.-Marcel to take the air, planning on the usual games. When they had arrived there, and had disported themselves for a while in their games, they chanced to find some excellent wine, sweet to drink, in a tavern there. A disagreement arose there between the drinking students and the innkeepers concerning the reckoning for the wine, and they began to strike one another and pull each others' hair. The men of the neighborhood came and rescued the innkeepers from the hands of the students, inflicting wounds on their clerical adversaries, who were well and thoroughly lambasted, and were forced to flee. They returned injured to the city, and urged their friends to revenge them. The next day they all came with swords and cudgels to St.-Marcel, and breaking into the home of an innkeeper, smashed all his wine jugs, and poured out the wine on the floor of the house. They then wandered around the streets, and they fiercely attacked whatever men or women they found and left them half dead with their injuries.

The prior of St.-Marcel complained to the bishop and queen. The queen called in the provost and guards:

> They, being inclined to pursue every sort of cruelty, went out with their arms
> at the city gates, and outside the city walls they came upon a large number of
> students playing, who were wholly guiltless of the violence I have recounted....
> The guards rushed upon the crowd, seeing them unarmed and innocent,
> killing some and wounding others.[21]

The masters protested this assault on clerical privileges first by suspending teaching, and when this proved ineffective, by dissolving the university. Many of the faculty and students left Paris for elsewhere, and not until two years later did teaching resume, and then only because the pope intervened, compelling the crown to enforce the students' privileges. Such conflicts between town and gown recurred repeatedly at medieval universities. The attitude of town dwellers like Pierre le Normant toward the students was ambivalent: on the one hand, the scholastic population was a great stimulus to the local economy, but on the other hand, the students themselves posed an ongoing problem for civil order.[22]

Friars

The rise of the university drew to the left bank a new type of cleric, the friar, who emerged in the thirteenth century in response to a growing interest in improving religious standards in secular society. The friars belonged to a religious order like the monks, but where monks sought spiritual perfection by withdrawing from the world, the friars' mission was the spiritual improvement of the public at large through preaching. The friars also differed from monks in that they were bound to collective as well as individual poverty. A monastery was free to own property, but a friary was supposed to be dependent on borrowed resources and donated provisions. Because they lived on the charity of others, the friars were also called the mendicant orders: the friars literally went from door to door soliciting donations.

There were two principal mendicant orders. The Dominicans were founded by St. Dominic in 1216. Dominic had been a cathedral canon, and from the outset his order was a priestly and scholarly organization. This contrasted with the Franciscans, founded by St. Francis about six years earlier. Francis was the son of an Italian merchant, and his original followers were enthusiastic laymen more concerned with personal piety than with the details of theology. As the century progressed, the Franciscans acquired a larger priestly element, and by 1300 they had gained a reputation for scholarship akin to that of the Dominicans. There were other smaller mendicant orders for men—the Augustinians and the Carmelites—and allied orders for women, such as the Poor Clares, founded by St. Clare, an associate of St. Francis.

Like the monks, the friars were committed to an austere communal life. The Franciscans wore a plain gray or brown habit, in imitation of the rough sackcloth tunic worn by St. Francis. The Dominicans wore a white habit underneath a black scapular. Both major orders founded friaries, similar in design and layout to monasteries. The friar, unlike the monk, was not tied to the cloister; travel was a normal part of his routine, whether to beg, preach, or offer or receive education. The mobility of friars tended to make the medicant orders rather cosmopolitan, with an international population in any given friary.

The membership of the mendicant orders reflected the revival of urban life. Where the monks traditionally were drawn from the aristocracy, the friars found their most fertile recruiting grounds among the upper levels of urban society. Urban in origin, the friars also gravitated toward the towns in fulfillment of their mission. The towns offered the greatest concentration of people to hear their preaching, and because many country folk came to market in the towns, the friars could reach an audience beyond the urban residents themselves. Friaries were therefore mostly founded in towns, and by the mid-thirteenth century there were friaries in most major cities.

SAINT FRANCIS OF ASSISI. Berto di Giovanni (Italian), ca. 1500–1510. Here, the friar holds a book and a cross-staff and wears the brown habit of the Franciscan order. His bare feet testify to his ideal of austerity, poverty, and piousness.

In Paris, both the Dominican and Franciscan friaries were located on the left bank, as were several lesser mendicant orders. Since the friars' reason for existence was to provide spiritual guidance for the lay population, education of their own membership was a high priority. Within a few years of their arrival in Paris, the friars were playing a leading role in the life of the university. Many of the principal intellectual figures of medieval Europe were friars, quite a few of them associated with Paris; among these were the theologian Thomas Aquinas and the scientist Roger Bacon.

The Periphery: The City and Beyond

City Defenses

The perimeter of Paris was defined by the walls that symbolized the city's political identity. In the late twelfth century, King Phillip Augustus had undertaken a massive project to surround the settlements on both banks with a substantial stone wall. Its construction was similar to the outer wall of a castle. The walls were six to ten feet thick and over thirty feet tall, with battlements and a walkway around the top, and mural towers spaced at 200-foot intervals, within arrow shot of one another. Principal access was through a half-dozen gatehouses on each bank, with additional posterns for the convenience of local pedestrian traffic. The right bank wall was built at the expense of the citizenry of Paris, but on the left bank, which was less developed, the cost was covered by the king himself. From surviving royal accounts we know that the left bank wall was nearly a mile and a half long and cost 50 *sous* per yard of length, and that the gates cost 120 *livres* each; its total cost was

over 7000 *livres*. Additional security for Paris was provided by the castle known as the Louvre, constructed in about 1200 just outside the southwest corner of the right bank wall. There were also smaller fortifications within the walls, including the royal palace, the Grand Châtelet, and the Petit-Châtelet. Castles were a common feature of large medieval towns, serving at once to protect this valuable property on the lord's behalf and as a symbolic reminder of the lord's authority.

As in a castle, the gates and mural towers of Paris probably served as stations for the town watch. The

PRESENT-DAY PHOTOGRAPH OF A SEGMENT OF THE CURTAIN WALL BUILT AROUND PARIS *by King Phillip Augustus near the end of the twelfth century.*

watch was drawn from the tradesmen of Paris, although some trades had the right to send their employees in place of the householder himself, and if Pierre le Normant served as a juror of the craft, he would have been exempted from this service. Each night at curfew (6 P.M. in winter, 7 P.M. in summer), the tradesmen assigned to duty were required to make their way to the Châtelet and present themselves to the royal officers in charge of the watch. At dawn the next morning, a horn was sounded to signal the end of the watch. Between curfew and sunrise, town gates were kept shut. An English law of the period mandated a guard of four to twelve men at each gate, and similar arrangements probably were in place at Paris. During the night the inhabitants of the town were expected to remain indoors; if found on the streets, they were stopped by the watch, who were required to ensure that no one went out without legitimate business. The defenses of Paris were particularly magnificent for their age, reflecting the importance of the city and its feudal overlord. Lesser towns were slower to build stone walls. Earthen ramparts and wooden pallisades were still in use in many places during the twelfth century, although by the late thirteenth century stone walls had become common for fortified towns. Walls were principally a feature of larger towns, since small market towns lacked the resources for such major works projects.

In times of war, a wall helped protect the city, its inhabitants, and its resources. In times of peace, a wall defined the city as a space distinct from the surrounding countryside, and it controlled traffic in and out, allowing the authorities to restrict access to the city, and facilitating the collection of import and export duties. Duties were levied at the gate on goods brought into the city: the rates at Paris depended on the merchandise, but were typically 2 to 4 *deniers* for a wagonload, 1 to 2 *deniers* for a cartload, and ½ to 1 *denier* for a horseload.

The Suburbs and *Banlieue*

In those parts of Paris that were further from the Cité, especially on the left bank and in neighborhoods more remote from the main thoroughfares, urban development was less intense. Even in the latter part of the thirteenth century there was still some agriculture within the city walls, mostly vineyards and vegetable gardens, but apparently some meadows as well. The population of Paris in the late thirteenth century included a few vinedressers, gardeners, mowers, and drovers. Outside the walls, urban development fell off sharply. This pattern of settlement, a fairly compact urban area in close contact with agricultural land, was typical of the medieval town. Suburban settlement in the modem sense did not exist, and a medieval town dweller was no more than a few minutes' walk from the farmer's fields.

Outside the walls there were also a few clusters of urban development, most of them grouped around religious establishments that had been founded outside the city in earlier centuries, such as St.-Germain-des-Prés, St.-Victor, St.-Martin-des-Champs, St.-Pol, and St.-Honoré. These medieval suburbs were essentially small towns of their own, with a lively and diverse economic life. As Paris grew, they were drawn into its orbit while retaining their independent economic and political identities. Even further beyond the walls were other villages and small urban communities that fell within the city's sphere of influence—there were about 120 such communities that were to some degree under the jurisdiction of Paris in the late thirteenth century. This zone of influence, called the *banlieue*, was common in medieval cities and generally covered a radius of several miles. The *banlieue* ensured that the town had control over its short-term food supplies, and Pierre Le Normant was required to share his privileges with bakers of the *banlieue*, although he jealously guarded them against encroachments from outside:

> It happened in the time of the late king . . . that the bakers of Corbeil and elsewhere rented granaries in the Grève and elsewhere to sell their bread during the week, which they may not and must not do. The bakers of Paris complained to the king . . . and pointed out to him the great profit that the king had from the bakers, paying the taxes that the bakers are required to pay to the king, and the king confirmed the decree of his grandfather, and commanded that no baker living outside of the *banlieue* should carry bread or have it carried for sale in Paris, except on Saturdays . . . unless there was

adverse weather, that is a great frost or flooding, on account of which the bakers of Paris were unable to feed the city of Paris.[23]

The medieval city was a dynamic environment that offered enormous possibilities to those with the enterprise and good fortune to profit from urban opportunities, but it was always precariously perched at the very limit of the infrastructure by which it was sustained.

8

THE MEDIEVAL WORLD

I N THE PRECEDING CHAPTERS WE HAVE LOOKED AT THE LIVES OF specific types of medieval communities. This chapter will step both away and inward: it will pull back from the local setting to consider how medieval people interacted with their world at large, and also move into the inner life of the individual to see something of how medieval people thought and felt.

THE OUTER WORLD

Geography and the Natural World

The medieval experience of the exterior world took place from a perspective profoundly different from that available to people today. Both physically and conceptually, medieval people saw their world from ground level. Elevated vantage points were rare. The view from the top of the keep at Dover Castle or from the summit of the towers of Notre-Dame was as high above the ground as an individual might get, and even that experience was limited to a few people. Mountaintops provided broad panoramas, but the point of view was still land based. While today we can see the world from above and interpret its shape on a grid of lines running north to south and east to west, medieval people saw their world from the surface, and related places to each other by landmarks, relative directions, and times of travel.

WORLD MAP FROM A PSALTER, *created 1265. Jesus is featured above the map, giving a blessing with his right hand. Christian maps from the Middle Ages had the East, rather than North, situated on top.*

This ground-level view of the world was reflected in medieval cartography. Maps were extremely rare, and used almost exclusively by scholars. Few medieval maps attempted to represent actual geography; they were usually schematic diagrams that interpreted the physical earth as a manifestation of divine order. The typical medieval representation of the earth was as a disk, with east at the top and Jerusalem in the center, the upper half representing Asia, the bottom left corner Europe, and the bottom right Africa. Scholars did not actually believe that Europe looked like a quarter circle, nor did they even think the world was flat as represented on the map. The map was merely a diagram that helped organize the scholar's understanding of the world.

For medieval people, the physical world was larger, more mysterious, and more dangerous than it is today. Inhabited areas might be highly developed, but at their margins lay expanses of wasteland—forests, marshes, moors—that were lonely, dark, and pathless. These were places of real danger, far from the possibility of human assistance. Outlaws and robbers often made their abodes in such places, and the popular imagination also peopled them with mysterious creatures not of human kind—giants, dragons, and fairy folk—much as today we fill the vast and mysterious void of space with extraterrestrials.

The forces of nature were difficult to counteract and almost impossible to explain. Little could be done in the face of major floods or fires. Even ordinary fluctuations of weather meant the difference between prosperity and famine. Given the chaos with which medieval people felt themselves surrounded, it is hardly surprising that they created what order they could through astrology, Galenic medicine, and highly schematized maps. Even if these systems for understanding the world were of limited use in acquiring real control over the elements, they at least offered people a comforting sense of order and empowerment.

Travel

The world was significantly larger in an age when limited technology and infrastructure made travel a laborious and sometimes dangerous undertaking. Most people were obliged to journey on foot, and such travel was slow under the

TRAVELERS ON THE ROAD TO SEVILLE, SPAIN. *Illustration by Georg Hoefnagel (Dutch), ca. 1612.*

best conditions. A traveler on foot might cover two miles in an hour in the winter and three in the summer; a typical day's journey might be about twenty miles. The only alternative on land was animal transport. A rider traveled on a horse or donkey, which were also used as pack animals. Riding was the fastest mode of transport available; a rider could easily travel thirty or thirty-five miles in a day, and if he was in a hurry he could cover twice as much. Pack animals traveled at similar speeds and were particularly useful on mountain roads and in rough terrain where wheeled vehicles could not pass. The well-to-do normally traveled on horseback, riding their own horses or a hired mount. A peasant householder might own a horse or donkey, but even if it could be spared from farm labor, it probably was needed to carry goods rather than a rider.

Carts and wagons, usually pulled by horses or oxen, were more restricted by the condition of the roads, but under good conditions they were more efficient than pack animals. A four-wheeled wagon with a pair of horses could haul as much as 1,300 pounds about twenty-five miles a day. Like horses, carts and wagons could be hired, usually with a driver to operate them; the cost in the late thirteenth century was about 4d. a day. Aristocratic ladies sometimes traveled in covered wagons; the experience must have been rough, as these wagons do not appear to have had much in the way of a suspension system. Large trains with substantial numbers of carts, such as an army or an aristocratic household with its possessions, tended to move slowly, and might cover only ten to twelve miles in a day.

The rate of travel depended on the nature and condition of the roads. Many Roman roads were still in use, but they had decayed from centuries of inadequate maintenance, and their stone foundations were covered by a thick layer of soil. More recent roads were not as well constructed, and many routes were served by little more than dirt tracks. In adverse weather, roads became muddy and difficult to pass. Riders in particular lost their advantage of speed when the road was poor or when they left the road for rougher country.

Routes of travel were highly sensitive to natural topography. Rivers were a major obstacle, and roads were sited to take advantage of such crossings as were available. Bridges were comparatively rare, since even a wooden bridge was expensive to build and maintain. Most bridges were built near major settlements having the means to sustain them. Where bridges were lacking, the river might be forded at a shallow point. This could be risky, since sometimes the current proved too strong, and men, beasts, and goods were lost in the water. In some places, a ferry carried passengers for a fee. Mountains also impeded traffic, obliging travelers to wind their way laboriously up and down each side. Travel routes tended to follow the contours of the land, running along river valleys rather than across them; a village might be in closer contact with a town some distance away in the same valley than with one closer to hand but on the other side of a substantial river or mountain ridge.

The challenges of travel were heightened by the danger of attack. Many roads passed through thinly populated areas that served as havens for highwaymen. For safety, it was generally considered prudent for travelers to find companions for the journey; many people traveled in the company of relative strangers for the sake of mutual protection, although there was always some risk in taking up with unknown company. Those who could afford it hired armed escorts to ensure their security. In some cases, security was provided by the feudal lords through whose territory the roads passed, since it was in their interest to encourage commerce and travel through their lands. Some lords even recompensed merchants for losses sustained at the hands of highwaymen. To reduce the risk of attack, the sides of the road might be cleared of trees and brush, depriving highwaymen of convenient hiding places: an English law of 1285 required that the roads between market towns be cleared for 200 feet on either side, although the law was probably not effectively enforced.

Commercial lodgings for travelers were relatively rare. A town might have inns, but an ordinary village would have none. A fully equipped monastery had facilities for visitors where a traveler could expect a bed and a meal before setting on his way again. A traveling aristocrat and his party might seek lodgings with a fellow aristocrat. Otherwise, the traveler might be left to make private arrangements with some household on the way, or seek shelter under a hedgerow or in some unsupervised building.

Water Routes

Travel by water was a less common experience than travel by land. Swimming was an unusual skill, and travelers generally chose land routes when they were available. Yet some journeys could not be made safely or quickly by land, and for the transportation of large quantities of goods, boats were often the fastest, cheapest, and most reliable option. A boat could carry far more cargo than a cart, it could travel in the rain when dirt roads became little more than mud baths, and with favorable winds and currents it could be self-propelling. The rivers of medieval Europe were busy highways, constantly plied by small merchant boats; when winds and currents were adverse, the boats were towed by draft animals on the shore. A boat might cover eighty miles in a day traveling downstream.

TRISTAN AND ISOLDE TRAVELING BY BOAT. *Illumination from an English manuscript, ca. 1450–1500.*

Medieval seagoing vessels were tiny by modern standards. A typical merchant vessel might have a displacement of 100 tons, measuring some sixty feet from stem to stern and twenty feet across, roughly comparable to a modern tugboat. Many were even smaller, although some of the largest Mediterranean ships reached 800 tons. Most had square-rigged sails, limiting their ability to sail toward the wind, but many were also equipped with oars. The rate of travel depended on the weather, but with favorable winds a ship at sea might sail 100 miles in a day. The crossing from England to the west coast of France might take four days, and the journey from Venice to Jaffa (the port that served Jerusalem) lasted a month. During this time most travelers lived in fairly cramped conditions on the lower decks of the ship. Regulations governing the carrying of pilgrims from Marseilles in 1253 stipulated that ordinary passengers were to be allotted a space of a mere twenty-five by sixty-five inches. Passage to the Holy Land might cost 60 *sous* for a cabin in the relative comfort of the fore- and sterncastles, 40 *sous* between decks, 35 *sous* on the lower deck, or 25 *sous* in the hold. Passengers had only such food as could be preserved on board. Salt meat was a common fare, as were biscuit, cheese, beans, lentils, and dried fruit. The journey did carry some risk. Piracy was endemic on the seas, particularly in the Mediterranean where Christians and Muslims preyed freely on one another's shipping, enslaving any whom they took captive. Even without human intervention, heavy weather could sink the ship.

Purposes of Travel

Given the challenges of travel in the Middle Ages, we might expect that people avoided it if at all possible. In fact, although few medieval people spent much of their time on the road, most traveled at some point in their lives, and for many, travel was a recurring feature of ordinary existence. The reasons were many. For villagers, the journey to the nearest market town was a frequent experience; they also made annual journeys to nearby fairs. Laborers traveled in search of work, and some people, like merchants, carters, and sailors, made their living by travel. The aristocratic household traveled among its various manors to look after their administration and to spread the burden of supporting the household. Aristocrats were also called upon to travel in discharge of their military service and in their role as political leaders. The clergy also traveled, whether in search of education or professional advancement, or to discharge business for the church or a lay patron.

Not all travel was for material or pragmatic purposes. The custom of pilgrimage was a distinctive element in medieval wayfaring life, reaching its peak in the High and late Middle Ages. Although only a small portion of the population actually went on pilgrimage, their experiences had a significant impact on medieval culture. Many pilgrimages were local in character, as travelers visited nearby religious establishments that held sacred relics, many of which were reputed to possess miraculous properties. More ambitious pilgrims undertook expeditions to visit a major holy site, such as Rome, Jerusalem, or Santiago de Compostela in northwestern Spain. In many ways, pilgrimage in the Middle Ages played a role not unlike that of tourism today. It was an expression of curiosity and wanderlust, an attempt at self-improvement, an expression of a person's evaluation of their own social status. Pilgrims even bought souvenirs at the shrines they visited. Travelers to the shrine of Saint Thomas à Becket at Canterbury in thirteenth-century England could purchase tiny tin bottles containing holy water mixed with a fragment of the saint's blood. Visitors to other shrines brought back cheap cast badges of tin bearing images symbolic of the shrine: a cockleshell for Santiago de Compostela, a palm leaf for Jerusalem, keys for Rome.

Last, we should remember that in an age before electricity was harnessed, all long-distance communication required travel. We have already seen in the life of Eleanor de Montfort at Dover that the aristocratic household relied heavily on couriers. Those who could not hire a messenger might have to wait until a traveler could be found who was headed for the right destination and was willing to carry the message. In any case, the speed of communication was limited by the speed of the messenger. The practical difficulties involved in communication made information haphazard and unreliable, and we might reasonably imagine people in the medieval world living in a perpetual "fog of war" in which the course of current events was never entirely clear. Part of the reason that people were willing to accommodate unknown travelers in their homes is doubtless because such outsiders satisfied some of their hunger for news of the wider world, and according to one English proverb of the twelfth century, "From mill and from market, from smithy and from nunnery are tidings brought."[1]

TIME

Time, like space, was perceived from within rather than from without. Medieval people navigated through time by a complex system of signposts based on natural cycles, religious rituals, and cultural traditions. The seven-day week was

"JUNE" ILLUMINATION FROM A BOOK OF HOURS.
*Jean Bourdichon (French), ca. 1489. A peasant,
lightly dressed for the summer heat, carries a scythe
for haymaking and a cask of water. At the top of the
illustration, the name of the month is decorated with
flourishes, with the feast days written below. The
astrological sign of Cancer appears in the sky.*

a part of ordinary life, since Sundays, and in many cases Saturday afternoons, were occasions of leisure. The week also determined the schedule of local markets and fasting days (Wednesdays, Fridays, and Saturdays, on which the church forbade people to eat meat). The twelve-month Roman calendar that we use today was less important to medieval people. Laypeople tended to organize their year around the cycle of religious holy days—days that served as occasions for secular merrymaking as well as religious observations. The countess of Leicester's daily accounts from Dover fixes dates as "the Monday before the feast of St. Margaret" and "the eve of St. Botolph." Manor courts in Cuxham were held "on the next Friday after the Conversion of St. Paul" or "on Wednesday the morrow of St. Augustine." Even in the more modern urban environment of Paris, the bakers paid their taxes to the king at Christmas, Easter, St. John's Day, and Martinmas. The repertoire and sometimes the actual dates of holy days varied from place to place, but the following calendar gives a general idea of the annual cycle. Major feasts, such as would be observed as a holiday and require a fast on the previous day, are indicated in boldface.

JANUARY

1	**The Circumcision of Christ**
6	**Epiphany (Twelfth Day)**
13	Sts. Hilary and Remigius
15	St. Maurus
16	St. Marcellus
20	Sts. Sebastian and Fabian
21	St. Agnes
22	St. Vincent
25	The Conversion of St. Paul

FEBRUARY

1	St. Bridget
2	**The Purification (Candlemas)**
3	St. Blase
5	St. Agatha
10	St. Scholastica
14	St. Valentine
16	St. Juliana
22	St. Peter's Chair
24	**St. Matthias the Apostle**

Movable Feasts

Shrove Tuesday: The day before Ash Wednesday.

Ash Wednesday: The Wednesday before the sixth Sunday before Easter. This day marked the beginning of Lent, a period of penitence observed by abstinence from meat.

MARCH

1	St. David
2	St. Chad
7	Sts. Perpetua and Felicity
12	St. Gregory
20	St. Cuthbert
21	St. Benedict
25	**The Annunciation**

APRIL

4	St. Ambrose
14	Sts. Tiburcius and Valerian
19	St. Alphege
23	St. George
25	**St. Mark the Evangelist**
26	St. Cletus
28	St. Vitalis
30	St. Erkenwald

Movable Feasts

Maundy Thursday: The Thursday before Easter.

Good Friday: The Friday before Easter.

Easter: The first Sunday after the first full moon on or after March 21; if the full moon was on a Sunday, Easter was the next Sunday. Lent ended at Easter. The days after Easter were often observed as holidays as well.

MAY

1	**Sts. Phillip and James**
3	**The Discovery of the Cross (Holy Rood Day)**
6	St. John at the Lateran Gate

19	St. Dunstan
25	St. Urban
26	St. Augustine
31	St. Petronilla

Movable Feasts

Rogation Sunday: Five weeks after Easter.

Ascension: The Thursday after Rogation Sunday.

Pentecost (Whitsun): Ten days after Ascension. There was often a holiday for several days after Pentecost.

Trinity Sunday: One week after Pentecost.

JUNE

1	St. Nichomedus
11	St. Barnabas the Apostle
15	Sts. Vitus and Modestus
17	St. Botolph
18	Sts. Mark and Marcellus
19	Sts. Gervase and Protase
22	St. Alban
24	**St. John the Baptist (Midsummer)**
29	**The Death of Peter and Paul the Apostles**
30	**The Commemoration of Paul the Apostle**

JULY

15	St. Swithun
17	St. Kenelm
20	St. Margaret
22	**St. Mary Magdalene**
23	St. Apollinarius

25	**Sts. James the Greater and Christopher**
26	St. Anne
31	St. Germanus

AUGUST

1	**St. Peter in Chains ("St. Peter ad Vincula" or Lammas)**
5	St. Oswald of Northumbria
10	**St. Lawrence**
15	**The Assumption of the Virgin**
24	**St. Bartholomew**
28	St. Augustine of Hippo
29	The Beheading of St. John the Baptist

SEPTEMBER

1	St. Giles
8	The Nativity of the Virgin
14	The Exaltation of the Cross
21	**St. Matthew**
22	St. Maurice
29	**St. Michael (Michaelmas)**

OCTOBER

1	Sts. Germanus and Remigius
2	St. Leger
9	St. Denis
14	St. Calixtus
18	St. Luke
21	The 11,000 Virgins
24	St. Magloire
25	Sts. Crispin and Crispianus

28	Sts. Simon and Jude
31	St. Quentin

NOVEMBER

1	**All Saints** (Hallowmas)
2	All Souls
6	St. Leonard
11	**St. Martin of Tours** (Martinmas)
13	St. Brice
20	St. Edmund
22	St. Cecilia
23	St. Clement
25	St. Katherine
30	**St. Andrew**

DECEMBER

6	**St. Nicholas**
7	St. Ambrose
8	The Conception of the Virgin
13	St. Lucy
21	St. Thomas the Apostle
25	**The Nativity of Christ (Christmas)**
26	**St. Stephen**
27	**St. John the Evangelist**
28	**The Holy Innocents (Childermas)**
29	St. Thomas of Canterbury
31	St. Silvester

The eve, vigil, or night of a feast was the day before; the morrow or second day was the day after, the third day was two days after, and so on.

The reckoning of years was also less orderly. The custom of numbering years from the birth of Christ was known, but in secular society, years were as likely numbered in relation to the local secular authority. Cuxham accounts are dated "in the seventh year of the reign of King Edward" or "in the tenth year of Edward," and even the accounts of the countess of Leicester number the years by the reign of the king against whom she is at war. January 1 was sometimes reckoned as the first day of the new year, but customs varied. In England until the twelfth century, the year was usually reckoned to begin at Christmas, but from the latter part of the century it became more common to begin the year on March 25, the feast of the Annunciation. At about the same time, the French shifted from reckoning the new year at Christmas to beginning it at Easter.

Medieval reckoning of the time of day was hampered by technological factors as well as by general cultural attitudes. Clocks began to appear in the thirteenth century, but they were extremely rare, and even in the fourteenth century they were still found only in the largest cities. The only other accurate means of telling time was a sundial, astrolabe, or similar astronomical device. For most people, hours and minutes were irrelevant. Time was reckoned instead by church bells ringing the canonical hours of the Divine Office. The lamp makers of Paris were required to stop work on Saturday "at the first strike of Vespers sounded at St.-Merry," and the carpenters had to stop "once None is sounded on the great bell of Notre-Dame." Otherwise, the markers of time were those of nature: cockcrow, dawn, morning, midday, afternoon, evening, dusk. This mode of reckoning time meant that the day had a substantially different shape from season to season, depending on the local hours of daylight at the time of year. It also meant that every locality was its own time zone: midday came to Cluny before it reached Paris, and to Dover before it came to Cuxham. Ordinary medieval people rarely had occasion to measure hours, minutes, or seconds, but when necessary, they might describe a period as "the time it takes to walk a mile," or "the time it takes to recite ten Pater-Nosters."

The Inner World

Literacy

The medieval approach to space and time was in part a reflection of the limited role of the written word. Literacy was highly restricted in the Middle Ages. It has been estimated that in 1500, 90 percent of men and 99 percent of women were still unlettered, and the figure must have been significantly higher in earlier centuries. Even those who belonged to the tiny literate minority operated within an overwhelmingly oral world, and when writing was used, it was commonly considered a secondary act. A legal document served as a permanent record of an oral transaction, and a written epic poem was a by-product of an art form that was primarily oral.

Medieval Minds

The relatively small scope for the written word in medieval society accounts for some of the characteristic features of medieval culture. In the oral world of the Middle Ages, things, not concepts, were the points of reference. Abstractions are not inherently memorable; they thrive principally in a literate culture where they can be committed to the memory of the page. The culture of the medieval world focused instead on what could be seen, felt, heard, and therefore remembered without the aid of the written word. People, objects, places, and memorable events served as the fixed points in the medieval universe, and in this sense everything in the medieval world was relative. Concrete things and events did not exist in an absolute grid of reference, but were themselves the points of reference in a world organized as a network of relationships.

This emphasis on the concrete pervaded medieval society. A villager's community was not so much an abstract political entity as a network of relationships connecting visible people and places: he was born into the social network of the family, itself embodied not only in people but in the physical house and landholding; he was subject to the personal authority of the manor lord, who was himself identified with the visible establishment of the manor house; he belonged to a parish represented by the parish church and priest. The

THE HAY HARVEST. Jörg Breu the Elder (German), ca. 1521. Pen and black ink with gray wash on paper. Community—and working together—was a vital part of medieval village life.

villager's relationships to these other points in the social network were themselves expressed in physical form. Cuxham's villeins handed over a couple of loaves of bread and a few hens to the manor lord at Christmas, a tax so trifling that it can best be understood as a symbol of the relationship rather than as a serious economic transaction. The peasant reckoned time not on a grid of months and days, but as a circuit marked by holy days as irregular mileposts. Similar social modes governed life within the aristocracy, and even in a monastery, with its high level of literacy, or in the town, with its more fluid social arrangements, concrete places and symbolic ceremonies were still used to structure the social world.

This reliance on a network of relationships among concrete points of reference made the world of medieval people at once simpler and more complex than our own. On the one hand, they were not subject to the myriad divisions and distinctions that carve up modern lives. People's private and public identities were generally one: a tradesman's house was also his workshop, a villager's cottage was integral to the landholding that supported him, an aristocrat ate and worked in the great hall of his castle or manor house. The religious community of the parish was often indistinguishable from the economic community of the village and the legal community of the manor. Medieval culture was pervaded by a powerful principle of unity that hearkened back in many ways to an earlier stage in the evolution of human society.

On the other hand, we should not think of medieval people as simple folk who led uncomplicated lives. The peasant householder's comprehensive and integrated mode of farming required a diverse knowledge of every aspect of agriculture and husbandry, and his wife was expected to have mastered a wide range of skills including dairying, gardening, and herbal lore. Their relationship to the manor lord was a complex exchange of mutual rights and responsibilities that had evolved over centuries. They needed to keep track of an intricate calendrical system without the advantage of a written calendar, and they used an equally bewildering array of weights and measures. The legal system in which they were regular participants was a variegated and often confused patchwork of traditional customs and jurisdictions. Similar complexities applied to the lives of people in other walks of life.

The emphasis on the concrete in the medieval world, and the attendant sense of holism, are doubtless a large part of what attracts us to the period. Underneath our veneer of literacy, we are still a tribal species, and although we have remade our world with documents, institutions, and principles, we still have a deep-seated craving for rituals, relationships, and symbols. We deliberately keep our working and personal lives apart, yet the division this creates within us will probably never be entirely comfortable. In the lives of medieval people we see a unity that we miss in our own. Meanwhile, the images and relationships that structured medieval life are deeply imbedded in the culture we have inherited from the Middle Ages, and continue to resonate even when the world that gave them their meaning can only be seen dimly across the centuries.

ACKNOWLEDGMENTS

I would like to express my thanks to David Hoomstra for his illustrations of Cuxham, Dover, and Cluny; to Patrick Florance for his maps of Cuxham, Dover, and the Juiverie; to Robert MacPherson for his insights on mail; to Paula Marcoux for her perspectives on food preservation; and to Charles and Kate Hadfield for their assistance during my foray to Dover and Cuxham.

ENDNOTES

Abbreviations

EETS—Early English Texts Society

EHR—*English Historical Review*

HMSO—His/Her Majesty's Stationary Office

Introduction

1. Cited in J. R. Hale, *The Evolution of British Historiography* (Cleveland: World Publishing Co., 1964), 36.

Chapter 1

1. F. J. Furnivall, ed., *Hali Meidenhad*, EETS original series 18 (London: EETS, 1922), 52.

2. G.-B. Depping, ed., *Réglemens sur les arts et métiers de Paris rédigés au 13e siècle et connus sous le nom du Livre des métiers d'Étienne Boileau* (Paris: Crapelet, 1837), 179.

Chapter 2

1. Depping, *Réglemens*, 20, 31, 37, 41, 43.

2. *Maternal Mortality: A Global Factbook* (Geneva: World Health Organization, 1991).

3. Josiah Cox Russell, *British Medieval Population* (Albuquerque: University of New Mexico Press, 1948), 180–81, 189.

4. Karl Michaelsson, *Le Livre de la taille de Paris l'an 1296*, Acta Universitatis Gothoborgensis 64:4 (Göteborg: University of Göteborg, 1958), 47.

5. Shulamith Shahar, *Childhood in the Middle Ages* (London and New York: Routledge, 1990), 63.

6. Shahar, *Childhood*, 85.

7. Gerald of Wales, *Giraldi Cambrensis Opera*, ed. J. S. Brewer (London: HMSO, 1861), 1.21.

8. Depping, *Reglemens*, 67, 93.

9. Ibid., 53, 127.

10. Ibid., 49.

11. Ibid., 58.

12. David Nicholas, *The Growth of the Medieval City from Late Antiquity to the Early Fourteenth Century* (London and New York: Longman, 1997), 212.

13. Jacques de Vitry, *The Exempla or Illustrative Stories from the* Sermones Vulgares *of Jacques de Vitry*, ed. Thomas Frederick Crane (London: Folklore Society, 1890), 112.

14. Pierre J. Payer, *Sex and the Penitentials: The Development of a Sexual Code 550–1150* (Toronto: University of Toronto Press, 1984).

15. F. J. Furnivall, ed., *Hali Meidenhad*, EETS original series 18 (London: EETS, 1922), 36.

16. G. G. Coulton, *Medieval Village, Manor, and Monastery* (Cambridge: Cambridge University Press, 1925), 99.

Chapter 3

1. N. J. G. Pounds, *The Medieval Castle in England and Wales* (Cambridge: Cambridge University Press, 1990), 195.

2. John Schofield and Alan Vince, *Medieval Towns: The Archaeology of Medieval Britain* (London: Leicester University Press, 1994), 103, 115.

3. Ibid, 106.

4. Depping, *Réglemens*, 59, 97–98.

5. James Craigie Robertson, ed., *Materials for the History of Thomas Becket* (London: HMSO, 1877), 3.20–21.

6. *Acta Sanctorum: Junii* (Paris and Rome: Victor Palme, 1867), 5.557.

7. Emilie Amt, *Women's Lives in Medieval Europe: A Sourcebook* (New York and London: Routledge, 1993), 101.

8. Barbara Hanawalt, *The Ties That Bound. Peasant Families in Medieval England* (New York and Oxford: Oxford University Press, 1986), 40; Maurice Beresford and John Hurst, *Wharram Percy: Deserted Medieval Village* (London: Batsford/ English Heritage, 1990), 44. On covering the fire with ashes, see: Udalric, "Antiquiores Consuetudines Cluniacensis Monasterii," in J.-P. Migne, ed. *Patrologia Latina 149* (Paris: Garnier, 1882), cols. 728, 729.

9. Udalric, "Consuetudines," col. 727.

10. Gerald of Wales, "Descriptio Kambriae," in James F. Dimock, ed., *Giraldi Cambrensis Opera Omnia*, Rolls Series 21:6 (London: HMSO, 1868), 1.11.

11. Urban Tigner Holmes, *Daily Living in the Twelfth Century, Based on the Observations of Alexander Neckham in London and Paris* (Madison, WI: University of Wisconsin Press, 1952), 165.

12. Schofield and Vince, *Medieval Towns,* 197, 198, 200. On medieval medicine, see also:

Beck, R. Theodore, *The Cutting Edge: Early History of the Surgeons of London* (London: Lund Humphries, 1974).

Gordon, Benjamin Lee, *Medieval and Renaissance Medicine* (New York: Philosophical Library, 1959).

Hunt, Tony, *Popular Medicine in Thirteenth-Century England: Introduction and Texts* (Cambridge: D. S. Brewer, 1990).

Rubin, Stanley, *Medieval English Medicine* (New York: Barnes and Noble, 1974).

Siraisi, Nancy A., *Medieval and Early Renaissance Medicine: An Introduction to Knowledge and Practice* (Chicago: University of Chicago Press, 1990).

Talbot, C. H., *Medicine* in *Medieval England* (London: Oldbourne, 1967). 64

13. On medieval money, see:

d'Avenel, Le Vicomte G., *Histoire économique de la propriété, des salaires, des denrées, et de tous les prix en général depuis l'an 1200 jusqu'en l'an 1800,* 2d ed., 5 vols. (Paris: Ernest Leroux, 1913).

Rogers, James E. Thorold, *A History of Agriculture and Prices in England* (Oxford: Clarendon Press, 1882).

Spufford, Peter, *Money and Its Use in Medieval Europe* (Cambridge: Cambridge University Press, 1988).

Spufford, Peter, Wendy Wilkinson, and Sarah Tolley, *Handbook of Medieval Exchange,* Royal Historical Society Guides and Handbooks 13 (London: Royal Historical Society, 1986).

14. On weights and measures, see:

Hall, Hubert, and Frieda J. Nicholas, *Select Tracts and Table Books Relating to English Weights and Measures,* Camden Miscellany 15 (London: Camden Society, 1929).

Zupko, A., *A Dictionary of English Weights and Measures from Anglo-Saxon Times to the Nineteenth Century* (Madison: University of Wisconsin Press, 1968).

Chapter 4

1. Principal sources on Cuxham are:

Harvey, P. D. A., A *Medieval Oxfordshire Village: Cuxham 1240 to 1400* (Oxford: Oxford University Press, 1965).

———, *Manorial Records of Cuxham, Oxfordshire circa 1200–1349,* Oxfordshire Record Society 50 (London: HMSO, 1976).

Mowat, J. L. G., *Sixteen Old Maps of Properties in Oxfordshire* (Oxford: Clarendon Press, 1888).

After Cuxham came into the hands of Merton College in the late thirteenth century, the manor had an institution rather than an individual for its manor lord, but the general contours of the manorial structure remained in place.

2. Harvey, *Manorial Records*, 111.

3. Ibid., 110.

4. Ibid., 618.

5. Ibid., 111.

6. Ibid., 109–10.

7. Ibid., 111.

8. Ibid., 109.

9. Ibid., 612–13.

10. Ibid., 619.

11. Ibid., 607, 109.

12. *Husbandry,* in *Waiter of Henley's Husbandry,* ed. E. Lamond (London: Longman's, Green and Co., 1890), 75.

13. R. H. Hilton, *Economic Development of Some Leicestershire Estates in the Fourteenth and Fifteenth Centuries* (London: Oxford University Press, 1947), 145–46.

14. Harvey, *Manorial Records*, 713.

15. Jaqueline Fearn, *Thatch and Thatching,* Shire Album 16 (Princes Risborough, Bucks.: Shire Publications, 1995), 29.

16. *Rotuli Parliamentorum* (London: n.p., 1783), 1.243–65.

17. Nathaniel J. Hone, *The Manor and Manorial Records* (London: Methuen, 1906), 230.

18. Historical Manuscripts Commission, *Calendar of the Manuscripts of the Dean and Chapter of Wells* (London: HMSO, 1907–14), 1.332.

19. *Waiter of Henley's Husbandry*, 9.

20. Anne Iker-Gittleman, ed., *Garin Ie Loherenc* (Paris: Champion, 1996), 11. 8268–74.

21. Peter the Venerable, "Opera Omnia," in J.-P. Migne, ed., *Patrilogia Latina* 189 (Paris: Garnier, 1890), col. 146.

22. Edward Miller and John Hatcher, *Medieval England-Rural Society and Economic Change 1086–1348* (London and New York: Longman, 1978), 151.

23. Miller and Hatcher, *Medieval England, 101–2.*

24. George Caspar Homans, *English Villagers of the Thirteenth Century* (Cambridge, Mass.: Harvard University Press, 1942), 273, 448 n.25.

25. Miller and Hatcher, *Medieval England*, 104–5.

26. Harvey, *Manorial Records, 611.*

27. Ibid., 611.

28. Ibid., 618.

Chapter 5

1. Principal sources on Dover are:

   Brown, R. A., *Dover Castle* (London: English Heritage, 1974).

   Brown, R. Allen, H. M. Colvin, and A. J. Taylor, *The History of the King's Works*, vol. 2, *The Middle Ages* (London: HMSO, 1963).

   Coad, J. G., *The English Heritage Book of Dover Castle and the Defences of Dover* (London: Batsford, 1995).

   Colvin, H. M., ed., *Building Accounts of King Henry III* (Oxford: Clarendon Press, 1971).

   Cook, A. M., D. C. Maynard, S. E. Rigold, "Excavations at Dover Castle, Principally in the Inner Bailey," *Journal of the British Archaeological Association* 32 (1969), 54–104.

   Macpherson, E., and E. G. J. Amos, "The Norman Waterworks in the Keep of Dover Castle," *Archaeologia Cantiana* 43 (1931): 167–72.

   Turner, H. T., *Manners and Household Expenses of England in the Thirteenth and Fifteenth Centuries* (London: Roxburghe Club, 1841).

2. N. J. G. Pounds, *The Medieval Castle in England and Wales*, 205.

3. *Close Rolls of the Reign of Henry III. A.D. 1247–1251* (London: HMSO, 1922), 505; *Close Rolls of the Reign of Henry III. A.D. 1261–1264* (London: HMSO,1936), 151.

4. *Close Rolls of the Reign of Henry III. A.D. 1254–1256* (London: HMSO, 1931), *34; Calendar of the Liberate Rolls Preserved in the Public Records Office. Henry III. Vol. 4: 1251–1260* (London: HMSO, 1959), 245.

5. *Liberate Rolls 1251–1260*, 135; *Close Rolls 1247–1251*, 476.

6. *Calendar of the Liberate Rolls Preserved in the Public Records Office. Henry III, Vol. 3: A.D. 1245–1251* (London: HMSO, 1937), 119.

7. *Close Rolls 1247–1251*, 8.

8. On the costs and schedule of construction at Dover, see: R. Allen Brown, "Royal Castle-Building in England, 1154–1216," *EHR* 70 (1955): 390, 393, 394. Brown, Colvin, and Taylor, *The History of the King's Works*, 75, 630, 632. For comparative costs and durations, see: Pounds, *The Medieval Castle,* 20, 102, 149, 176; John R. Kenyon, *Medieval Fortifications* (Leicester and London: Leicester University Press, 1990), 39. On maintenance and operating costs, see: Pounds, *The Medieval Castle,* 122–23, 139.

9. *Calendar of the Liberate Rolls Preserved in the Public Records Office. Henry III, Vol. 1: 1226–1240* (London: HMSO, 1916), 217.

10. *Liberate Rolls 1226–1240*, 217.

11. Francisque Michel, ed., *Histoire des Ducs de Normandie et des Rois d'Angleterre* (Paris: J. Renouard, 1840), 177–78.

12. *Calendar of the Liberate Rolls Preserved in the Public Records Office. Henry III, Vol. 2: 1240–1245* (London: HMSO, 1930), 258.

13. *Close Rolls of the Reign of Henry III. A.D. 1242–1247* (London: HMSO, 1916), 219; *Liberate Rolls 1251–1260*, 255; *Calendar of the Patent Rolls Preserved in the Public Record Office. Henry III, Vol. 5: A.D. 1258–1266* (London: HMSO, 1910), 319.

14. *Patent Rolls 1258–1266*, 168.

15. Colvin, *Building Accounts*, 49.

16. *Liberate Rolls 1251–1260*, 240.

17. *Calendar of the Patent Rolls Preserved in the Public Record Office. Henry III, Vol. 4: A.D. 1247–1258* (London: HMSO, 1908), 399.

18. *Close Rolls of the Reign of Henry III. A.D. 1231–1234* (London: HMSO, 1905), 105; *Close Rolls 1254–1256*, 272; *Close Rolls 1261–1264*, 52; *Calendar of the Liberate Rolls Preserved in the Public Records Office. Henry III, Vol. 5: 1260–1267* (London: 138 HMSO, 1961), 188; *Patent Rolls 1258–1266*, 63; *Liberate Rolls 1251–1260*, 323, 324, 440, 446; *Liberate Rolls 1260–1267*, 188.

19. *Liberate Rolls 1226–1240*, 477.

20. *Liberate Rolls 1226–1240*, 456, 477.

21. *Close Rolls of the Reign of Henry III. A.D. 1251–1253* (London: HMSO, 1927), 188. For accounts of the services owed to Dover, see Hubert Hall, ed., *Red Book of the Exchequer*, Rolls Series 99 (London: HMSO, 1896), 615–18, 706–12, 717–23; J. H. Round, "Castle Guard," *Archaeological Journal* 59 (1902): 144-59; F. W. Hardman, "Castleguard Service of Dover Castle, " *Archaeologia Cantiana* 49 (1938): 96–107.

22. A. Ballard, "Castle Guard and Barons' Houses," *EHR* 25 (1910): 713–14.

23. *Liberate Rolls 1226–1240*, 468; *Liberate Rolls 1240–1245*, 99, 129; *Liberate Rolls 1251–1260*, 493; *Close Rolls of the Reign of Henry III. A.D. 1259–1261* (London: HMSO, 1934), 441; *Close Rolls of the Reign of Henry III. A.D. 1256–1259* (London: HMSO, 1932), 354.

24. *Liberate Rolls 1260–1267*, 105.

25. *Patent Rolls 1247–1258*, 430.

26. *Liberate Rolls 1260–1267*, 106.

27. *Close Rolls of the Reign of Henry III. A.D. 1234–1237* (London: HMSO, 1908), 424.

28. *Close Rolls of the Reign of Henry III. A.D. 1237–1242* (London: HMSO, 1911), 456.

29. P. W. Hammond, *Food and Feast in Medieval England* (Stroud, Gloucestershire: Sutton, 1993), 95.

30. Mary Bateson, *Medieval England* (New York: Putnam's; London: Unwin, 1904), 314.

31. *Liberate Rolls 1260–1267*, 218.

32. *Liberate Rolls 1260–1267*, 53.

33. On the chapel staff, see: *Liberate Rolls 1226-1240*, 391; *Liberate Rolls 1240–1245*, 129, 146, 173; *Liberate Rolls 1245–1251*, 33,54, 122–23,112, 162, 311; *Liberate Rolls 1260–1267*, 84; *Patent Rolls 1247–1258*, 502; *Close Rolls 1259–1261*, 205.

34. *Liberate Rolls 1251–1260*, 11.

35. *Patent Rolls 1247–1258*, 399; *Patent Rolls 1247–1258*, 418.

36. *Calendar of Fine Rolls Preserved in the Public Record Office, Vol. 1: Edward I. A.D. 1272–1307* (London: HMSO, 1911), 33, 107.

37. *Liberate Rolls 1226–1240*, 456.

38. Pounds, *The Medieval Castle*, 83.

39. Jaques de Vitry, *The Exempla*, 53 (#115).

40. *A Collection of Ordinances and Regulations for the Government of the Royal Household* (London: Society of Antiquaries, 1790), 37.

41. S. Glixelli, "Les *Contenances de Table*," *Romania* 47 (1921): 28. For an Italian example of the same period, see: Bonvesin da la Riva, "De quinquaginta curialitatibus ad mensam," in *Poeti del Duecento*, ed. Gianfranco Contini (Milan and Naples: Riccardo Ricciardi, 1960), 703–12.

Chapter 6

1. Principal sources on Cluny are:

   Bruel, F. L., *Cluni, 910–1910: Album historique et archéologique précédé d'une étude résumée et d'une notice des planches* (Mâcon: Protat, 1910).

   Conant, Kenneth, *Cluny: les églises et la maison du chef d'ordre* (Mâcon: Protat, 1968).

   Evans, Joan, *Monastic Life at Cluny 910–1157* (Oxford: Oxford University Press, 1931).

   Peter the Venerable, *Opera Omnia,* in J.-P. Migne, ed., *Patrilogia Latina 189* (Paris: Garnier, 1890), cols. 1–1072.

   Udalric [Ulrich], "Antiquiores Consuetudines Cluniacensis Monasterii," in J.-P. Migne, ed., *Patrilogia Latina* 149 (Paris: Garnier, 1882), cols. 634–778.

2. Peter the Venerable, "Opera," cols. 876-77.

3. Peter the Venerable, "Opera," col. 419.

4. Ordericus Vitalis, *The Ecclesiastical History of Ordericus Vitalis,* ed. Marjorie Chibnall (Oxford: Clarendon Press, 1973), 3.119.
5. Udalric, "Consuetudines," col. 709.
6. Gerald of Wales, *Giraldi Cambrensis Opera Omnia,* ed. J. S. Brewer. Rolls Series 21 (London: HMSO, 1861), 1.51.
7. Peter the Venerable, "Opera, " col. 1044.
8. Udalric, "Consuetudines," cols. 703–4, 711, 707.
9. Charles Homer Haskins, *Renaissance of the Twelfth Century* (Cambridge, MA: Harvard University Press, 1927), 83–84.
10. *The Rule of St. Benedict in Latin and English*, ed. and trans. Abbot Justin McCann (Westminster, MD.: Newman Press, 1952), 6.

Chapter 7

1. *Paris sous Phillippe-le-Bel d'après des documents originaux, et notamment d'après un manuscrit contenant le rôle de la taille imposée sur les habitants de Paris en 1292,* ed. H. Geraud (Paris: Crapelet, 1837), 143 col. a.

The other Parisian *taille* rolls are:

Michaelsson, Karl, *Le livre de la taille de Paris l'an 1296.* Acta Universitatis Gothoburgensis 64:4 (Göteborg: University of Göteborg, 1958).

———, *Le livre de la taille de Paris l'an 1297.* Acta Universitatis Gothoburgensis 67:3 (Göteborg: University of Göteborg, 1962).

———, *Le livre de la taille de Paris l'an de grace 1313.* Acta Universitatis Gothoburgensis 57:3 (Göteborg: Wettergren and Kerberg Forlag, 1951).

By 1313, neither Pierre nor any of his family were to be found in the Juiverie. Other key primary sources on Parisian life include:

Lespinasse, R. de, ed., *Les métiers et corporations de la ville de Paris* (Paris: Imprimerie Nationale, 1886—1897).

Réglemens sur les arts métiers de Paris rédigés au 13e siècle et connus sous le nom du Livre des métiers d'Étienne Boileau, ed. G.-B. Depping, (Paris: Crapelet, 1837).

Secondary sources include:

Berty, Adolphe, *Les trois ilots de la Cité compris entre les rues de la licorne, aux fèves, de la lanterne, du haut-moulin et de Glatigny.* Révue Archéologique, nouvelle serie 1 (Paris: Didier, 1860).

———, *Topographie historique du vieux Paris,* 6 vols. (Paris: Imprimerie Nationale, 1885–1897).

Boussard, Jacques, *Nouvelle histoire de Paris. De la fin du siège de 885–886 à la mort de Phillippe Auguste* (Paris: Hachette, 1976).

Cazelles, Raymond, *Nouvelle histoire de Paris. De la fin du règne de Phillippe Auguste à la mort de Charles V 1223–1380* (Paris: Hachette, 1972).

Franklin, Alfred, *Les rues et les cris de Paris au 13e siècle* (Paris: Willem et Daffis, 1874).

Friedman, Adrien, *Paris, ses rues, ses paroisses du moyen âge à la revolution* (Paris: Plon, 1959).

Geremek, Bronislaw. *Le salariat dans l'artisanat parisien aux 13e–15e siècles,* trans. Anna Posner and Christiane Klapisch-Zuber (Paris and the Hague: Mouton, 1968).

2. On the populations of medieval cities, see: David Nicholas, *The Growth of the Medieval City from Late Antiquity to the Early Fourteenth Century* (London and New York: Longman, 1997), 178.

   On the population of Paris, see: Anne Terroine, *Un bourgeois parisien du 13e siècle. Geoffroy de Saint-Laurent,* 1245?–1290, ed. Lucie Fossier (Paris: Centre National de la Recherche Scientifique Èditions, 1992), 103.

3. On crime in medieval Paris, see: Bronislaw Geremek, *The Margins of Society in Late Medieval Paris,* trans. Jean Birrell (Cambridge: Cambridge University Press, 1987).

4. Jacques Rossiaud, "The City-Dweller and Ufe in Cities and Towns," in *The Medieval World,* ed. Jacques Ie Goff, trans. Lydia G. Cochrane (London: Collins and Brown, 1990), 143.

5. Geraud, *Paris sous Phillippe-le-Bel,* 142–43.

6. Franklin, *Rues, 17.*

7. Ibid., 18.

8. Amaury d'Esneval, "Images de vie universitaire parisienne dans l'œuvre d'Ètienne Langton (vers 1150–1228)," *Bulletin de la Societé de L'Histoire de Paris et de l'Ile de France* 103-4 (1976–1977): 35.

9. On Notre-Dame, see Allan Temko, *Notre-Dame of Paris* (New York: Viking, 1955). David Macaulay's *Cathedral: The Story of Its Construction* (Boston: Houghton Mifflin, 1973), offers an excellent sense of the architecture and technology of the Gothic cathedral.

10. *Reglemens,*9–10.

11. Ibid., 177.

12. Ibid., 7–8.

13. Ibid., 12.

14. Cazelles, *Paris,* 87.

15. *Reglemens,* 116.

16. Franklin, *Rues,* 11.

17. *Reglemens*, 16.
18. Ibid., 139.
19. On fairs, see Ellen Wedemeyer Moore, "Medieval English Fairs: Evidence from Winchester and St. Ives," in *Pathways to Medieval Peasants,* ed. J. A. Raftis (Toronto: Pontifical Institute of Mediaeval Studies, 1981), 283–300.
20. On the Jews in Paris, see L. Rabinowitz, *Social Life of the Jews of Northern France in the Twelfth to Fourteenth Centuries,* 2d ed. (New York: Hermon Press, 1972).
21. Matthew Paris, *Chronica Majora,* ed. Henry Richards Luard. Rolls Series 57 (London: HMSO, 1876), 3.166–67.
22. On medieval universities, see: Rashdall, Hastings, *The Universities of Europe in the Middle Ages,* ed. F. M. Powicke and A. B. Emden, 3 vols. (Oxford: Clarendon Press, 1936).; Thorndike, Lynn, *University Records and Life in the Middle Ages* (New York: Octagon, 1971).
23. Depping, *Reglemens,* 15–16.

Chapter 8

1. James Morton, ed. and trans., *The Ancren Riwle. A Treatise on the Rules and Duties of Monastic Life, Edited and Translated from a Semi-Saxon Manuscript of the Thirteenth Century,* Camden Society 57 (London: Camden Society, 1853), 89.

GLOSSARY

AKETON A padded cloth tunic worn for protection in combat.

ALMONER An administrative officer responsible for distributing charity.

ALMONRY A building in a monastery used as a charitable residence for the poor.

BAILEY A large enclosed area within a castle.

BARBICAN A fortified enclosure outside a gate, designed to protect it.

BATTLEMENTS or CRENELLATIONS Openings at the top of a fortified wall to allow defenders to shoot through.

BOLTER A person who sifts flour through a sifting-cloth.

BRAIES A type of loose trousers worn as underwear.

CANON One of a body of priests serving in a cathedral or in a community of priests living under a monastic-style rule.

CHAMBER *See* solar.

COIF A simple linen cap or bonnet worn by men.

CONFESSION A religious ceremony in which the individual confesses his sins to a priest.

CONFIRMATION A religious ceremony admitting an individual as a full member of the church.

COTTAGER A peasant who holds a cottage but no lands in the village fields.

CRENELLATIONS *See* battlements.

CUSTUMAL A code of institutional by-laws.

DEMESNE Land kept in the feudal lord's hand rather than let out to tenants.

DIOCESE An administrative region of the church under the authority of a bishop, a bishopric.

DIVINE OFFICE A formalized cycle of daily worship services observed in monasteries and other religious institutions.

DOVECOTE A building for housing doves.

DROP-SPINDLE A small rod bearing a circular weight at one end, used for spinning: the fiber would be attached and the spindle would be suspended and rotated so that it would twist the fiber and pull it out as it descended to the ground.

FALLOW LAND Land left unplanted for a season.

FEE or FIEF A holding of land traditionally held in return for military service.

FULLING The process of cleansing newly woven cloth.

GRAMMAR SCHOOL A school roughly comparable to a modern secondary school, providing education in Latin language and literature.

GRANGE A manor owned by a monastery and used to supply agricultural produce for the monastery.

HABIT A uniform overgarment worn by members of the regular clergy.

HALL A room in a castle, manor house, or other house, used for meals, business, and other public activities.

HERIOT A death duty, typically the deceased's best beast, paid to a villein's lord.

HOLDING A parcel or quantity of land rented to a tenant; the right to rent a holding was often salable or heritable, and bordered on a kind of ownership. Also called a tenement.

HONOR A fief consisting of a number of subordinate feudal manors; a barony.

HURDLE A flat object made of sticks woven into a basket-like surface.

JOURNEYMAN A tradesman who has finished his apprenticeship and is entitled to practice his trade freely but does not possess a shop of his own.

JUROR An administrative official in a Parisian trade guild.

KEEP A large fortified tower at the heart of a castle.

LAY BROTHER A resident of a monastery living a semi-monastic life but not participating in the Divine Office.

LIMEWASH A liquid derived from limestone and water, used to coat buildings. Once dry, it creates a hard protective surface.

LITURGY The ceremonies and customs of worship used by the church.

MANGONEL A siege engine used to hurl large stones.

MANOR The smallest unit of feudal landholding, often corresponding to a village and sufficient to support a knight and his household.

MASTER A teacher at a university; also, a tradesman who is the head of his own establishment.

MATINS A worship service held in the morning as part of the Divine Office.

MENDICANTS Regular clergy living a communal life but not restricted to a cloister, and belonging to an order devoted to communal as well as individual poverty.

MINING The digging of tunnels underneath a castle wall in order to bring it down.

MURAL TOWER A tower built into a fortified wall.

OBLATE A child living in a monastery or nunnery and training to be a monk or nun.

OUTWORK A small fortification lying outside the main walls of a castle.

PADSTONE A large flat stone supporting a building.

PALISADE A fortified wall made of wood.

PANNIER A basket worn on the back, often used by bakers to carry bread.

PIMENT A spiced wine mixed with honey.

POSTERN A small gate in a fortified wall.

PRIVY A latrine.

RECTOR The legal owner of the property of a parish church and its income.

REEVE A manorial officer, usually a serf, responsible for overseeing the business affairs of the manor.

REGULAR CLERGY Men or women living a communal life under an established rule of organization and conduct.

SALLY PORT A small gate in a castle wall designed to allow defenders to attack a besieging force.

SCAPULAR An open, sleeveless garment worn as part of a clerical habit.

SECULAR CLERGY Clergymen responsible to ministering for the public at large.

SELION A strip of plowed land belonging to an individual villager.

SERF A commoner standing in a position of personal bondage to a feudal lord. Called a villein in England.

SOLAR A building or room used as a private withdrawing area and as sleeping quarters. The room is sometimes also called a chamber.

TABLES The family of games played on a backgammon board.

TALLY STICK A stick marked with notches as a means of accounting.

TENEMENT *See* holding.

TONSURE Shaving of the hair from the crown of the head, used as the distinguishing mark of the clergy.

TREBUCHET A siege engine used to hurl large objects.

TURRET A rounded tower built into a fortification.

VALET In medieval French, either a servant or a journeyman.

VASSAL An aristocrat standing in a position of personal subordination to a feudal lord.

VILLEIN *See* serf.

WATTLE and DAUB. A style of wall filling made of interwoven sticks covered with a mixture of clay, dung, and straw.

WINNOW To separate grain from chaff with a fan or winnowing basket.

SELECTED BIBLIOGRAPHY

General

Barber, Malcolm. *The Two Cities: Medieval Europe, 1050-1320.* London and New York: Routledge, 1992.

Delort, Robert. *Life in the Middle Ages.* Trans. Robert Allen. Lausanne: Edita, 1973.

The Dictionary of the Middle Ages. New York: Scribner, 1982.

Evans, Joan, ed. *The Flowering of the Middle Ages.* New York: McGraw Hill, 1966.

Goetz, Hans-Werner. *Life in the Middle Ages from the Seventh to the Thirteenth Century.* Trans. Albert Wimmer. Ed. Steven Rowan. Notre Dame and London: University of Notre Dame Press, 1993.

Haverkamp, Alfred. *Medieval Germany 1056-1273.* Trans. Helga Braun and Richard Mortimer. Oxford: Oxford University Press, 1988.

Holmes, Urban Tigner. *Daily Living in the Twelfth Century, Based on the Observations of Alexander Neckham in London and Paris.* Madison: University of Wisconsin Press, 1952.

Le Goff, Jacques, ed. *The Medieval World.* Trans. Lydia G. Cochrane. London: Collins and Brown, 1990.

Miller, Edward, and John Hatcher. *Medieval England-Rural Society and Economic Change 1086-1348.* Social and Economic History of England. London and New York: Longman, 1978.

Moorman, John R. H. *Church Life in England in the Thirteenth Century.* Cambridge: Cambridge University Press, 1945.

Storey, R. L. *A Chronology of the Medieval World 800 to 1491.* Oxford: Helicon, 1973.

Trevisa, John. *On the Properties of Things: John Trevisa's Translation of Bartholomeus Anglicus' De Proprietatibus Rerum,* gen. ed. M. C. Seymour. Oxford: Clarendon Press, 1975.

Zacour, Norman. *An Introduction to Medieval Institutions.* New York: St. Martin's Press, 1969.

Women

Amt, Emilie. *Women's Lives in Medieval Europe: A Sourcebook.* New York and London: Routledge, 1993.

Gies, Frances, and Joseph Gies. *Women in the Middle Ages.* New York: Crowell, 1978.

Jewell, Helen. *Women in Medieval England.* Manchester and New York: Manchester University Press, 1996.

Power, Eileen. *Medieval Women.* Cambridge: Cambridge University Press, 1975.

Shahar, Shulamith. *The Fourth Estate: A History of Women in the Middle Ages.* Trans. Chaya Galai. London and New York: Methuen, 1983.

Williams, Marty Newman, and Anne Echols. *Between Pit and Pedestal: Women in the Middle Ages.* Princeton, N.J.: Markus Wiener, 1994.

The Life Cycle

Alexandre-Sidon, Daniele. "Du drapeau a la cotte: vetir l'enfant au moyen age (13e.-15e. s.)." In *Le Vêtement: Histoire, archéologie et symbolique vestimentaires au moyen âge.* Paris: Leopard d'Or, 1989: 123-168.

Gies, Frances, and Joseph Gies. *Marriage and the Family in the Middle Ages.* New York: Harper and Row, 1987.

Hanawalt, Barbara. *Growing Up in Medieval London: The Experience of Childhood in History.* New York and Oxford: Oxford University Press, 1993.

Herlihy, David. *Medieval Households.* Cambridge, Mass. and London: Harvard University Press, 1985.

McLaughlin, Mary Martin. "Survivors and Surrogates: Children and Parents from the Ninth to the Thirteenth Centuries." In *A History of Childhood,* ed. Lloyd deMause. New York: Psychohistory Press, 1976: 101-181.

Orme, Nicholas. *From Childhood to Chivalry: The Education of the English Kings and Aristocracy 1066-1530.* London and New York: Methuen, 1984.

Payer, Pierre J. *Sex and the Penitentials: The Development of a Sexual Code 550-1150.* Toronto: University of Toronto Press, 1984.

Russell, Josiah C. "How Many of the Population Were Aged?" In *Aging and the Aged in Medieval Europe,* ed. Michael Sheehan. Toronto: Pontifical Institute of Medieval Studies, 1990: 119-127.

Shahar, Shulamith. *Childhood in the Middle Ages.* London and New York: Routledge, 1990.

———. *Growing Old in the Middle Ages,* trans. Yael Lotan. London and New York: Routledge, 1997.

Swanson, Jenny. "Childhood and Childrearing in *Ad Status* Sermons by Later Thirteenth-Century Friars" *Journal of Medieval History* 16 (1990): 309-331.

Trevisa, John. *On the Properties of Things: John Trevisa's Translation of Bartholomeus Anglicus' De Proprietatibus Rerum,* gen. ed. M. C. Seymour. Oxford: Clarendon Press, 1975.

Material Culture

Alexander, Jonathan, and Paul Binski, eds. *Age of Chivalry: Art in Plantagenet England 1200-1400.* London: Royal Academy of Arts, 1987.

Blair, John, and Nigel Ramsay, eds. *English Medieval Industries.* London: Hambledon Press, 1991.

Charleston, R. J. *English Glass and the Glass Used in England circa 400-1940.* London: Unwin, 1984.

Clark, John, ed. *The Medieval Horse and Its Equipment:* Medieval Finds from Excavations in London, 5. London: HMSO, 1995.

Eames, Penelope. *Furniture in England, France and the Netherlands from the Twelfth to the Fifteenth Century.* London: Furniture History Society, 1977.

Egan, G. *The Medieval Household: Daily Living c. 1150-1450.* Medieval Finds from Excavations in London, 6. London: HMSO, 1998.

Hornsby, Peter, Rosemary Weinstein, and Ronald Homer. *Pewter: A Celebration of the Craft 1200-1700.* London: Museum of London, 1990.

Ladurie, Emmanuel Le Roy. *Montaillou.* New York: Braziller, 1978.

London Museum. *Medieval Catalogue.* London: HMSO, 1967.

Lovillo, Jose Guerrero. *Las Cantigas. Estudio arqueológico de sus miniaturas.* Madrid: Consejo Superior de Investigaciones Cientificas, 1949.

McCarthy, Michael R., and Catherine M. Brooks. *Medieval Pottery in Britain A.D. 900-1600.* Leicester: Leicester University Press, 1988.

MacGregor, Arthur. *Bone, Antler, Ivory, and Horn: The Technology of Skeletal Materials Since the Roman Period.* London: Croom Helm, 1985.

Mercer, Eric. *Furniture 700-1700.* New York: Meredith Press, 1969.

Architecture

Barley, Maurice. *Houses and History.* London and Boston: Faber and Faber, 1986.

Chapelot, Jean, and Robert Fossier. *The Village and the House in the Middle Ages.* Trans. Henry Cleere. London: Batsford, 1985.

Dyer, Christopher. "English Peasant Buildings in the Later Middle Ages (1200–1500*).*" *Medieval Archaeology* 20 (1986): 19-45.

Grenville, J. *Medieval Housing.* The Archaeology of Medieval Britain. London and Washington, D.C.: Leicester University Press, 1990.

Schofield, J. *Medieval London Houses.* New Haven and London: Yale University Press, 1994.

Wood, Margaret. *The English Mediaeval House.* London: Phoenix House, 1965.

Wrathmell, Stuart. *Wharram: A Study of Settlement on the Yorkshire Wolds VI. Domestic Settlement 2, Medieval Peasant Farmsteads.* York University Archeological Publications 8. York: York University, 1989.

Clothing and Accessories

Boucher, François. *2000 Years of Fashion.* New York: Abrams, 1957.

Cowgill, J., M. de Neergard, and N. Griffiths, eds. *Medieval Finds from Excavations in London.* Vol. 1, *Knives and Scabbards.* London: HMSO, 1987.

Crowfoot, E., F. Pritchard, and K. Staniland, eds. *Medieval Finds from Excavations in London.* Vol. 4, *Textiles and Clothing.* London: HMSO, 1992.

Cunnington, Q. W. and P. Cunnington. *Handbook of English Medieval Costume.* London: Faber and Faber, 1952.

———. *The History of Underclothes.* London: Faber and Faber, 1981.

Davenport, Millia. *The Book of Costume.* New York: Crown Publishers, 1948.

Egan, G., and F. Pritchard, eds. *Medieval Finds from Excavations in London.* Vol. 3, *Dress Accessories.* London: HMSO, 1991.

Grew, F., and M. de Neergard, eds. *Medieval Finds from Excavations in London.* Vol. 2, *Shoes and Pattens.* London: HMSO, 1988.

Houston, Mary G. *Medieval Costume in England and France.* London: Black, 1939.

Kelly, Francis M. *A Short History of Costume and Armour.* London: Batsford, 1931.

Kohler, Carl. *A History of Costume.* London: Harrap, 1928.

Lester, Katherine Morris, and Bess Viola Oerke. *Accessories of Dress.* Peoria, Ill.: Manual Arts Press, 1954.

Norlund, Poul. "Buried Norsemen at Herjolfsnes." *Meddelelser om Groenland 67* (1924): 87-192.

Piponnier, Françoise, and Perrine Mane. *Dress in the Middle Ages.* Trans. Caroline Beamish. New Haven and London: Yale University Press, 1997.

Piton, Camille. *Le Costume civil en France du 13e au 19 siécle.* Paris: Flammarion, 1913.

Food

Hammond, P. W. *Food and Feast in Medieval England.* Stroud, Gloucestershire: Sutton, 1993.

Henisch, Bridget Ann. *Fast and Feast: Food in Medieval Society.* University Park: University of Pennsylvania Press, 1976.

Mennell, Stephen. *All Manners of Food: Eating and Taste in England and France from the Middle Ages to the Present.* Oxford: Blackwell, 1985.

Scully, D. Eleanor, and Terence Scully. *Early French Cookery: Sources, History, Original Recipes and Modern Adaptations.* Ann Arbor: University of Michigan Press, 1996.

Wilson, C. Anne. *Food and Drink in Britain from the Stone Age to Recent Times.* London: Constable, 1973.

Village Life

Astill, G. G., and A. Grant. *The Countryside of Medieval England.* Oxford: Blackwell, 1988.

Beresford, Maurice, and John Hurst. *Wharram Percy: Deserted Medieval Village.* London: Batsford/English Heritage, 1990.

Britton, Edward. *The Community of the Vill: A Study in the History of the Family and Village Life in Fourteenth-Century England.* Toronto: Macmillan of Canada, 1977.

Duby, Georges. *Rural Economy and Country Life in the Medieval West.* London: Edward Arnold, 1968.

Gies, Frances, and Joseph Gies. *Life in a Medieval Village.* New York: Harper and Row, 1990.

Hanawalt, Barbara. *The Ties That Bound: Peasant Families in Medieval England.* New York and Oxford: Oxford University Press, 1986.

Hartley, Dorothy. *Lost Country Life.* New York: Pantheon, 1979.

Homans, George Caspar. *English Villagers of the Thirteenth Century.* Cambridge, Mass.: Harvard University Press, 1942.

Ladurie, Emmanuel Le Roy. *Montaillou.* New York: Braziller, 1978.

Miller, Edward, and John Hatcher. *Medieval England—Rural Society and Economic Change 1086-1348.* Social and Economic History of England. London and New York: Longman, 1978.

Raftis, J. A., ed. *Pathways to Medieval Peasants.* Papers in Mediaeval Studies 2. Toronto: Pontifical Institute of Mediaeval Studies, 1981.

Walter of Henley's Husbandry. Ed. E. Lamond. London: Longman's, Green and Co., 1890.

Wrathmell, Stuart. *Wharram: A Study of Settlement on the Yorkshire Wolds, VI. Domestic Settlement, 2: Medieval Peasant Farmsteads.* York University Archeological Publications 8. York: York University, 1989.

Castle Life

Blair, Claude, *European Armour circa 1066 to circa 1700.* New York: Macmillan, 1959.

Bradbury, Jim. *The Medieval Archer.* Woodbridge, Suffolk: Boydell Press, 1985.

Edge, David, and John Miles Paddock. *Arms and Armour of the Medieval Knight.* New York: Defoe, 1988.

Gies, Joseph, and Frances Gies. *Life in a Medieval Castle.* New York: Harper and Row, 1979.

Kenyon, John R. *Medieval Fortifications.* The Archaeology of Medieval Britain. Leicester and London: Leicester University Press, 1990.

Labarge, Margaret Wade. *A Baronial Household of the Thirteenth Century.* London: Eyre and Spottiswoode, 1965.

Laking, Sir Guy Francis. *A Record of European Arms and Armour Through Seven Centuries.* 5 vols. London: Bell, 1920-1922.

Nicolle, David C. *Arms and Armour of the Crusading Era 1050-1350.* 2 vols. White Plains, N.Y.: Kraus, 1988.

Norman, A. Vesey. *Arms and Armour.* New York: Putnam's, 1964.

Oakeshott, R. Ewart. *The Archaeology of Weapons.* New York: Praeger, 1960.

Pounds, N. J. G. *The Medieval Castle in England and Wales.* Cambridge: Cambridge University Press, 1990.

Monastic Life

Brooke, Christopher N. L. *The Monastic World 1000-1300.* London: Elek, 1974.

Coppack, G. *The English Heritage Book of Abbeys and Priories.* London: Batsford, 1990.

Greene, J. Patrick. *Medieval Monasteries.* The Archaeology of Medieval Britain. Leicester, London, and New York: Leicester University Press, 1992.

Knowles, David. *The Monastic Order in England.* Cambridge: Cambridge University Press, 1941.

Knowles, David, ed. and trans. *The Monastic Constitutions of Lanfranc.* London and New York: Nelson, 1951.

Lawrence, C. H. *Medieval Monasticism: Forms of Religious Life in Western Europe in the Middle Ages.* London and New York: Longman, 1984.

McCann, Abbot Justin, ed. and trans. *The Rule of St. Benedict in Latin and English.* Westminster, Md.: Newman Press, 1952.

Milis, Ludo J. R. *Angelic Monks and Earthly Men: Monasticism and Its Meaning to Medieval Society.* Woodbridge, Suffolk: Boydell, 1992.

Power, Eileen. *Medieval English Nunneries c. 1275 to 1535.* Cambridge: Cambridge University Press, 1922.

Town Life

Gies, Joseph, and Frances Gies. *Life in a Medieval City.* New York: Harper, 1981.

Le Goff, Jacques, ed. *La ville mediévale.* Histoire de la France urbaine 2. Paris: Seuil, 1980.

Nicholas, David. *The Growth of the Medieval City from Late Antiquity to the Early Fourteenth Century.* London and New York: Longman, 1997.

Platt, Colin. *The English Medieval Town.* London: Seeker and Warburg, 1976.

Reynolds, Susan. *An Introduction to the History of English Medieval Towns.* Oxford: Clarendon Press, 1977.

Schofield, John, and Alan Vince. *Medieval Towns.* The Archaeology of Medieval Britain. London: Leicester University Press, 1994.

Travel

Friel, Ian. *The Good Ship: Ships, Shipbuilding, and Technology in England 1200-1520.* London: British Museum Press, 1995.

Gardiner, Robert, ed. *Cogs, Caravels, and Galleons: The Sailing Ship 1000-1650.* Conway's History of the Ship. London: Conway, 1994.

Hutchinson, Gillian. *Medieval Ships and Shipping.* London: Leicester University Press, 1994.

Marsden, Peter. *Ships of the Port of London: Twelfth to Seventeenth Centuries A.D.* London: English Heritage, 1996.

Ohler, Norbert. *The Medieval Traveller.* Woodbridge, Suffolk: Boydell, 1989.

Entertainments

Gleason, Harold. *Examples of Music Before 1400.* Rochester, N.Y.: Eastman School of Music, 1942.

McLean, Theresa. *The English at Play in the Middle Ages.* Windsor Forest, Berks.: Kensal Press, 1983.

Murray, H. J. R. *A History of Chess.* Oxford: Clarendon Press, 1913.

Sargent, Brian. *Minstrels: Medieval Music to Sing and Play.* Cambridge: Cambridge University Press, 1974.

———. *Minstrels 2: Medieval Music to Sing and Play.* Cambridge: Cambridge University Press, 1979.

Wood, Melusine. *Historical Dances.* London: Imperial Society of Teachers of Dancing, 1952.

Illustrated Books

There are a large number of illustrated books on the Middle Ages aimed at a slightly younger readership; the following are some of the best.

Corbishley, Mike. *The Middle Ages.* New York: Facts on File, 1990.

Gravett, Christopher. *Knight.* Eyewitness Books. New York: Knopf, 1993.

———. *The World of the Medieval Knight.* New York: Peter Bedrick Books, 1996.

Langley, Andrew. *Medieval Life.* Eyewitness Books. New York: Knopf, 1996.

Macaulay, David. *Castle.* Boston: Houghton Mifflin, 1977.

———. *Cathedral: The Story of Its Construction.* Boston: Houghton Mifflin, 1973.

Nicholle, David. *Medieval Knights.* New York: Viking, 1997.

Quennell, Marjorie, and C. H. B. Quennell. *A History of Everyday Things in England.* London: Batsford, 1957.

Sancha, Sheila. *The Luttrell Village.* New York: Crowell, 1982.

———. *Walter Dragun's Town: Crafts and Trade in the Middle Ages.* New York: HarperCollins, 1987.

Novels

Marston, Edward. *The Dragons of Archenfield.* New York: St. Martin's, 1995.

———. *The Lions of the North.* New York: St. Martin's, 1996.

———. *The Ravens of Blackwater.* New York: Fawcett, 1996.

———. *The Wolves of Savernake.* New York: Fawcett, 1995.

Pargeter, Edith. *The Brothers of Gwynedd Quartet.* North Pomfret, Vt.: Trafalgar, 1990.

———. *The Heaven Tree Trilogy.* New York: Warner, 1993.

———. *The Marriage of Meggotta.* New York: Viking, 1979.

Penman, Sharon Kay. *The Queen's Man*. New York: Holt, 1996.

Peters, Ellis. *Brother Cadfael's Penance*. New York: Mysterious Press, 1994.

————. *The Confessions of Brother Haluin*. New York: Warner, 1988.

————. *Dead Man's Ransom*. New York: Warner, 1984.

————. *The Devil's Novice*. New York: Fawcett Crest, 1983.

————. *An Excellent Mystery*. New York: Warner, 1985.

————. *The Heretic's Apprentice*. New York: Warner, 1990.

————. *The Hermit of Eyton Forest*. New York: Warner, 1989.

————. *The Leper of St. Giles*. New York: Fawcett Crest, 1981.

————. *Monk's Hood*. New York: Warner, 1992.

————. *A Morbid Taste for Bones*. New York: Warner, 1977.

————. *One Corpse Too Many*. New York: Warner, 1994.

————. *The Pilgrim of Hate*. New York: Warner, 1982.

————. *The Potter's Field*. New York: Warner, 1991.

————. *The Raven in the Foregate*. New York: Warner, 1997.

————. *The Rose Rent*. New York: Fawcett Crest, 1988.

————. *St. Peter's Fair*. New York: Warner, 1992.

————. *The Sanctuary Sparrow*. New York: Fawcett Crest, 1981.

————. *The Summer of the Danes*. New York: Warner, 1992.

————. *The Virgin in the Ice*. New York: Fawcett Crest, 1982.

Undset, Sigrid. *The Master of Hestviken*. New York: Knopf, 1970.

Recordings

The Dufay Collective. *A Dance in the Garden of Mirth: Medieval Instrumental Music*. Chandos, 1994.

————. *Miri It Is: Songs and Instrumental Music from Medieval England*. Chandos, 1995.

Other Media

Common Life in the Middle Ages. The Western Tradition Series 21. Santa Barbara: Intellimation, 1989.

The Crusades. New York: A&E Home Video, 1995.

The Feudal Order. The Western Tradition Series 20. Santa Barbara: Intellimation, 1989.

The Lion in Winter. Los Angeles: New Line Home Video, 1968.

The Luttrell Psalter: Everyday Life in Medieval England. Films for the Humanities and Sciences, 1992.

Medieval London: 1066-1500. Princeton, N.J.: Films for the Humanities and Sciences, 1976.

Medieval Realms CD-ROM: Britain 1066 to 1500. London: British Library, 1994.

Medieval Women. Green Bay, Wise.: Center for Television Production, University of Wisconsin-Green Bay; Chicago: International Film Bureau, 1987.

The Middle Ages. The Western Tradition Series 19. Santa Barbara: Intellimation, 1989.

The Return of Martin Guerre. Los Angeles: Embassy Home Entertainment, 1984.

The Sorceress and the Friar. New York: Mystic Free Video, 1988.

Visual Sources

Ashdown, Charles Henry. *British and Foreign Arms and Armour.* London: T. C. and E. C. Jack, 1909.

Atlas des anciens plans de Paris. Paris: Imprimerie Nationale, 1880.

Bateson, Mary. *Mediceval England: English Feudal Society from the Norman Conquest to the Middle of the Fourteenth Century.* New York: G. P. Putnam's Sons; London: T. F. Unwin, 1904.

Berty, Adolphe, *Les trois îlots de la Cité compris entre les rues de la licorne, aux fèvres, de la lanterne, du haut-moulin et de Glatigny.* Revue Archeologique, nouvelle serie 1 (Paris: Didier, 1860).

Burnham, Dorothy. *Cut My Cote.* Toronto: Royal Ontario Museum, 1973.

Clinch, George. *English Costume.* Chicago and London: Methuen, 1910.

Conant, Kenneth. *Cluny: les églises et la maison du chef d'ordre.* Mâcon: Protat, 1968.

de Honnecourt, Villard. *Album de Villard de Honnecourt, architecte du 13e siécle.* Paris: Imprimerie Imperiale, 1858.

Demay, G. *Le costume au moyen age d'apres les sceaux.* Paris: D. Dumoulin, 1880.

Dieudonné, A. *Manuel de numismatique française.* Paris: Picard, 1916.

Gay, Victor. *Glossaire Archéologique.* Paris: Librairie de la Société Bibliographique, 1887.

Géraud, H. *Paris sous Philippe-le-Bel d'apres des documents originaux, et notamment d'après un manuscrit contenant le rôle de la taille imposée sur les habitants de Paris en 1292.* Paris: Crapelet, 1837.

Grew, F., and M. de Neergard, eds. *Medieval Finds from Excavations in London.* Vol. 2, *Shoes and Pattens.* London: HMSO, 1988.

Hartley, Dorothy, and Margaret M. Elliot. *Life and Work of the People of England: A Pictorial Record from Contemporary Sources: The Eleventh to Thirteenth Centuries.* London: Putnam's, 1931.

Hinton, D. A. *Archaeology, Economy and Society: England from the Fifth to the Fifteenth Century.* London: Seaby, 1990.

Hottenroth, Friedrich B. *Le costume chez les peuples anciens et modernes.* New York: E. Weyhe, 1900.

Kohler, Carl. *A History of Costume.* London: Harrap, 1928.

Le Goff, Jacques, ed. *La ville mediévale.* Histoire de la France urbaine 2. Paris: Seuil, 1980.

Maciejowski Bible. *Old Testament Miniatures.* Ed. Sydney C. Cockerell and John Plummer. New York: Braziller, 1969.

Manesse Manuscript. *Minnesänger.* Ed. Kurt Martin. 4 vols. Baden-Baden: Woldemar Klein Verlag, 1960.

Norlund, Poul. "Buried Norsemen at Herjolfsnes." *Meddelelser om Groenland 67* (1924): 87-192.

Paris, Matthew. *The Illustrated Chronicles of Matthew Paris: Observations of Thirteenth-Century Life.* Ed. and trans. Richard Vaughan. Stroud, Gloucestershire: Alan Sutton, 1993.

Power, Eileen. *Medieval Women.* Cambridge: Cambridge University Press, 1975.

Quennell, Marjorie, and C.H.B. Quennell. *A History of Everyday Things in England.* London: Batsford, 1918.

Ruding, Rogers. *Annals of the Coinage of Great Britain.* London: J. Hearne, 1840.

Salzman, L. F. *English Industries of the Middle Ages.* Oxford: Clarendon Press, 1923.

Santarem, Manuel visconde de. *Atlas composé de mappemondes, de portulans et de cartes hydrographiques et historiques depuis le 6e jusqu'au 17e siécle.* Paris: E. Thunot, 1849.

Turner, T. Hudson. *Some Account of Domestic Architecture* in *England from the Conquest to the End of the Thirteenth Century.* Oxford and London: Parker, 1874.

Viollet-le-Duc, E. *Dictionnaire raisonné de l'architecture.* 10 vols. Paris: Morel, 1875.

———. *Dictionnaire raisonne du mobilier français.* 6 vols. Paris: Gründ and Maguet, 1914.

von Landsberg, Herrod. *Hortus Deliciarum.* New Rochelle, N.Y.: Caratzas Brothers, 1977.

INDEX

candles. *See* lights and lighting

canons, 12–13, 163, 224, 229–230, 241

castles and fortifications, xvi, 101–102, 121–157, 226, 230, 250–251; construction, illustrated, 121; functions of castles, 122–123; garrison life, 136–144; household, 144–157; inhabitants of castles, 136–157; layout and environment, 124–136

Cathars, xvii, 14

cathedrals, 12, 83, 108, 228–230, 241. *See also* canons; churches and chapels

cats, 55, 98, 157

cemeteries. *See* burial and cemeteries

cereals. *See* grains

cheese, 57, 59, 69, 143, 154, 181. *See also* dairy work and produce

children, 19–30, 56, 93, 147; care of, 16, 22–26; in clergy, 27–28, 169–170, 195–196; education of, 26–30; of serfs, 8; work of, 26–30, 70, 91

Christianity, vii, x, xvi, 13, 14–15, 159–160. *See also* church and religion; monks and monasteries

Christmas, 109, 182, 184, 268; as administrative term, 85, 137, 232, 269; as holiday, 111, 144, 235, 246; religious observations on, 107. *See also* holidays and holy days

church and religion, ix, 11–15, 31–34, 82–83, 151. *See also* clergy; parishes; pope; prayers; sacraments

churches and chapels, 37, 106–107, 130–131, 133, 134, 136, 151, 166, 177, 223–225. *See also* cathedrals

Cîteaux and Cistercians, 163, 179, 182

cities. *See* towns

cleaning. *See also* laundry; washing

clergy, 11–13, 16–17, 27–28, 83, 86. *See also* bishops; canons; church and religion; friars; monks and monasteries; nuns and nunneries; pope; priests

cloister, 171, 172–177, 229–230

cloth and cloth production, 16, 25, 41–43, 71. *See also* dyes; embroidery; linen; thread and spinning; wool

clothing, 41–51; clerical and monastic, 169–170, 182–183, 195, 248; university students, 245–246. *See also* belts; braies; cloth and cloth production; gloves; headgear; hose; shirts; shoes and footwear; thread and spinning

Cluny, xiv, 54, 116, 161–199; clothing at, 182–183; daily routines at, 190–195; diet at, 180–181; illustrations of, 161, 173, 179; layout and architecture, 172–180; organization of, 163–167; silence in, 187–188, 189–190. *See also* clergy; friars; monks and monasteries

combs, 40. *See also* hair

commoners, 2–4, 7–10, 11, 15–16. *See also* craftsmen and tradesmen; laborers; peasants; poverty and the poor

communion, 15. *See also* Mass; sacraments

confession, 31. *See also* sacraments

confirmation, 26. *See also* sacraments

cooking and food preparation, 26, 29, 53, 58–59, 93–94, 99, 103–104. *See also* dairy work and produce

craftsmen and tradesmen, 39–40, 205–207, 251; in castles, 131, 144; education and training of, 29–30;

income and standards of living of, 70–
71, 210–211; location in towns, 220,
222; in monasteries, 177; surgeons and
apothecaries as, 64; in villages, 89–92.
See also apprentices; guilds; shops

crime, 11, 208, 259. *See also* law

crossbows. *See* archers and archery

Crusades, xv, xvi–xvii, 2, 142, 240

cups. *See* tableware

Cuxham, xii, 75–119, 263, 269, 271;
geography of, 78–81; inhabitants
of, 77–78, 115–119; manorial
organization of, 82–88; tradesmen and
laborers in, 89–92; as village example,
75; women in, 92–95

D

daily schedules, 53, 58, 70, 147–157, 183,
190–195, 235, 245–246, 251

dairy work and produce, 16, 26, 57, 61,
94, 104, 111, 154. *See also* butter;
cheese

dancing, 113–114, 157

de Montfort, Eleanor, 122, 124, 145–157

death and mortality, 20, 23, 35,
36–37, 185, 204. *See also* burial and
cemeteries

demesne land, 8, 83, 84, 104–105, 106

dentistry, 64. *See also* medicine

dinner. *See* meals

disease. *See* health

Divine Office, 160, 166, 169, 170, 176,
186, 188, 190–191, 196

doctors. *See* physicians

dogs, 98, 104, 223

Dover Castle, xii, 121–122; inhabitants
of, 136–157; layout and environment
of, 124–136

drinks, 59–60, 146, 166. *See also* ale and
brewing

dyes, 43, 48, 49. *See also* cloth and cloth
production

E

Easter, 184, 239, 265; as administrative
term, 137, 145, 232, 269; folk
traditions at, 13; as holiday, 111, 235,
246; religious observation of, 107. *See
also* holidays and holy days

economy, 215

education, 26–30, 170, 197, 241,
249. *See also* literacy and writing;
universities

eggs, 57, 60, 69, 154, 181. *See also* food

Eleanor de Montfort. *See* de Montfort,
Eleanor

embroidery (needlework), 16, 27, 49,
50, 149, 196. *See also* cloth and cloth
production

England, x, xiv–xvii, 7, 9, 65, 67, 203. *See
also* Cuxham; London; Oxford

entertainments, 155–157. *See also* dancing;
games and sports; music

Epiphany (Twelfth Day), 111, 232, 264

etiquette, 4, 27, 153–154, 186–187

F

fairs, 115, 239–240. *See also* markets;
shops

families. *See* households

fashion, 4, 44, 49–50

fasting, 58, 154. *See also* Lent; monks and
monasteries, diet of monks; weekly
schedules

festivities, 21, 33. *See also* holidays and
holy days

headgear, 47–48, 49. *See also* clothing; hoods

health, 62–64. *See also* hygiene and grooming; medicine; plague (Black Death); sanitation; vermin

heating, 52–54, 185. *See also* fire and fires

Henry II, king of England, xv, xvi, 125, 135

Henry III, king of England, xv, 123, 125, 128, 132

herbs. *See* medicine; spices and seasonings

holidays and holy days, 181, 263–269; as days of rest, 113, 235, 246; eves of, 58, 154, 269; religious observation of, 107; in rural year, 109, 110, 111, 112, 113. *See also* Christmas; Easter; Epiphany (Twelfth Day); festivities; Lent; Martinmas; Michaelmas; Midsummer (St. John's Day); Pentecost

honey, 22, 60, 105, 181. *See also* cooking and food preparation; food; spices and seasonings; sugar

hoods, 46, 47. *See also* headgear

horn, 40, 231

horses, 68, 104–105, 130, 146, 147, 166, 257–258. *See also* animals

hose, 44–46, 47, 69. *See also* clothing

households, 22, 31, 98, 99–101, 106, 146–147, 210

houses and buildings, 101–106, 108, 236; in castles, 130–136, 147–151; design and materials of, 40–41, 96–99; in monasteries, 175–180; of peasantry, 36, 95–101; rental of, 68, 212; in towns, 210–213, 215. *See also* castles and fortifications; cathedrals; churches and chapels; kitchens and kitchen utensils

humors, 62–63

hunting, 156

hygiene and grooming, 24, 54–55, 62, 154, 175–176, 184–185, 195. *See also* etiquette; sanitation; tonsure

I

incomes. *See* wages and incomes

inflation, 75

inheritance, 3, 4, 7–8, 22, 31, 86, 88, 92–93

iron, 39–40, 90, 91. *See also* metals

Islam. *See* Muslims and Islam

Italy, x, 14, 67, 203, 204, 205, 226, 242

J

jewelry, 50

Jews, 14, 159, 240

John, King of England, xv, xvi, 125, 128

journeymen, 206–207

K

kings, xiii–xvii, 123, 133–134, 144, 226–227; in feudal hierarchy, 3–4, 6–7, 10, 82

kitchens and kitchen utensils, 103–104, 131, 135, 175. *See also* cooking and food preparation; food

knights, xvi, 130, 146; in feudal hierarchy, 2–4, 7, 82, 136–137; income of, 70; military role and equipment of, ix, xvii, 2–3, 7, 82, 122, 137–139; Templars, 163, 224; training of, 27, 29; wages and incomes, 140

knives, 40, 46, 99, 153, 174, 183

mills and millers, 59, 77, 78, 83–84, 89–90, 132, 215

money, viii, ix–x, 9, 32, 33, 164; currency values, xiii, 65–68; gold, xvii, 65, 67. *See also* prices; wages and incomes

monks and monasteries, ix, xvi, 12–13, 27–28, 36, 75, 159–199, 224–225; abbots, 160, 162, 164, 165, 167, 172, 181, 193; children and, 169–170; clothing of monks, 182–183; communal life, 188; diet of monks, 180–181; etiquette, 186–187; functions of monasteries, 196–199; gear for monks, 183–184; illustrations of, 161, 168, 173, 179; lay brothers and laborers, 171–172; layout of monasteries, 172–180; monastic orders, 162–163; monastic routines, 190–195; monks singing, illustrated, 188; novices, 170–171; oblates, 169–170; organization of monasteries, 163–167; origins of monasticism, xvi, 159–160; recruiting and admitting monks, 167–171; silence in monasteries, 187–188, 189–190. *See also* abbots; clergy; Cluny; friars. *See also* Cluny; Divine Office

Montaillou, 50, 55

mortality. *See* death and mortality

music, 4, 25, 114, 170, 243. *See also* dancing

Muslims and Islam, xv, 14, 261

N

names, 21, 146, 203

napkins, 99

needlework. *See* embroidery

Normandy, xiv, 203

Notre-Dame de Paris, xvi, 227, 228–230, 235, 238

nuns and nunneries, 17, 27, 177, 195–196

nurses and nursing, 23, 56, 147

O

oats. *See* grains

old age, 22, 35–36, 185, 196, 232

Oxford, 76, 82, 108, 115, 242

P

paganism, 13, 14

Paris, xii, xvi, 15, 21, 29–30, 65, 171, 201–253; churches in, 223–225, 228–230; defenses of, 250–251; economy of, 214, 215, 230–240; episcopal complex, 227–228; feudalism and, 225–226; government of, 236; houses in, 210–213; inhabitants of, 203–210; map and plan of, 202, 218–219; photos and illustrations, 202, 212, 214, 218–219, 225, 227, 228, 237, 246, 250; streets, 215–222; suburbs of, 251–253

parishes, 20, 32, 106–109, 130–131, 270–271; administration of, 11–12, 13, 107–108; held by monasteries, 164; urban, 224. *See also* church and religion; clergy

pasturage, 81, 105

peas. *See* legumes

peasants, 7–10, 31, 32, 77, 83–101, 106, 109–119. *See also* laborers; manorialism; villages

Peasants' Revolt, xvii, 9

Pentecost, 184, 266

pepper. *See* spices and seasonings

Phillip II, King of France (Phillip Augustus), xiv–xv, xvi, 221, 222–223, 227, 237, 240, 250

Phillip IV, King of France (Phillip the Fair), xv, xvii, 207–208

physicians, 19, 64. *See also* medicine; surgeons

pilgrims and pilgrimage, 197, 207, 261–262. *See also* travel

pins, 40, 44, 48

plague (Black Death), vii, ix, xvii, 223. *See also* death and mortality; health; medicine

plows, 104, 106, 109–110

pope, xiv, xv, 12, 247. *See also* church and religion; clergy

population, ix, x, 76, 163, 201, 204–205

pouches. *See* purses and pouches

poultry, 83, 85, 94, 104; as food, 58; in towns, 211; women's care of, 16, 26

poverty and the poor, 36, 132, 153, 183, 193, 196, 208–210

prayers, 25, 150, 151, 153, 157. *See also* church and religion; Divine Office

prices, 29, 66, 125, 212, 238, 250, 258, 261. *See also* inflation; money

priests, 12, 27–28, 106, 107–109, 162, 166–167, 196, 248; administration of sacraments by, 20–21, 32–33, 37, 107; employed by aristocracy, 144; income of, 70, 144, 170–178; in villages, 27–28, 77, 106–109. *See also* church and religion; parishes

prisons, 11, 123, 134, 230

privacy and personal space, 56

purses and pouches, 44, 46

R

rats. *See* vermin

reading. *See* literacy and writing

rectory, 108

recycling, 40–41, 50–51

reeves, 77, 78, 117

religion. *See* church and religion

Richard I, King of England (Richard the Lionhearted), xvi, 125

rivers, 76, 214, 258. *See also* boats and ships

roads and bridges, 4, 214–215, 258. *See also* streets; travel

S

sacraments, 37. *See also* church and religion; communion; confession; confirmation; marriage; Mass

saints, 21, 197

salt, 58, 61, 69, 153, 154, 181. *See also* spices and seasonings

sanitation, 55, 100, 103; in castles, 127, 157; in monasteries, 175, 176, 179–180; in towns, 211, 213, 222–223

Saturdays. *See* weekly schedules

schools. *See* education; universities

science, 62–63

serfs, 8–9, 83–86, 204

servants and service, 22, 103, 140, 207, 209; in aristocratic households, 103, 146–147, 149–150, 152–154, 155; as life stage, 27, 30; in peasant households, 91–92; wages of, 70. *See also* laborers; squires

sexuality, 13, 33–34, 56. *See also* marriage

shaving. *See* hygiene and grooming

ships. *See* boats and ships

W

wages and incomes, 3–4, 23, 67, 116, 140, 144, 145, 170–178. *See also* feudalism; land and landholdings; money; prices

Wales, 55

warfare, ix, xvii, 2–4, 16, 121, 126–127, 137, 178. *See also* knights; military service; soldiers

washing, 24, 55, 154, 173, 177, 184–185. *See also* cleaning; hygiene and grooming; laundry; towels

water, 54, 76, 89, 124, 134, 135, 175, 179–180. *See also* rivers

weapons. *See* archers and archery; arms and armor

weekly schedules, 107, 183, 228, 236, 262–263; fasting and, 58, 154, 181, 263; labor service and, 85; leisure and, 113, 235–236, 263

weights and measures, 71–73

Wharram Percy, 76, 77, 98–99, 101, 102, 103, 114

wheat. *See* grains

widows, 17, 36, 48, 77–78, 95, 118, 207–208, 231. *See also* women and girls

William, duke of Normandy, xiii, 6

William the Conqueror, 6, 124

windows, 51–52, 98, 107, 136, 147, 175, 176, 229

wine, 60, 64, 72, 151, 155, 181, 196, 197, 230. *See also* drinks

women and girls, 15–17, 146–147, 156, 208–210, 270; childrearing and, 22–23, 26; clergy/monasteries and, 16–17, 172, 178, 187, 230; clothing of, 45–51; income of, 70; inheritance and, 22, 92–93; marriage and, 31–35; in mendicant orders, 248; work of, 26–27, 31, 64, 93–94, 152, 208–210. *See also* de Montfort, Eleanor; nuns and nunneries; widows

wool, 41–42, 43, 44–45, 49, 50–51, 69, 147–148. *See also* cloth and cloth production; clothing; thread and spinning

world map, 257

writing. *See* literacy and writing

Y

yearly schedules, 61, 70, 109–113, 235, 246, 263–269

IMAGE CREDITS

ABOUT THE AUTHOR

Jeffrey L. Singman is the author of several works on medieval and early modern Europe, including *Daily Life in Chaucer's England* (Greenwood, 1995), *Daily Life in Elizabethan England* (Greenwood, 1995), and *Robin Hood: The Shaping of the Legend* (Greenwood, 1998). Dr. Singman has worked at various living history sites, including Greenfield Village and Plimoth Plantation, and is now the Paul S. Morgan Curator at the Higgins Armory Museum and Adjunct Professor of Humanities at Worcester Polytechnic Institute in Massachusetts.